THE

SUCCESSFUL MERCHANT:

SKETCHES

OF THE

LIFE OF MR. SAMUEL BUDGETT,

LATE OF KINGSWOOD HILL.

BY

WILLIAM ARTHUR, A. M.

AUTHOR OF "A MISSION TO THE MYSORE, ETC."

NEW-YORK:
D. APPLETON & COMPANY,
346 & 348 BROADWAY.
M.DCCC.LVII.

PREFACE.

On the day that Mr. Budgett died I was in Bristol, staying with one whose heart was that day full. He who had just departed was naturally the subject of conversation, and the incidents of his early life were freely talked over. Just then the prospect of a long involuntary leisure was before me; and designs for improving it by literary occupation were already formed. But as the uncommon history of the deceased merchant was discussed, the thought arose that to make it the subject of a *Commercial Biography* would be the most useful application of the expected leisure. This design was more homely than those originally entertained, and at first, not very welcome; but after some time spent in observing and inquiring, the conviction of its superior usefulness was confirmed.

I therefore ventured to request permission from the family to acquaint myself with all the accessible details of his life, and to prepare them for the Public in the form which had suggested itself to me. The request was unexpected, but was kindly met; and without a trace of the vulgar reluctance to allude to the earlier stages of a remarkable rise, every particular was communicated and freely left at my disposal. A strong desire, indeed, was manifested to lay me under restraint as to any thing which might be construed into business display; but my design required freedom to show what Mr. Budgett had attained, and that I was obliged to use.

I saw him carried to his grave, and that day conversed with numbers of his neighbours and his men, none knowing my intentions. At long intervals, such conversations were repeated with many who had known him closely, some being aware and others not aware that a book was in contemplation; and certainly very seldom has a master been portrayed so much by the hand of his own men, or a citizen by that of his neighbours, as in the following pages.

Biographers, like portrait painters, are a suspected race: it is generally taken for granted that they paint men as they ought to be; while to the historian you must look for the delineation of men as they are. How far the infirmity of the race besets me would not be discussed impartially just here; but it may fairly be said that, in the picture you are asked to look upon, an effort has been made to insert, with a firm hand, every real scar. Some will say they are too slight; others will say they are too deep, and these they who most intimately knew the original.

The design of this volume is to furnish a work wherein an actual and a remarkable life is traced in relation to Commerce. It was never meant to enlarge the knowledge of the scholar, to mature the graces of the holy, or to hallow the retirement of the contemplative; but to be a friendly, familiar *book for the busy*, to which men from the counting-house or the shop might turn, feeling that it concerned them, and for which they might possibly be the better here and hereafter. Beyond this, one hope did arise,—that it might perhaps meet the eye of some whose leisure, abilities, and spirit would fit them to direct a more powerful literature or a sacred eloquence to the quickening of commercial life with the principles of Christian charity and uprightness. May God grant that, by the instrumentality of this humble book, some youths may be led to habits which will be "profitable to all things," some men lifted above the trammels of commercial selfishness, and some preachers or authors moved to labour to bring religion and business into closer union!

CONTENTS.

THE SUCCESSFUL MERCHANT.

CHAPTER I.

THE SPHERE WHEREIN HE MOVED.

"Lives of great men all remind us
We can make our lives sublime,
And, departing, leave behind us
Footprints on the sands of time;
Footprints, that perhaps another,
Sailing o'er life's solemn main
A forlorn and shipwrecked brother,
Seeing, shall take heart again."

LONGFELLOW.

KINGSWOOD is not a bewitching place. Going out from Bristol, you find the road skirted by rough cottages, prolific of a rough population. Here and there is a man whose complexion has just been painted in the coal-pit, or a woman in costume appropriate to other ages,—a long great-coat of dark-blue cloth, with manifold capes, like a coachman's, surmounted by a quaint black hat, with a low crown, and a leaf spreading widely all around, but lapped down about the ears. To the eye of a stranger, the neighbourhood seems to lie at a distance from our day. But a few modern houses, aspiring toward respectability, a modern church, and modern chapels, all in very good taste, show that a new spirit of improvement has broken in upon the old apathy of the place.

Just at the top of Kingswood Hill, about four miles from Bristol, a lane turns off from the main road. A few dozen yards down that lane, you find gates that indicate the entrance to a substantial residence. Passing inside, you are in grounds where shrubs and statues pleasantly contrast with the adjacent rudeness. To your left, is a handsome house. On a bright green lawn, just before the door, stand a fountain, an arbour of weeping ash, and a pedestal supporting a sun-dial. On the other side of the lawn, spangled groups of flowers appear through the transparent walls of a conservatory; and close by, in a large and handsome aviary, a silver pheasant holds court over a tribe of birds, some curious, some musical. Down a gentle slope, the grounds spread over a surface of about fifteen acres, where you see patches of plantation, a speck of water enlivened by some rare poultry, and a troop of sheep graced by a stag and fawn. Beyond this, the view stretches away up a rich valley, and then far on, over undulating lands, till, in the distance, the eye catches a lofty monument at Dursley, some twenty miles away. A cottage here and there decks the green fields, with its red tiles and walls of shiny white. The prospect convinces you that nature is not to be blamed for the roughness of the neighbourhood. The residence and grounds show, that some one was found who could appreciate the advantages which nature offered.

On Wednesday the 7th of May, 1851, just before the village clock struck twelve, you might have seen a strange, new foreground to the pleasant picture which lies in front of that dwelling. On the circular pathway before the door, about two hundred men stood ranged in order, two by two. Each figure was clad in a mourning cloak, each hat had a funeral band. A listless look you did not see, nor a head carried thoughtlessly. Those at the rear of the column were only boys; before these were youths; and so advancing, till, near its head, you found grey-haired men; and they appeared the saddest. That long column,—black, black, all black,—did look deeply mournful, in front of the pleasant lawns and the bright Gloucestershire valley, in their May-day leaf and bloom. The head of the column stood close by the portico of the house. A bier was there. A single glance would have told a stranger all;—the master of the place was gone, and his retainers had gathered to honour his burial.

Inside the gates, everything told you that the residence had lost its master. Outside, everything told you that the village had lost its chief man. The houses had their blinds drawn down; the shops were closed; the whole population seemed abroad and eager. A dense crowd stood round the gates; and all along the road, "to the place of sepulchre," for a quarter of a mile and more, was ranged an expecting throng. Never before, though familiar with Irish funerals, had I witnessed such an assembly at an interment—at least, never but once; and that was on the occasion when even the volatile heart of Paris was heavy for a day, while her whole population came forth to follow the bier of those who had perished in the frantic battle of June, 1848.

How natural it is, when one sees a funeral indicating wealth or influence, to think of Southey's forcible piece, and to watch among the attendants for tokens of the place the departed held in their hearts.

"These mourners here, who from their carriages
Gape at the gaping crowd. A good March wind
Were to be pray'd for now, to lend their eyes
Some decent rheum; the very hireling mute

> Bears not a face more blank of all emotion
> Than the old servant of the family!
> How can this man have lived, that thus his death
> Costs not the soiling one white handkerchief!"

It was not so here. As you looked along that numerous "following," from the men that bore the coffin to the boys that brought up the distant rear, you felt that it was not a pageant, but a mourning.

The procession entered a spacious chapel. Every nook was soon crowded, and a surplus throng remained without. While the solemn service was read, you could see, among the working men who had followed the bier, many a countenance very deeply shaded. A minister then addressed the multitude. He spoke of the deceased, not in graceful and balanced eulogies, but with a gush of hearty regard that was not to be framed up and gilded. He spoke of worth and bounties as of things that all present knew as well as he; and as he spoke, all faces gathered feeling. "Those hands," he cried, "have given away their hundreds upon hundreds;" and then, perhaps, you seldom saw so many *men* quite melted. Many an eye was full, and many an eye ran over.

Just as the coffin was lowered into the vault, a woman, standing behind me in the crowd, said, "Ah, poor man! hope he's gone happy!"

"Gone happy!" replied a neighbour; "if *he* isn't gone happy, what must *us* do?"

Turning away with the slowly retiring crowd, I said to a woman, "Have you often such funerals as this in Kingswood?" She looked at me in a style not at all complimentary to my intelligence, as if to say, "Where can *you* have spent your days, to ask a question like that?" Then exclaiming with special emphasis, "Niver!" she left me to better my information.

Joining a poor but thoughtful-looking man, I said, "This is a remarkable funeral." "Yes, sir; such a one as we never had in Kingswood before." Then, pausing, he added, sadly, "The best man in Kingswood gone to-day!"

A few days afterwards, meeting with an elderly man, whom I had seen as one of the retinue of mourners, I asked him if he had not been in the employment of the deceased merchant. "Yes, sir, for seventeen years." Then his countenance flushed, and he added, "Ah, sir! a great man fallen!" I coolly observed that I supposed he had been an important man in the neighbourhood. "In the neighbourhood!" replied the old man, "there wasn't his equal in all England. No tongue can ever tell all that man did." This man was about sixty years of age. His hair was grey; and as he thus spoke of his late master to a perfect stranger, the tears fell fast.

Ye cotton lords and corn lords! that would be no unworthy monument,—a man who had grown grey in your service, weeping at the mention of your name. But such a monument as that, like a Parian monument, costs a price It never comes unbought. And it must be paid for in your own lifetime, and with your own hand. Your will, or your survivors, may secure a marble that will droop and mourn over your grave for centuries; but if you would have a few warm tears from the heart of a poor man, neither heir nor will can buy them. "Rarely," said the 'Bristol Times' of that week, "has a neighbourhood suffered a greater loss in the death of a man than Kingswood in the decease of Mr. Budgett, whose charity was unbounded, and who distributed with discrimination and liberality, and without ostentation, fully £2,000 a year from his own pocket."

This estimate is too high as an average, whatever may have been the case in some particular year; but when a man is thus spoken of in his own vicinity, you can understand how some tears should fall at his removal.

And who was this man, whose death moved an entire neighbourhood, and wrung individual hearts? You might often have seen driving into Bristol, a man under the middle size, verging towards sixty, wrapped up in a coat of deep olive, with grey hair, an open countenance, a quick brown eye, and an air less expressive of polish than of push. He drives a phaeton, with a first-rate horse, at full speed. He looks as if he had work to do, and had the art of doing it. On the way he overtakes a woman carrying a bundle. In an instant the horse is reined up by her side, and a voice of contagious promptitude tells her to put up her bundle and mount. The voice communicates to the astonished pedestrian its own energy. She is forthwith seated, and away dashes the phaeton. In a few minutes the stranger is deposited in Bristol, with the present of some pretty little book, and the phaeton hastes on to Nelson Street. There it turns into the archway of an immense warehouse. "Here, boy; take my horse, take my horse!" It is the voice of the head of the firm. The boy flies. The master passes through the offices as if he had three days' work to do. Yet his eye notes everything. He reaches his private office. He takes from his pocket a memorandum-book, on which he has set down, in order, the duties of the day. A boy waits at the door. He glances at his book, and orders his boy to call a clerk. The clerk is there promptly, and receives his instructions in a moment. "Now, what is the next thing?" asks the master, glancing at his memorandum. Again the boy is on the wing, and another clerk appears. He is soon dismissed. "Now, what is the next thing?" again looking at the memorandum. At the call of the messenger, a young man now approaches the office door. He is a "traveller;" but notwithstanding the habitual push and self-possession of his class, he evidently is approaching his employer with reluctance and embarrassment. He almost pauses at the entrance. And now that he is face to face with the strict man of business, he feels much confused. "Well, what's the matter? I understand you can't make your cash quite right."

"No, Sir."

"How much are you short?"

"Eight pounds, sir."

"Never mind; I am quite sure you have done what is right and honourable. It is some mistake; and you won't let it happen again. Take this and make your account straight."

The young man takes the proffered paper. He sees an order for ten pounds; and retires as full of admiration as he had approached full of anxiety.

"Now, what is the next thing?" This time a porter is summoned. He comes forward as if he expected rebuke. "Oh! I have got such a complaint reported against you. You know that will never do. You must not let that occur again."

Thus, with incredible dispatch, matter after matter is settled, and all who leave that office go to their work as if some one had oiled all their joints.

At another time, you find the master passing through the warehouse. Here, his quick glance descries a man who is moving drowsily, and he says a sharp word that makes him, in a moment, nimble. There, he sees another blundering at his work. He had no idea that the master's eye was upon him, till he finds himself suddenly supplanted at the job. In a trice, it is done; and his master leaves him to digest the stimulant. Now, a man comes up to tell him of some plan he has in his mind, for improving something in his own department of the business. "Yes, thank you, that's a good idea;" and putting half-a-crown into his hand, he passes on. In another place he finds a man idling. You can soon see, that of all spectacles this is the one least to his mind. "If you waste five minutes, that is not much; but probably if you waste five minutes yourself, you lead some one else to waste five minutes, and that makes ten. If a third follow your example, that makes a quarter of an hour. Now, there are about a hundred and eighty of us here; and if every one wasted five minutes in a day, what would it come to? Let me see. Why, it would be fifteen hours; and fifteen hours a day would be ninety hours, about eight days, working time, in a week; and in a year, would be four hundred days. Do you think we could ever stand waste like that?" The poor loiterer is utterly confounded. He had no idea of eating up fifteen hours, much less four hundred days, of his good employer's time; and he never saw before how fast five minutes could be multiplied.

Turning from this energetic merchant to the establishment of which he is the head, you are astonished at its magnitude and order. "What business do you call yours?" would be your natural inquiry. "General Provision Merchants." And, verily, they do seem bent on making general provision. The warehouse is one hundred and eighty feet long, by three hundred and fifty at its greatest depth. You pass from office to office, from yard to yard, from loft to loft, and from loft to cellar, till you wonder how all this has been brought under one roof. Then you are led across the street to commence a similar process on a smaller scale, in a bonded warehouse. Even though you have travelled a good deal, you may find the tour of that warehouse a curious and instructive journey. Here you come upon a region of loaf sugar, where it is stored up, pile upon pile, as if seven years of saccharine famine had been foretold. There you light upon a tract of sugar tierces, before which you cease to wonder at the piles of loaf. "What!" you say to yourself, "are all these tierces to be melted away in tea-cups?" Then, thinking such masses must move off slowly, you ask, "How much does each tierce weigh?"

"Ten hundred weight."

"And do you sell many of them whole?"

"We sold two hundred and fifty last week."

Here, you come upon a territory overgrown with tea-chests; there, upon a colony of casks replenished with nutmegs, cassia, and all spicery. Again, you are environed with piled-up boxes of fruit; then, with a vast snowy region of flour. Presently, you are in a land of coffee; then, in a realm where treacle reigns alone, parading itself in hogshead after hogshead, and dozens of hogsheads, till you see there is more treacle in the world than you ever thought before. Now, you are wandering in a wilderness of cheeses; then, on lofts which groan under mountains of peas. Here, tobacco abounds; there, bacon. And, as if to mock your surprise at the large store of articles which rank among the necessaries of life, you find a heap of canary-seed, which, in a barn, would look respectable for a heap of corn. As you prosecute your journey, here you are in stables with stalls for forty or fifty horses; there, in a carpenter's shop; again, amongst a band of coopers. Below, you find a troop of waggoners, lading their capacious carts, and marching off to distribute the contents to steamboats and railways, in an array that would do no discredit to a military commissariat. In one office (through which you must needs pass to get into the warehouse), you have a clerk whose business is simply to learn your errand, and to direct you accordingly. In another, you have a salesman, surrounded by all manner of samples, and cheerfully at the service of any customer for cash. In another set of offices you have a large array of clerks. In each department you find a head man with his troop under him. Here, they are breaking up tierces of sugar, and mixing the different kinds. There, they are weighing flour. In this corner, you find a man before a solid heap of currants, which stubbornly retains the form of the cask, belabouring it with an instrument uncommonly like a fork in a stable yard. Here, they are with an order book, making up the items of an order. There, they are weighing and packing. In a central position, an inspector is placed in a counting-house glazed on all sides, from which he can look out on the whole stream of business, as it passes to and fro. In another place you find a monster coffee-roaster in full play. Again, you are in a room where some have dozen kinds of tea are ready to be tasted by one of the principals. Presently, you light upon a band who are hidden behind a drapery of flour bags, and, thus secluded, are repairing such bags as have suffered in the service. Near these, you see three boys seated at an anvil, hammering old nails straight. This, you are told, is one of the first steps in the establishment. On entering, a boy is set to this work. If diligent here, he is promoted to serve under the master bagmender. If he do well there, he is made a messenger. And then, his future position in the house depends entirely on his ability and application. "But," you are very likely to ask, "what are these old nails, which the boys are beating straight?"

"O! they are the old nails picked up about the concern."

"And are there old nails enough picked up about the concern to keep three boys employed?"

"Not constantly."

As you pass through the different scenes of labour, you find the men moving with great regularity. Every one is at work, yet there is no haste. You receive an impression of activity, rather than of bustle. You naturally inquire, "What are your hours of business?"

"The men come at six; some of the clerks at half-past seven. We leave just when we have done; the clerks about four; the porters at from five to half-past."

"'When you have done;' what do you mean by that?"

"We always do the day's work within the day; and we are at liberty to leave when it is done."

You would, perhaps, wish to know more about this doing the day's work within the day; but for that you must wait till we reach another chapter. At present, we are only looking round the premises and gathering general impressions.

In such an establishment one naturally observes the men, to form an idea of their health, their character, and their position as to comfort. That part of one's survey is often painful enough. In many a prosperous cotton or woollen factory, you see everything which, to an expert eye, tells of ill-health in some, disorderly habits in others, wretched homes in a third class; and in particular individuals, the whole of these evils unmistakably meet, for the air, the eye, the gait, the complexion, and the attire, record them as clearly as the most expressive pen. In great iron works, how painfully an observer feels that some of those brave and brawny fellows, who are performing such herculean labours for the general good, are sinking prematurely under the twin effects of fire and intoxication. In some of the arsenals whence issue our matchless Sheffield wares, how sad to look on those busy frames whose life is plainly wasting. In some of the mining districts of Cornwall, it is touching to observe how few old men are to be found in a crowd; and to see here and there a brave young miner bearing fearful tokens of underground accident. In the metropolitan warehouses, how often does the eye turn sad over a countenance where decay is appearing, or where dissipation is recorded. In all these spheres, happily, one may often trace proofs that masters are attentive to the well-being of those who labour under their eye. In many cases, late years have witnessed great advancement, both in comfort and in morals. But still, in such scenes of industry, there is often enough to make one mourn over the lot of those who are serving us all. You have seen hives of labour whence much sweet gain accrued, but one was little tempted to envy him into whose storehouse it came; for, to secure the honey, so many of the bees are sacrificed. Ye that are able to direct those who are only able to toil, ye have a right to goodly gain; but when you count your increase, forget not those by whose weary labours you were enabled to carry out your plans. Think what you can do for their health, their homes, their intellect, and their souls.

It is a great pleasure to go through a stirring house of manufacture, or of commerce, and see clean attire, healthy complexions, and cheerful looks. Sometimes, one is agreeably surprised to find out how far this is the case, even when the occupation and the atmosphere are very unfriendly. But the great warehouse in Nelson-street, Bristol, is exempt from the difficulties which some kinds of business present to cleanliness, cheerfulness, and health. There you see scarcely a face that raises a suspicion of drunken or disorderly habits; scarcely an attire but seems comfortable, according to the grade. You meet with many whose mien tells you explicitly, that they are thoughtful, intelligent men. And several who pass in white apron and cap, strike you at once as having the expression that indicates a mind to which the comforts and the virtue of piety are habitual. And keep your ear open as you may, you will not catch an oath or an unseemly word.

In your course round the premises, you meet with one large room, which contains no merchandise, and has no air of business. A large range of neat forms are its sole contents, except a table at the head. On the table, lie "Fletcher's Family Devotion," and "Wesley's Hymns." "What," you ask, in some doubt, "what is this place?"

"This is our chapel. A large number of men breakfast on the premises; and before breakfast, half an hour is allowed for family worship. Then the men assemble here for that purpose."

Family worship here! you are ready to exclaim; surely it would be wise and good, if a family feeling could be shed over such a vast establishment, and the hearts of the men be saved from feeling, in the haste of business, that all relations but those of commerce were forgotten. Some sacred link ought surely to hallow the intercourse of those whose lot it is, day after day, to toil side by side. How often it seems to be taken for granted, that when the business of a day is begun, in a large concern, all family scenes and all religious thoughts must wait till the day is over!

The morning after Mr. Budgett's funeral, I was in the warehouse before half-past seven o'clock. The various departments were in full play, and the waggoners packing their loads. At the half hour, the bell rang. I went into the chapel. It was soon filled with the men in their working dress. About eighty assembled. A son of the deceased principal sat at the table. He took up "Fletcher's Family Devotion," and read the portion of Scripture appointed for the 8th of May, with the accompanying reflections. The passage is that which records the wish of the daughters of Zelophehad. The reflections seemed as if they had been framed on purpose to follow the memorable scene in which they had all acted a part yesterday; turning upon the duty of honouring the memory of the departed.

The young merchant, himself affected by the circumstances, and by the coincidence of such a lesson coming on that particular morning, addressed the men in a few words of cordial, Christian advice. He then gave out a hymn, which was heartily sung. Next, he called upon one of them, by name, to pray. All knelt down, and the man prayed, with fervour and solemnity, for spiritual blessings to them all; for comfort to the bereaved family; and for the business, that God might make it prosper. When he ceased, the young master took up the strain; and thus men and master unitedly worshipped the great Disposer, who appoints the lot of all. About half an hour was spent in this religious service. Little would a man of the world think, in watching the vast trade going forward within those walls, and the vigour with which the whole machine moves, that time is daily found to pause and hearken to a voice from the unerring Guide, and bow down to call for blessings from the hand that can make everything to speed. And think you that those daily prayers have had no part in the rapid growth and healthy action of that establishment?

You naturally ask if one of the family always takes the lead in this act of "family prayer." "Oh! no; not always —if any of them are here; but if not, it goes on all the same. We have a regular plan, by which a certain number of the pious men take it in turn, two every morning."

Such is the establishment of which Mr. Budgett was the head. It stands there his monument. Its proportions record the extent of his views; its order, his power to systematise; its prompt and rapid action, his vigour; its moral tone, his piety. Thirty years ago, he was admitted a partner in a retail shop in a country village. Now, he has left what a local paper calls "the largest business in the West of England, and one which turns nearer millions than thousands in the course of the year." It does not turn "millions." Its returns, in one year, are not a million, perhaps not quite three-quarters of a million. But that, mark! is all brought in by a system of prompt payment. No bills; all cash. The rule in that great establishment is, that all purchases made within the month are paid for at the end of the month.

Such returns! such a stock! such a number of hands! You are ready to exclaim, "What a business stock-taking must be! How long does it occupy?"

"At twelve o'clock on a certain day we stop business; and, before twelve at night, the stock is taken, the balance struck, and the principals in their beds at Kingswood or at Clifton."

What was the history of the man who has left us such a monument?

CHAPTER II.

THE BORN MERCHANT.

> "Still let thy mind be bent, still plotting where,
> And when, and how, the business may be done."
>
> HERBERT.

COMMERCE is not one of the Muses. A bargain is not so beautiful a thing as a poem, an oratorio, a picture, or a flight of eloquence. Yet the bargain holds no mean place in the framework of this present world. It is the first *material* bond of human society. By it, the individual acquires what he could not produce, and is relieved of what he could not employ. By it, the best fruits of a skill possessed by one alone are distributed throughout the community; and the one, in serving the community, is advancing himself. By it, nation is linked with nation in a thousand beneficial connexions. By it, the dissimilar produce of climates lying wide apart meet in a single home; the temperate zone gathering winter comfort from the pole, and summer luxury from the equator. Much as we should regret the departure from our world of the poem, the picture, or the oration, that would not leave mankind so utterly at a loss as the departure of the less beautiful bargain. Without it, we could never behold a shop, a public conveyance, a factory, a ship, a railway, or an extensive town.

"The Iliad for War," cries the author of 'Friends in

Council,' and the Odyssey for wandering; but where is the great domestic epic?" A very fit question. And where is the great commercial epic? Arms, agriculture, love, travel, and adventure, all have had their ample offerings of song; but, in spite of Dyer's 'Fleece,' and Grainger's 'Sugar Cane,' and Phillips' 'Cyder,' with minor attempts to give commerce a poetic status, it has thus far held on its course in the world without any notable obligation to the lyre. Any subject, in its vulgar aspect, appears below the dignity and interest of poetry; but once that it has been seen by the eye of the poet, and that his numbers have set it forth, all will recognise its higher aspects. Commerce, in its petty details, is very far from poetry; so is a brigade of recruits on drill, lifting up and setting down first one foot and then the other, as the sergeant cries, "Left! right!—left! right!" But commerce, on the grand scale, is connected with the chief events of history, with all the noted terrestrial discoveries, all the scenes of nature, all the spheres of enterprise, all the triumphs of invention, all the manners of the nations. It is by the light of Commerce that, far away on the misty frontier of history, we first catch sight of Phœnicia, careering on the ancient seas; of Greece, receiving her colonies and her lights; of Carthage, spreading enterprise around the West; of Ancient Britain, emerging out of the unknown, and holding in her hand, as her modest contribution to the common store of mankind, a goodly supply of tin. It is Commerce that first tells us of bright rich lands in the distant East, beyond the range of western politics and wars; that brings thence gem, and spice, and silky robe, which, to northern eyes, look as if they came from some strange realm of light; that, displaying these, stirs up her first-born offspring, Enterprise, to stretch her flight for their native lands; that, at length, placing Enterprise on her own wings, bears her across the wide Atlantic, and lets her gaze on a new continent; then, carrying her round the African Cape, unfolds the real scene whence the great excitement came—the Taprobane, the Golden Chersonesus, the lands of cinnamon and peacocks; of pearl, ivory, and diamond; of muslin, sandalwood, and silk. It is Commerce which presides at the inauguration of the new age, when Europe founds empires beyond the sea, and east and west meet together in new rivalries and friendships, till the devotees of trade cover every eminence of Columbia with foreign standards, and transfer the gorgeous realm of the Great Mogul to masters who confess the creed of the Nazarene. And, sweeping her course from Tadmor to St. Francisco, what magic communities spring up in her train! Solomon's fair city, in the wilderness; the queenly daughter of Alexander, by the mouths of the Nile; Venice, emerging from the flat isles of the Po, beyond the range of the barbarians who then overswept all Italy's ancient glory; Bussorah, springing up by the Tigris, under auspices of the Crescent; the Low Countries, rising out of the sea, gathering the wealth of the Eastern Archipelago, striking down the banner of Spain, and lifting up the paralysed arm of Protestant England; the city of Clive and Hastings, by the ancient Ganges; with wonders endless, on the bays and streams of yonder new world, and here, in our Lancashire vales, on our Yorkshire hills, or in the districts where the great wise Hand has stored up our iron and our coal.

Again, her course amid the paths of nature is not less wonderful than among those of history. Now she is overwhelmed in the simoom, now refreshed on the oasis; now hemmed in by the icebergs, now drenched by the waterspout; now lashed by the monsoon, now enchained by the calm; now steadily wafted by the trade-wind, now broken upon the rock; now joyfully riding in the haven, now away on the open main, where sky and sea alone can meet her eye; now hasting through the hollow tunnel, where cloud, and tree, and wave are alike unseen; now chasing an invisible land by the mysterious track of the magnet; now reading in the conjunction, the transit, the eclipse, or the culminating sun, her instructions how to travel upon earth.

And all the feats whereof poetic rapture ever sang are surely to be matched by those which are daily displayed in the service of Commerce. The huntsman chasing tiger, elephant, lion, bear, ostrich and kangaroo; the diver seeking pearl; the fisherman vanquishing the whale; the miner undoing the bolts and bars of nature's treasure vaults; the mariner wrestling with both wind and sea; the engineer scooping the hill or spanning the strait; the caravan daring the sands; the fleet braving the waters; the bullock-train encountering the kloof; and all that ancient poets could find to originate ideas of Cyclops and supernatural powers, was little to the flaming wonders of one night's survey from Dudley Castle, or one day's study of the magic hives of Manchester.

Then, Commerce mounts her upon every steed; now on the camel, patient as a thing inanimate; now on the ship, active as a thing of life, with canvas wing and magnet scent; now on the fleet horse, now on the drowsy buffalo; now on the toiling wain, now on the flying engine; now on the steadfast mule, now on the quivering steam-boat; now she follows the fleet foot of the reindeer, now loiters on the dank canal; now skims in the slight canoe, now rolls in the thundering train; now whirrs on the wing of the carrier-pigeon, now clings to the writhing catamaran.

Commerce, too, has done much toward fulfilling its mission. It was ordained to bind man to man, province to province, and nation to nation, by the solid tie of common interests. "Had all nations found at home every thing necessary and agreeable, it is impossible to conceive to what extent their mutual alienation might have proceeded. China and Japan help us to an idea of that which, in such a case, would have constituted nationality." But God gave each individual a relish for all that is charming in creation, yet distributed the productions which all enjoy over the various zones of earth. Consequently, if the people of one land would partake of all they coveted, it was necessary to know and to deal with the people of other lands. Thence came that interchange of services by which we now see the beverage of Englishmen depending on the rains in China, the wealth of many a Chinese on the markets of England, the bread of many a family in Manchester on the weather of Carolina, the comfort of many a home in Leeds on the sheep of the Cape and Australia, the welfare of many a Spanish vine-grower on the rents of the English squire, the value of Norwegian pine on a vote at St. Stephen's, the prosperity of the Russian hemp-grower on the prosperity of England, and the robes of the Swedish ladies on the silk-worms of the south. Commerce is the appointed medium for making that universal in benefit which is local in production; for preserving in men a sense of dependence upon other men; and thus, for giving the most favoured nations a knowledge of the condition of others, an interest in their welfare, and a facility for that intercourse by which they may teach and elevate. It is not a spiritual or sentimental tie; but a material bond—a chain of gold, by which the hand of Providence has linked the interests of all men in a connexion which the most carnal eye may see; but which, when recognised, tends to facilitate all the errands of Christianity among the nations. It was through Commerce that Carey and Swartz were enabled to know India. and to reach it; that Morrison had his path made to China; that the Fetish tree of Guinea and the Kraal of South Africa were laid open to the eye of Christian pity; that the heart of zeal was told of cannibal feasts in New Zealand, and infant murder in the Polynesian isles. Of old, we see her ships and her dromedaries bearing the gold and the gems of the richest lands, to lay them as her offering at the gate of God's glorious temple on Zion. Thus may she be seen often twining ties of international amity; often calling forth the enlightened to teach the dark; and now convening all earth's tribes under one pure dome of crystal. But often, too, she appears perverted from her purpose; stirring man against man with a pitiless rivalry; rousing nation against nation, for lucre; letting loose all the bloodhounds of war; and, alas! alas! the whole curse of the slave-yell falls upon her head, the whole blood of the slave trade lies upon her skirts. Surely, if Commerce could find her poet, the poet could find his materials. Yet, we have no commercial epic!

And what is far more wonderful in a "nation of shopkeepers," we have no commercial biography. Our power abroad, our quiet at home, the stability of our government, the security of our towns, the value of our crops, are all so dependent upon commerce, that, nationally, it is our first interest and our leading characteristic. Our merchants have been a race of vast endeavour, and incredible achievement. They have built up a fabric that astounds us all, and our neighbours more than us. They have had, in their individual careers, the most wondrous vicissitudes, the highest romance of real life. They have ever furnished the noblest, the meanest, the most unaccountable, the most exemplary, the most eccentric specimens of character. Many of them have influenced contemporary history more than reigning princes; many of them have displayed more comical peculiarities than the queerest oddity of fiction. There is scarce a town of note, to which some one of the race has not bequeathed a tradition of wonderful success, accompanied by hated parsimony, by envied sumptuousness, or by benevolence univer sally extolled. Here, you have a mansion and park; there, a set of almshouses; yonder, a church or school; each with its short but pregnant tale of a remarkable man. Yet, with such a race in the midst of us, and such tokens of what they have been doing, we seek in vain for the Lives of the British Merchants. Booksellers look uncommonly wise when you ask for a volume of commercial biography. Johnson has taken care of the poets; Allan Cunninghame of the artists; Campbell of the Lord Chancellors: but no one has thought of the Lord Mayors; except, indeed, that worthy scribe who regaled our childhood with the pleasant story of "Whittington and his Cat." Divines, orators, men of science, of letters, of art, statesmen, generals, admirals, yea, even play-actors, have abounded in biographers; but the men who have reared factories more costly than a castle, who have given bread to more men than an ancient chieftain led out to war, who have created fleets that are sailing under every sky, who have raised an entire neighbourhood from indigent inaction to gainful enterprise, who have presided over the destinies of a whole exchange, who have built up a financial power before which foreign cabinets bend suppliantly,—no one has cared to trace for commercial posterity the course wherein these kings of commerce struggled and achieved.

When biographers have taken up a commercial man, they have dropped business as a leaden thing, a dead weight, that would sink the book; and so you float away with a fragrant cargo of philanthropy or public life. Mr. Knight gives us Gresham; but Gresham dealt in state finance, and the high service of kings. In the edifying biography of Allen, you see much of the beauty of holiness, nothing of the stern struggle of profit and loss. In the almost faultless biography of Buxton, you are now and then permitted to have a distant peep of the brewery, far away in the recesses of Brick Lane; and one day you are positively taken inside the gates,—but it is to eat beefsteaks with the Premier and the Lord Chancellor. In nearly all the religious biographies of those who have been in business, you see the inner man alone. Had Jacob's life fallen into the hands of a modern biographer, he would never have thought of telling us the contrivances by which he multiplied his wealth. That would not have been sufficiently intellectual, sufficiently ethereal,—or, indeed, sufficiently to Jacob's credit.

Arkwright produced an invention by which the British people have been more influenced politically, socially, and morally, than by all the expeditions in search of the North-West passage, all the orations of Curran, all the poems of Burns, all the pictures of West; yet, the aspiring apprentice who would trace that wonderful (I do not mean noble) man, must hunt in the 'Beauties of Derbyshire,' among the Cyclopedias, or in the faithful annals of the 'Gentleman's Magazine,' for some faint outline of his career. Should he go to a circulating library, and ask for the life of Arkwright, perhaps he may be favoured with an offer of the life of Charles Matthews. The first Sir Robert Peel, from an ambitious labouring lad, became a baronet, who employed fifteen thousand men, spoke often in Parliament, published political pamphlets, when the country was threatened with invasion gave ten thousand pounds to aid our overladen finances, raised half a regiment of volunteers, and bequeathed to England a son who became her most powerful statesman. Yet if a Lancashire boy feels, as he felt, that he has the capability of raising himself to station and power, he may go to the library, and instead of the life of the founder of the Peels, be offered one of Lady Hester Stanhope. Rothschild began by buying prints at Manchester, and ended by wielding a power which was felt by every king in Europe. Yet the young merchant who would study his habits of business, may, possibly, if he inquire for his biography, be offered that of Theodore Hook.

Nothing tends to form the rising members of any profession more than the biographies of those who have been eminent in the same line. The advantage of the finest models has long been before the eye of all the *alumni* of the theological, military, political, and artistic schools. Not so with the young men of commerce. Those of their predecessors who have accomplished the greatest wonders, are known only by a stray anecdote or a slight sketch. Every boy in the navy knows how Captain Brock took the Chesapeake; but what boy in the merchant service knows anything of the way in which Mr. Green created his superb mercantile fleet, with its noble accompaniment, his sailor's home? Every young author can learn precisely how many pounds a day Scott earned while writing the life of Bonaparte, how much Byron received from Murray for Manfred or for the Corsair; but though points so mercantile are worthy of record in the high regions of poetry, none can tell by what transactions, successes, and plans the Barings built up their power. Turn where you will, you see wonders of commerce, the origin of which is recent, the history of which would be instructive; but which are known only by flying traditions. At Leeds, you see Marshall's mills rising up as by magic, giving employment directly or indirectly to thousands, raising many to comfort, some to affluence, spreading competence and education around, giving that great borough a representative, and adorning the banks of Conistone and Ullswater with new mansions and demesnes. Yet, who of us can tell how that wonderful structure arose? But we are all well taught in the momentous fact that Lord Byron kept his figure slim by living on potatoes and vinegar. At Stockport we see the mills of another Marshall, performing, in cotton, prodigies akin to those of the former in flax; yet what working man who wants to rise can con over the narrative of how the founder of that establishment began, and rose, and weathered the storm, and pressed on, till he was the largest cotton manufacturer in Europe? But we are all instructed in the portentous truth, that when Oliver Goldsmith presented himself to a Bishop for ordination, he was arrayed in scarlet breeches.

"Commerce is a dirty thing," we have heard literary lips say. Yes, in dirty hands, it is a dirty thing; and in rude hands, a rude thing; and in covetous hands, a paltry, pelfy thing. Nevertheless, it is a thing on which those who despise it are largely dependent. Without it, the author would have no market for his works; the intellectual gentleman, no bookshop; the grand lady, no sumptuous furniture; the fop, no finery; the idler, no dainties. And, what is far more important, it is the thing in which the bulk of our countrymen are spending their lives, and in which the bulk of future generations will spend their lives too,—the thing on which their earthly hopes will depend, in which their souls will be tempted, exercised, chained down to the dust, or prepared for immortal joy. If literature has any work in this world at all, it is to refine and elevate every sphere of human life; to be the companion, and friend, and teacher of every rank of men. It cannot, therefore, without being faithless to its mission, pass lightly over that sphere wherein the most numerous and most energetic class of the community are trained in youth and tried in manhood. No theme is dull, if not handled with dulness; no theme low, if the writer exalts it. The pen of Wordsworth can chain you to the track of an old Cumberland beggar, until you almost count the nails in his footprint, and feel the dust from his meal-wallet. The moss-trooper, the smuggler, the buccaneer, are all chosen subjects of lofty authors; but to depict an actual man, whose life has been spent in the struggles, the reverses, the glossy frauds, and the sordid triumphs, of downright purchase and sale, seems a task far too practical for a pen from the ethereal plume of genius. Galt, even when under taking to portray the curious life of Grant Thorburn, must needs enshroud it in the fiction of 'Laurie Todd.'

"Who would ever think of writing the life of the moiling pelf-worm, who works and wriggles through the dust, thinking of nothing but making his way? True, who would? But who would think of writing the life of the commonplace soldier, who wheels to right or left, loads, presents, fires, and fixes bayonet? or of the scribbler who palms a book upon the world? or of the spouter who perpetrates dull speeches? The ignoble is ignoble in any sphere; the great is great in any. Commerce, like other spheres, has had its marvellous men; and to the moralist, no class he could handle would afford such innumerable points on which important light might be shed upon life's actual ways, wherein the plodding and the practical are ever tempted to sell truth and integrity for gold. But from them the literati seemed to have turned away. *The* TERRA INCOGNITA *of the learned is ordinary life.* The Chronicles of the Stock Exchange, the History of Banking, the Bankers' Magazine, and some prints devoted to economical questions, all show that literature has at length set out to explore that region of reputed desert.

For business men, as a class, literature has done little. They can lay their hands on few books that are not likely to estrange them from their avocations just in proportion as they charm them. The young men of any other profession, beside the dry study of principles, may at the same time relax their minds, and rouse up all their professional aspirations by the lives of some who have trodden the very path on which they are starting, and found it the way to eminence. Not so the young merchant, of whatever grade. For the lives of the great, he must go out of his own line, and perhaps learn to despise it, when he might have learned its value, and had all his views ennobled. Thus many business men dread books, just as literary men dread business. The two things have been at enmity. The literatus has looked down on the man of figures and facts, with counting-house taste and cash-box imagination. The merchant has looked down on the man of lofty ideas and light pockets, redundant in sentiment, but lacking in common sense. You can hardly ever find a business man who has any just notion of the mercantile value of genius, or a literary man, who has any appreciation of business. How seldom does a millionaire take any pains to encourage letters; or a scholar care to analyse the life of a merchant, whatever mental power he may have displayed, whatever impulse he may have given to the improvement of international or internal relations, whatever influence he may have exerted on the history of a kingdom. Consequently little light has been shed into the recesses of commerce from higher spheres. Men of business have been left to form their own codes of morals, with a millionth part of the criticism, from the erudite, on the moral correctness of this principle and of that mode of transaction, that has been spent on the letter *h*, the Greek article, or the digamma. The politics of commerce are now, perforce, a favourite study; but the *morality of purchase and sale*, the effect of business upon character, the relation which art, science, and literature bear to commerce, are points on which business men are little indebted to those whose calling it is to instruct. Had it been otherwise, the mercantile class might have been great gainers, in enlarged views, in refined pleasure, in appreciation of the efforts and the utility of the higher orders of mind, and also in clear views of the moral principles of trade.

But more attention to practical life, on the part of literary men, would be as rich in benefit to themselves as to men in business. In handling that subject, they would grow wiser, and would impart more wisdom. They would discover that fictitious characters were no more necessary to furnish interest, pleasure, amusement, surprise, and sadness, than fictitious landscapes are necessary to furnish mountain, forest, water, and sky. They would constantly find moral problems, which might engage the most subtle dialectitians, and yet would interest the stock-jobber and the shopman.

To the lawyer who has constantly to handle commercial transactions, to the judge who has to pronounce upon them, to the statesman who has to balance conflicting mercantile interests, to the schoolmaster who has to train men for business life, a knowledge of all its aspects would be invaluable. But to the preacher, above all, who has constantly to deal with men immersed in trade, it is of an importance not to be calculated that he should know the life which all the week long his hearers are leading—its temptations, its glosses, its rivalries, its depressions, its joys; its anxieties, which cast the care of the soul into the shade; its ambitions, which outweigh the claims of truth and right. Ignorant of these he must leave many to flounder in temptation, whom he might be the means of extricating; many to be worried with care, when he might win their attention to better things; many to sink under their load, to whom he might have given a timely solace; many to go on in a course of gainful sin, whose conscience he might have reached and aroused. Too often, the man of business feels that the remarks from the pulpit only show that his case is not at all understood. There are few preachers of whom it could be said, as I have heard it said of Dr. M'Neile, that after some of his sermons his hearers felt as if he had served his time to every trade in the town. Dr. Chalmers, too, endeavoured worthily to bring the strong light of his Christian eloquence to elucidate the pathway which is ever so crowded, however it may be forgotten by the learned.

I have now to tell you of a genuine son of English com

merce; not of one who, like Gresham, was by birth a prince of the blood in the empire of trade; but of one who, beginning in the ranks, fought his way up to eminence: not of one who took his stand among the archers of speculation, and, drawing his bow at their brilliant target, chanced to strike the gold; but of one who rose by sheer dint of working, systematising, and extending his own legitimate business: not of one who accumulated by the simple power of retention,—getting, griping, holding, and never giving; but of one who was as apt to scatter as to increase: not of one in whom early influence and education had combined the polish of aristocratic circles with the pursuits of commercial life; but of one who was, to the last, the keen, bustling, downright man of business: not of one who was so absorbed in trade that he never had a spare thought or a spare moment for recreation, friendship, the interests of others, the culture of his mind, or the care of his soul; but of one who, while passionately earnest in business, had always a heart for a friend, a hand for the poor, an hour for good works, a relish for a book, and a lively solicitude for the things that never pass away: not of one who amassed and left behind him a fortune, making a wonder in itself; but of one who did not care to die rich: not of one who moved in the high walks of cosmopolitan philanthropy; but of one whose work was wrought near his own door, among the colliers and the lane-side cots of a poor and unpolished neighbourhood. Such is the tale I have to tell; do be patient, and follow me.

The little Somersetshire town of Wrington has been known to the great world only through one name. It was there that the sage eye of John Locke first opened to the light. How strange, that, age after age, the natives of Wrington should pass away unknown, and a single individual stand up before mankind a prodigy and an ornament, greeted everywhere by the noble and the wise with admiring obeisance. That one illustrious reputation, overshadowing those numbers of humble names, speaks to us very weightily of a hand which silently frames our powers and allots our sphere.

It was in this same quiet little town of Wrington, that Samuel Budgett received his birth; on the 27th of July, 1794. But his recollections brought up to him no trace of his native town. It was to the village of Backwell, whither his parents had removed, that his first gleams of memory referred; and these "were very faint." When only five years old, his parents again removed; fixing this time at Nailsea. Here it is that his recollection begins fully to retain events. Of some of these we have records in his own words. A young friend, to whom, late in life, he had become much attached, and who knew how to estimate the remarkable man whose intimacy she had gained, set her heart on preserving his own animated narratives of the leading occurrences in his career. She was able to carry out her purpose only as far as regarded his earliest years; then opportunities never recurred till disease and death closed the lips from which she would, otherwise, have collected many a tale pregnant with interest and with lessons. Our opportunities of laying his own words before the reader will be so few, that some of these early recitals, which might otherwise have been passed over, may be given, to permit the man to make his own impression.

It may generally be assumed, that those events of childhood which leave a permanent impression on the memory, have had considerable influence in moulding the character. Adventures which are trivial as possible in their external history, may be so frequently present to the early reflections, and may mingle with so much of early thought, that their place in the inner history is altogether disproportioned to their seeming importance. Mr. Budgett thus narrates "the very first recollection of importance" which he preserved :—

"The very first recollection of importance I have, is that of a Mr. Taylor, an Irish gentleman, coming to lodge in my father's house, and offering to undertake the education of the children; and although my parents were both extremely kind and indulgent, so far was it from producing, as it ought to have done, anything like hope or pleasure, I remember distinctly such fear was produced in my mind (although I am not aware that he ever spoke an unkind word to me), that, for a short time, annihilation seemed preferable to life itself: and life became a complete burden, from no other cause than the idea I had formed of his warmth of temper. My mind, however, was completely relieved when the proposition was not accepted. This circumstance left an indelible impression, and produced great care, in after life, to prevent a recurrence of the kind in the case of my own children."

This first glimpse at his character brings to light two things;—an extreme sensitiveness, a painful heart-sinking timidity; and a habit of treasuring up a lesson from the past, to apply it to the emergencies of the future. The former of these characteristics was probably physical; the latter was one of his great elements of power and success. The terror he had felt was not looked back upon with a smile, as a mere childish folly; but was carefully preserved in view, as a guard against allowing similar distress to be coupled in the mind of one of his own children with their education.

The next of his early recollections is this :—

"About the same time, I remember a remarkable dream of my father's. After having lost a black mare for some weeks, supposing it to have been stolen, he had given up all search; and when he awoke one morning, he said, 'Betsy, I have dreamt that I found the mare at Kingston Seamore, grazing on the Moors; and the dream is *so* distinct, I'll go and see.' He soon obtained a horse, and rode off. My mother having told us of it, we were in full expectation, toward evening, of my father's return; and a little before dusk, as we were all looking out, big with expectation and hope, the gate flew open, and in rode my father on the horse with which he left home in the morning, and leading the black mare in his right hand, with his pocket-handkerchief filled with a quantity of crabs and other live fish which he brought home for our amusement. The delight and glee which we all felt on his arrival, at his success, and on beholding for the first time animals of this kind crawling on the large stones before our door, may more easily be conceived than described, and left an impression which will *never* be effaced, as one of the most wonderful events that could happen; particularly as during the loss of the horse, the children participated in the feelings of the parents, supposing we were well nigh ruined."

This again brings to light one of the most powerful elements in forming his character and fixing his pursuits,—a lively sympathy in the concerns of his family. Few boys of five or six would feel so intensely about the injury arising to their parents from the loss of a horse, that its recovery should form, ever after, one of the chief events of early life. But we shall abundantly see, as we proceed, that this early activity of family affection was a true index of his heart.

Perhaps this adventure of the lost mare also affected his character in another way. Here, at the outset of life, his feelings had been intensely wrought upon in connexion with a horse. The horse had been made to appear a treasure and a friend. In after life, he was remarkable for his love of horses; and we shall find his benevolence making a singular use of that peculiarity. Perhaps the loss of the black mare at Nailsea was the secret of that fancy to which some of his poor neighbours at Kingswood were indebted for the gift of a good horse.

What child has not his escapes? They too often leave important traces both in the physical and mental history. Besides a terrible accident in a tanpit, where he was hardly rescued from drowning, he had a mishap which left a mark upon his countenance to the end. He thus describes his most memorable escape:

"We then lived in a large and respectable house, belonging to the late James Davis, Esq., of Bristol, having large entrance-gates on the left hand of a long yard opposite the house door. On the right hand was a very nice cherry orchard; on the left hand, going from the cherry orchard to the alcove, was a flight of steps leading to the kitchen garden; at the bottom of which was a bathing pond: and on one occasion, when this was emptied, a large quantity of mud had collected at the bottom, which was drawn away by a cart with three horses. As the cart was moving on, when loaded, from the pond, I (being between five and six years of age) ran before the wheel, and falling on my back, the broad wheel passed over the top of my right thigh, across my body, over the left shoulder, grazing my chin, and has left a mark to this day. My father took me up and carried me in, supposing me dead; but on being bled, I recovered, and was soon better."

Such a shock was not calculated to abate the sensitiveness from which he so much suffered.

"In 1801," he says, "we removed to Kingswood. I remember, there, father and mother taking a shop, which was termed 'the great shop on the *cassy*' (causeway)." Two years afterwards, this shop was left in the hands of a brother, many years older than he, and the son of another mother. On this occasion the family removed to Coleford, "where," he says, "my parents opened a small general shop."

The same benevolent Power which sends amongst mankind some qualified, by special genius, to advance their knowledge, manners, or polity, also sends some qualified, by special genius, to advance their commercial development. Such a man was Samuel Budgett. He was born a merchant, just as other men have been born poets, painters, or mathematicians. Genius lies in intuition and impulse,—an inborn aptitude to perform a certain thing, and an inborn desire to perform it. Dr. Johnson's definition, "a mind of large general powers, accidentally determined in some particular direction," applies to the highest order of the human mind; but shoots above the majority of those who possess proper genius, which often exists, remarkably, in persons not gifted with "large general powers," and not capable of pre-eminence in any direction but the one to which their "genius" leads them. Large general powers may take their direction accidentally; genius does not. It always sets its possessor on his own particular path. An old lady in Nottinghamshire, who happens to imagine that dead people dwell in the moon, has only to provoke the boy-lord of Newstead Abbey, when he breaks out,—

> "In Nottingham county, there lives at Swan Green,
> As cursed an old lady as ever was seen;
> And when she shall die, which I hope will be soon,
> She firmly believes that she'll go to the moon."

There it was; the impulse to put his passion into verse, and the ability to do it. The old lady might have provoked all the other boys in Nottinghamshire, and not found one, whatever were his general powers, who would have vented his irritation in that form. So Watts, when whipped for rhyming, begged pardon in rhyme. So Pascal, when still carefully prevented from seeing mathematical books, is found working demonstrations on the floor, with charcoal, calling his lines *bars*, and his circles *rounds*. So Chantrey, sent to sell milk, is busy carving heads on a walking-stick. So Jackson, set upon a tailor's board, is perpetually drawing pictures with his chalk. So Arkwright, deep in dyeing wigs, is planning the perpetual motion. So James Watt, placed at a tea-table, is pondering the properties of steam. Thus it ever is; if a man has naturally the power of genius, he spontaneously exerts it. The power would be useless without the impulse. In the case before us, the power was specially commercial, and the impulse took that bent. Just as other boys naturally betook themselves to rhyming, sketching, or making models; so Samuel Budgett naturally betook himself to making bargains. That was his sphere, and he entered upon it early.

At Coleford, when about ten years of age, he began to display his mercantile predilections, and to lay the foundations of his habits and his fortune. His own account of his first essay in merchandise, and his first possession of money, is very straightforward.

"The first money I ever recollect possessing, was gained iu the following way. I went to Mr. Milks, of Kilmersdon, to school, a distance of three miles. One day, on my way, I picked up a horse-shoe, and carried it about three miles, and sold it to a blacksmith for a penny. That was the first penny I ever recollect possessing; and I kept it for some time. A few weeks after, the same man called my attention to a boy who was carrying off some dirt opposite his door; and offered, if I would beat the boy, who was a bigger boy than myself, to give me a penny. I did so; he made a mark upon it, and promised, if I would bring it to him that day fortnight, he would give me another. I took it to him at the appointed time, when he fulfilled his promise, and I thus became possessed of threepence; since which, I have never been without, except when I gave it all away."

One would not have imagined, in seeing the little school boy stop and look at the old horse-shoe, that the turning point of his life had come. But so it was. He converts that horse-shoe into his first penny, and never wants a penny more. Had he not picked it up; had he "never thought," as people so naturally say; or, having thought of it, had he felt ashamed to offer such a thing for sale; or had he set it down as too much trouble to carry an old horse-shoe for three miles, probably he would not have had a penny for many a day, and would have often "been without" afterwards. Do you think, young man, that *you* could use such an opportunity to any purpose? If so you may rely upon finding a horse-shoe in your path, some day. Those men whom we see often without a penny, have, all of them, passed by the horse-shoe on their path when they were boys. And those other men, who, from nothing, are rising up rapidly above their neighbors, have all had the sense to seize the horse-shoe, and turn it into the foundation of a fortune. Paths vary, but every boy, if his eyes are open, will certainly find the horse-shoe in his path, at one point or another.

Mr. Budgett was one day riding in a lane near his own residence, when he saw a boy following the track of a hay-cart and picking up the tufts of hay that fell. He at once put his hand in his pocket, and gave the boy a shilling. Doubtless he bethought him then of his own horse-shoe, and hoped his young neighbor was finding his.

And that is an expressive note which closes the record of his first fortunes, "Since which, I have never been without, *except when I gave it all away*." Mark it, for we shall find something to call it to mind.

Here is the history of his second attempt at making money:—

"The next addition to my stock of money was, when one of my sisters, in drawing treacle, had let it run over; and a considerable quantity was wasted. After taking up what she thought was worth saving, and being about to wash away the remainder, I ran to my mother and said, "Mother, may I scrape up that treacle, and sell it for myself?" Having gained her consent, I set to work, scraped it up as clean as possible, and sold it for three halfpence. Thus, by little and little, my fund became augmented, until I had enough to pnrchase 'Wesley's Hymns,' and I considered myself a rich and happy boy."

In this case, again, we see his impulse to convert to gain that which others would let run to loss. The "little and little" of which he speaks, was little and little indeed. A surviving brother describes him as perpetually trading. When at school he found that for a half-penny he got only six marbles, but for a penny fourteen. By buying a pennyworth, and selling to his comrades two different half-pennyworths, he earned two marbles honestly; and so drove a profitable trade. Lozenges were also in request at school; and he found that a similar law of commerce obtained in lozenges as in marbles,—the large purchaser had an advantage over the small. Therefore he bought in pennyworths and sold in half-pennyworths, ever making head. This trade returned a good profit on the capital, and was, moreover, perfectly safe. But it seems in the nature of the merchant to make large and hazardous adventures as his funds thrive. Accordingly, the growing means of our juvenile tradesman tempted him to seek a larger sphere. One day, on the way to school, he encountered a woman bearing a basket of cucumbers. He asked the price, and to her surprise, and his brother's discomfiture, would know the price of the whole store. It was in vain for his brother to remonstrate; he would buy, and he would sell. The old woman finding him really in earnest, concluded a bargain, and the cucumbers became his own. It was not a very likely investment for the capital of a school-boy; but his energy made it answer. The cucumbers were all sold, at, I think, the notable profit of ninepence.

Yet the boy who had this singular passion for trade, and with it a tenacious care of money, had his heart set on something nobler than a plentiful store of pelf. When, "by little and little," his original penny had swollen to some shillings, he invests it all in a purchase that can yield no return but poetry and devotion,—the two things one would least expect to find dwelling in the same heart with this marvellous love of traffic. You see the little merchant counting over his profits, and think what a lover of money he will be. You then see him making haste to exchange it for 'Wesley's Hymns;' and as he eagerly clasps his new purchase, you are ready to think that it, also, is to sell and get gain. But, no; it is to read, and learn, and sing. And lo! with this possession, he feels himself "a rich and happy boy." There is something more in that young heart than appetite for gold.

From this original trade in small wares, he proceeded to deal in live stock. "I still went on to accumulate, by seizing every opportunity; such as buying a few eggs or chickens, a young donkey or pig." The adventure of the young donkey so lies at the base of his mercantile character, and was wont to be recounted by himself with such zest, that it is well we have it in his own words.

"I was one day coming from Leigh, when about twelve years of age, and saw a man walking along with an old donkey and a young one. I asked the price of the young one. He said, Two-and-sixpence. I tried to see if he would take less; but finding he would not, got a cord, put it round his neck, paid the two-and-sixpence, took it home and kept it a few days; then sold it to a Mrs. Ellis for five shillings; but she said she had no money, but would pay in the course of the week. I objected to leave it without security. But here a difficulty arose, as she had no security to offer, but a pair of new stays which had just cost ten shillings. 'Oh!' said I, 'there is nothing like that, because it is easily carried.' So, on receiving them, I carried them all through the village in my hand, and said, 'Mother, here's a pair of stays. I have sold the donkey; Mrs. Ellis will call and pay five shillings; be sure and not let her have the stays without the money.' The donkey, however, unfortunately died; and she wished to have the stays returned without the money; but in vain, as I believed the death was occasioned by want of proper treatment; and by that I learnt, 'A bird in the hand is worth two in the bush.'"

This principle of the bird in the hand may seem manageable enough in the case of an amateur merchant not yet in his teens; or even, perhaps, in the tiny transactions of a village shop. But many would pronounce it quite inapplicable to extensive wholesale transactions; at least, in an age when lengthened credit is so essential a part of commercial economy. Few would attempt so to apply it, and fewer still would carry out the attempt. But you can already discover in the boy-merchant a power to push his purpose. He intends to have the money for his donkey. His neighbour cannot pay, just then. Any ordinary boy would abandon his point, and take the promise. But he had made up his mind to be paid, and paid he must be, no matter whether in shillings or in stays. Perhaps had all gone smoothly in this case, he might afterwards have been less strict. But it soon proves that the stays in hand are his only protection from the loss of his entire two-and-sixpence. That was a lesson he was not the man to forget. It was treasured up, like the lessons of other early events. "A bird in the hand is worth two in the bush," becomes one of his standing axioms. And when he has become one of the most extensive merchants in England, the principle taught by the death of the donkey is strengthened and elevated by a conviction that a system of cash payments, introduced generally into commerce, would save thousands of families from ruin, and would save the country in times of depression from those series of bankruptcies which follow each other like a train of explosions in a mine. True, he encounters immense difficulty in pursuing this course. Every day presents temptations to depart from it. Many a large and safe customer will not submit to conditions which other houses do not impose. His natural passion for a vast commerce is strong. Endless opportunities of extension open, if he will only forego his rule. But, no; he settled it when a boy: "A bird in the hand is worth two in the bush." Now that he is a man, he may doubt whether he could not widen his sphere, and multiply his gain by a "more liberal" course; but his system has been smiled upon by Providence, and he is convinced that one example of success, on such a system, may be an incalculable public benefit; therefore, to the day of his death, if you transact with him you must transact in cash.

Most of the maxims by which men of original mind guide their course are derived from their own observation. We have already seen that this was the case with the principle which led Mr. Budgett to aim at a system of cash payments; it was also the case with the principle upon which he relied for success in that difficult course. Among his reminiscences of boyhood, no single one more completely displays the born merchant than the following, in which we find him philosophising with acumen and advantage on the business habits of others:—

"I remember, about 1806 or 1807, a young man called on my mother, from Mr. D——, of Shepton, to solicit orders in the grocery trade. His introduction and mode of treating my mother were narrowly watched by me, particularly when she asked the price of several articles. On going in to my father, she remarked there would be no advantage in dealing with Mr. D——, as she could not see that his prices were any lower than those she was in the habit of giving. I slipped aside, and began to think, 'Why, that young man might have got my mother's trade if he had known how; if, instead of mentioning so many articles, he had just offered one or two, at a lower price than we have been in the habit of giving, she would have been induced to try those articles; and thus he would have been introduced, most likely, to her whole trade. Beside, his manner was rather loose, and not of the most modest and attractive kind.' I believe the practical lesson then learnt has, since that, been worth to me thousands of pounds,—namely, Self-interest is the mainspring of human actions; you have only to lay before persons, in a strong light, that what you propose is to their own interest, and you will generally accomplish your purpose."

Little did the unsuccessful traveller imagine that the very little boy whom he had seen in the shop was pondering the causes of his ill success, and eliciting a principle which would prove to him a spring of commercial power. He saw the precise point in which the man failed,—he had not shown his mother that in dealing with him she would serve herself. Had he done so, she would certainly have become his customer. He at once educes a general principle from this individual fact:—All buyers will feel as his mother feels; they buy not to serve the person from whom they purchase, but to serve themselves: the reason of this is, that "Self-interest is the mainspring of human actions;" and the practical use of this fact is, that "you have only to show people that what you propose is to their own interest, and you will generally accomplish your purpose." He now settles it in his mind, that in his future dealings with men it will be necessary that he provide himself with a case, which, when fairly looked at, will convince them that their interest lies in purchasing from him. It may be difficult to obtain such a case; but if he can only enlist self-interest on his side, he counts infallibly on success. In this, as in other cases, he tenaciously held by his early conclusion. His axiom was, that you had no firm basis of success, but the conviction on the part of others, that, in coming to you, they promoted their own ends. Therefore, he resolutely endeavoured so to construct his system that a rule should never be sacrificed to a customer; but that the customer should be told that such was the rule of the firm, and if it were not to his advantage to deal with them, they should be sorry for him to do so.

His system of cash payments seemed, at first sight, to be in conflict with the principle of engaging self-interest on his behalf. His customers would think he denied them advantages which others conceded. But firmly persuaded in his own mind that the reverse was the case, he relied on the goodness of his ground, and thought he could "show them, in a strong light," that on his system they obtained advantages much more substantial than those conferred by the usual term of credit.

Thus did he pass his early boyhood, gaining at once profits from trade and principles from experience; laying up a store of money, and laying up a far more valuable store of maxims. By the time he had reached his fourteenth year, he was an old merchant in practice and in sagacity; and thirty pounds in sterling cash was the fruit of his boyish barter. The time now came when he must set forth into the world. He was apprenticed to his elder brother at Kingswood. One would expect that he would march forth to his apprenticeship exulting in his wealth, and full of visions as to the golden days to come. Already his penny had become thirty pounds; that is, his original capital multiplied seven thousand two hundred times. What might not his present capital become, if used with equal ability? Such would be the calculations, such the emotions, one would naturally look for in this boy, as he turned his steps to face the world. But how does his own simple record of what then happened falsify our anticipations :—

"By the time I left Coleford for Kingswood, when I was between fourteen and fifteen years of age, I had saved thirty pounds, which I presented to my parents; which they intended returning, but were incapable."

This recalls to one's mind that singular note with which he closes the account of his first penny, "and I was never without afterwards, except when I *gave it all away*." What! *he* give "all away"—the boy that would carry a horse-shoe three miles to make a penny; that would trade and save, and save and trade, till pence became shillings, and shillings pounds; that would take Mrs. Ellis's stays, rather than trust her, lest he should lose his crown;—this boy give away! One would have expected him to be a copper-hearted little miser. Perhaps you would; but he was not a miser, he was a merchant. His passion was for trade, not for gold. The joy of the miser is a great hoard; the joy of the merchant, a successful transaction. You may find one man who is both miser and merchant; another who is miser and no merchant; and another who is merchant and no miser. Samuel Budgett was the latter; a merchant by nature, a merchant in extreme; but his soul was as far above the soul of a miser as the soul of a philosopher is above that of a pedant. While a due sense of the value of money is an absolute pre-requisite to commercial success, an excessive love of it is a drawback rather than a fitness for high mercantile adventure. The danger of Mr. Budgett did not lie in an excessive love of money, but it did lie in an excessive love of a good bargain.

It was, certainly, a remarkable combination of character, by which this boy had the keen love of trade and the rigid care of money that enabled him to gather so fast, and yet the heart which made him feel "rich and happy" when he had parted with his first bright store for the sacred lyrics of Charles Wesley, and which impelled him, when on the eve of apprenticeship, to take the whole of his thirty pounds and "present it to his parents," turning to face the world without even the parent penny that sprang from his old horseshoe! As he sets forth on the hard path of life, fresh from this filial offering, who does not see beauty and blessing resting on the head of the penniless apprentice? When he took that tempting thirty pounds which exalted him above his comrade boys, and laid it all in the hand of his good mother, it was the best venture of his life. Young man! rely upon this, *No investment under the sky is so sure as a parent's blessing*. Temporal welfare is made over to the dutiful son, by "the first commandment with promise." Show me the young man whose hat has lost its nap, whose coat is dim and bare, whose gloves are far worn, who walks when his comrades ride, who entertains no one, who sees few sights, who never has a spare shilling, but whose mother at home, every now and then, drops a tear over new tokens of his self-denial; and far, far rather would I purchase the prospects of that young man, than of one whose hat is bright, his coat new, his gloves spruce, who can jaunt to-day and entertain to-morrow, but whose mother, when neighbours inquire for her boy, says he was well when last she heard, hiding in the solitude of her aching heart how long it is since a letter came.

What, then, were the natural elements, and what the early influence from home, from religion, from school, or from early associations and occurrences, that went to form the character of this remarkable boy?

CHAPTER III.

THE BASIS OF CHARACTER.

"In every work that he began . . . . . . he did it with all his heart and prospered."
2 CHRON. xxxi. 21.

THE chief causes that unite to give a man the stamp which the world calls his character, are, natural qualities, parental and family influence, school training, early adventures and associates, and above all, religious impressions. The last none can ever trace except the man himself; but they modify the other constituents of character with a power limited only by their own intensity.

As to natural qualities, the most prominent feature in Mr. Budgett's case has been already dwelt upon, namely, his commercial genius. A swift intuition of character and of probabilities was the most obvious source of his power. With a rapidity almost incredible he read a man or unravelled a complex set of circumstances. He soon acquired great confidence in this intuition, seldom hesitating to act upon it either as to an individual or as to a transaction. And all his friends would closely watch that man whom his first glance distrusted, and would prosecute hopefully that transaction which he declared promising.

With this faculty was most happily combined an uncommon logical power of tracing out in strict sequence, step by step, the probable result of a chain of circumstances. He could arrange, in his own mind, beforehand, the separate turns and details of a negotiation; and put down on paper the points that weighed on this side and those that weighed on that, and then mark precisely the line where he could act with advantage. I have had before me a calculation of this kind, made late in life, which remarkably shows that though always ready to act upon his rapid intuition when circumstances compelled him so to do, he was equally disposed, when opportunity allowed, to forecast every step he took. In fact so far did he carry the latter habit, that he never issued from his library for a day's duty without having arranged on paper all the steps to be taken that day; and never went to converse on any important matter, without having noted down the points to be raised. In thus checking and disciplining intuition, often lies the difference between a wise man and a rash one. A man finds that often his first impressions prove correct, and his first impulses right. He also sometimes finds that when he has allowed subsequent consideration to reverse his first impression, or subsequent persuasion to check his first impulse, he was wrong. He thence concludes that he is always right in his first impressions and first impulses. "I never am dissuaded from my own judgment but I repent of it afterwards," is his sage reflection; and on he goes, following his own judgment alone, till, at the end of life, he and his judgment have made a pitiful career. If you are at all inclined to think you have a good portion of sense, I would strongly advise you not to take it for granted. True, you may have at hand several instances in which you were right. But some of us have a better memory for the cases in which we are right than for those in which we are wrong. Take the wisest man you know; and when you find your opinion differing from his, *do not forget the fact.* Watch how that matter turns out.

If you find that you are generally right in such cases, then begin humbly to believe that God has given you a fair understanding as one of the talents for which you must account. But if you find you were wrong, first make the full deduction necessary from your self-confidence, and then try and find out what beguiled you, that you may take a juster view at a future time. Again, when great events occur about which you are much excited, either in the family, the business, the church, or the state, *remember the side you took, and the anticipations you formed when the matter was yet undecided.* Then when the issue is known, test your judgment by facts. Be honest: see whether you are right three times out of four; and if not, be very humble; but if so, be humble still, yet hopeful that when you have deliberately judged you are probably not far wrong. You have often met with people who, happen what will, always say, "I knew that would be it." Happy prophets they! whose foresight is always paulo-post-future. If you have, or think you have, a strong intuition, take care! Genuine intuition is allied to foresight; but even such an intuition must only have a limited sway. If left absolute, it overrides all the faculties of mind, all the opportunities of life; if reduced by check, restraint, and counsel to a limited sway, it may reign with vast advantage. Mr. Budgett's intuition was trained by caution and forecast till it was fit to be trusted.

He had also, in the highest degree, the power to concentrate his attention on one point. He cared not how rapid the succession of his engagements might be. He would go through as many as you pleased; but pass to a new one he would not while the one in hand was incomplete. No sooner was this dismissed than out came his quick "now what is the next thing?" but of the "next thing" he never thought till the former one was finished. This rapid discernment, this power of forecasting, this fixity of attention on one thing, seem to constitute the chief *intellectual* features of his mercantile ability.

That ability was under the constant impulse of an invincible desire to act and to succeed. He seemed born under a decree to *do*. Doing, doing, ever doing, his nature seemed to abhor an idleness, more than the "Nature" of the old philosophers abhorred a vacuum. An idle moment was an irksome moment; an idle hour would have been a sort of purgatory. No sooner was one engagement out of hand than his instinct within him seemed to cry out, "Now what is the next thing?" Even in taking a ride, he must be learning or teaching something. In his letters, he sometimes bitterly complains that he had not sufficiently improved his time; and among such of his memoranda as escaped destruction at his own hand, one note tells of a joyless and uncomfortable Sabbath,—"and no wonder, for I did not rise till half-past five o'clock."

His, with an emphasis almost tremendous, was "life in earnest." One of his letters to a friend, written when he was twenty-one, has the following remarks on the way to learn the value of time:—

"You think that if you were obliged to labour from morning till night without interruption, this would teach you the value of time. Is not this a mistake? Can anything so effectually teach us its value as a deep conviction that it is *not our own*, but an important talent put into our hands, for which we must give a strict account at the great, the general audit of all our accounts with our Maker? If so, of how little importance is it to us what may be the nature or quantity of our engagements, so long as we may secure at the last the blest plaudit of "*Well done!*" from Him whose approbation alone it is that gives real value to everything in earth or heaven."

As his intuition was guarded by forecast, so was his activity by caution and perseverance. "Never attempt, or accomplish;" was one of his constant maxims. And consequently he would not attempt anything till he saw that it might be achieved. He would not wait till it was easy; enough that it was not impossible. That settled, the path was plain; to work! and let it be done. Once set out in an undertaking, nothing roused him so much as what ordinary men would call "impossibilities." Only set impossibilities before him, and his heart rose up resistless and went on. Such was his own power that he believed every one could make his way as he had done. Not long before his death, he heard some one saying he wished for more money. "Do you? then I do not, I have quite enough. But if I did wish for more I should *get* it." He would often say that place him in what position you might he could work his way on; ay, leave him without a shilling, still he could rise. His faith in the power of perseverance was unbounded. In speaking to some of the poorest young men in the neighbourhood, and urging them to self-improvement, he declared that there was no reason why they might not every one of them be worth ten thousand pounds. Sir Fowell Buxton placed his confidence in "ordinary powers and *extraordinary application.*" So do most men who accomplish much, either for themselves or others. The man who has genius without perseverance may run the career of a rocket, but can never be a star; he that has perseverance without genius will be a bright and steady star, but can never be a sun; he that has genius and perseverance will be the sun of his own system.

From what has been said about his habit of preconcerting a negotiation and of applying only to one thing at a time, it is scarcely needful to add, that love of system was as deeply rooted in his character as activity or perseverance.

Critics sometimes censure writers of fiction for allowing their heroes to appear in aspects inconsistent one with the other. I cannot say how fictitious heroes ought to be modelled. They, perhaps, had better be all proportionate and statuesque. But as to the actual men and women we meet with here in this world of families, churches, markets, and amusements, they are very far from being a rigidly symmetrical race. Indeed, they are a different race altogether,—a wayward, ill-proportioned, unaccountable race, constantly making us say, "Well, he was the last man in the world I should have expected to do that!"—a race framed to no one standard, responding to no one ideal, conformable to no one model;—a race over which a terrible distortion must have come since it sprang forth from the Creator's hand. Let the critics have it as they will, nothing is so natural in a man as contradictions. A painful heart-sinking sensitiveness does not seem to fit at all well on the rapid intuition, the endless activity, the inflexible perseverance, the strict order, which we have already noted. Yet, there it was. You remember the terror inspired by the hot-tempered gentleman who was likely to become his tutor. That was "the very first recollection of importance," in his life. Another of his first recollections shows how nervously excitable he was in childhood:—"I remember going to chapel and hearing Adam Clarke preach. But the singing so affected me, I burst into tears; and although I cried as gently as possible, I could not refrain. My father took me up and carried me out, talked kindly to me, and told me I need not be terrified. But it had so affected me, that I was obliged to be taken home." He also said, in speaking of his childhood, "A cross word appeared worse than a blow; and beneath it I often felt crushed, crushed." His ideas of himself were singularly low. In his letters, he speaks to his familiar friends as immeasurably beneath them. Mentally and religiously, he seemed to hold himself inferior to all. With this sinking heart, he often trembled at the outset of an enterprise which brought him into the presence of others; but let them only raise serious difficulties, above all let them be haughty or harsh, and then all his tremor fled, and he flushed up with the determination to conquer.

The habit of deducing a general lesson from a particular occurrence has already been noticed, but must be distinctly borne in mind as one of the notable springs of his power. From the pain he felt at the thought of a fiery dominie, he learned a lesson on education; from the death of the donkey, one on credit; from the failure of the traveller in his mother's shop, one on the necessity of adapting yourself to the interest of others; and so he generalised as he went along, and stored up the result for service at a future day. That result came forth in those maxims by which he regulated his business course, and which he would ever maintain at the cost of immediate loss. Some men glide amongst events like sand in a glass, bearing no trace of what they have passed through. They are no wiser for a hundred lessons, no more modest for a hundred failures, no more cautious for a hundred errors. Others pass through events like waters through the soil, carrying with them a tinge of all they traverse. On some life is lost: death alone can make them wiser. On others no event falls fruitless; there is for them an improvement and an instruction in all things. To the unwise the past is an exploded match, that has flashed and missed, and is useless. To the wise the past is a steady light, shedding beams on the path of the future. Young man! if you do not learn from the things that befall yourself, grey hairs will be no glory to you.

Any one would say that he who combined all these qualities would be a remarkably shrewd man, quick to descry an advantage and resolute to press it. This was strikingly the case with Mr. Budgett, and formed the chief deduction from the benevolence of his character. In business he was keen —deliberately, consistently, methodically keen. He would buy as scarcely any other man could buy: he would sell as scarcely any other man could sell. He was an athlete on the arena of trade, and rejoiced to bear off the prize. He was a soldier on the battle-field of bargains, and conquered he would not be. His power over the minds of others was immense, his insight into their character piercing, his address in managing his own case masterly, and, above all, his purpose so inflexible that no regard to delicacy or to appearances would for a moment beguile him from his object. He would accomplish a first rate transaction, be the difficulty what it might. That secured, his word was as gold, and generosity was welcome to make any demand on his gains. But in the act of dealing he would be the aptest tradesman in the trade. To those who only met him in the market this feature of his character gave an unfavourable impression. They frequently found themselves pressed and conquered, and naturally felt sore. To those who knew all the excellence and liberality which lay beneath this hard mercantile exterior, it appeared the peculiarity and the defect of an uncommonly worthy man, yet still a defect and a peculiarity.

Mr. Budgett justified, to his own mind, this habit of keen trading. His natural inclination led him to it. His natural ambition was for commercial conquest. Such being the case, it was not difficult to find maxims which appeared to consecrate keen dealing. These maxims were such as these: —In whatever calling a Christian is found he ought to be the best in his calling; if only a shoeblack, he ought to be the best shoeblack in the neighbourhood. Again, It is your duty to buy in the cheapest market and sell in the dearest. Again, The seller must not pretend to judge of the buyer's business, nor the buyer of the seller's business. Each man knows his own concerns. The buyer will not give more for goods than they are worth to him, and the seller will not take less for goods than is equal to their value to him.

Against the first of these maxims there can be no possible objection, provided its application is duly guarded. To aim at excellence is an unquestionable duty. He that can see others excel him in his own line without endeavouring to improve, is inert and ignoble. But from what motive must he aim at excellence? Is it for his personal advantage that he may shine and gather? or is it from a sense of duty to God that he may fulfil his calling in the sphere wherein Providence has placed him; and from a sense of duty to his neighbour, that he may, to the utmost of his ability, perform his part in the common service of man? The gospel leaves no doubt on this question. To improve our talent that we may gratefully and faithfully fulfil the trust which the great Master has committed to us, that we may effectually perform our part in the labour and toil of our struggling human family, —this is the spirit of Christ. To improve our talent that we may outrun, eclipse, and conquer others, that we may enrich and exalt ourselves,—this is the spirit of the world. Diligence may be animated by either of these opposite spirits. Right and wrong may walk in the same track and be covered with the same mantle. You are endeavouring to excel; but, as you think, not from any ambitious motive. The test of that lies here: How do you *use* your proficiency? Do you habitually use it so as to *magnify* God's great law of loving your neighbour as yourself? Or do you habitually use it so as to convince your neighbour that if you can advantage yourself you disregard him? To *acquire* proficiency in your calling is your bounden duty to God and man. But that proficiency acquired, you must use it only in such a way as will honour God's authority, and as will respect your neighbour's rights. If a merchant, it is doubtless your duty to be the best merchant possible. But is he the best merchant who, having superior tact, relentlessly uses that superior tact, in every transaction, to thwart and outdo others, regardless whether or not he shall appear to them inconsiderate and unkind? He may be the ablest merchant; but that is all. The best shoeblack does not mean the shoeblack who manages to worry people out of the greatest amount of money, but the shoeblack who does his work in the best possible way, and then only seeks a just and reasonable reward. The best cabman is not the man who drives in the best style and then teases you till you overpay him, but the man who drives in the very best style and is content with his just wages. So the best merchant is not the man who best understands his business and contrives to bargain others out of their reasonable profits, but he who best understands his business and never takes advantage of any man's ignorance, of any man's necessity,—who never forgets that the interests of others are as sacred as his own. The best merchant is he whose business talent is of the highest order and improved to the highest pitch, but never used so as to dishonour God or wrong man.

"But who ever thinks about God in business? I think about God at church; but in business one has something else to think about. Men in a market are not likely to think about God." Perhaps not; but men in a market have great need to think about God. No bargain is ever made in which God is not concerned. He is the eternal and the universal guardian of justice. You never can exclude Him from any matter in which the rights of his offspring are involved. Against all who would wrong you, he takes your part. Against you, he takes the part of all you would wrong. Over all the rights of his creatures his own hand is evermore spread as a buckler. No man can wound your rights without smiting that hand. You can wound no man's rights without smiting it. See that you smite it not, for that great right hand of justice holds a tremendous sword.

The maxim, "It is my duty to buy in the cheapest market, and to sell in the dearest;" has a manifest basis of truth. It would be wrong for a merchant to go and buy tea at eighteenpence per pound when he knew another market where he could get the same tea for fourteen. It would be wrong for him to neglect a market where the price was eighteen, and to sell in one where it was fourteen. In either of these cases, he would display a negligence which, if habitual, must end in ruin. But it is one thing to go to the cheapest market, and another thing, when there, to set your heart on buying so cheaply that you will wrench from the anxious seller every hope of an honest profit.

"But the buyer must not pretend to be judge of the seller's business. He knows at what price it will answer his purpose to sell; the buyer knows at what price it will answer his purpose to buy. Every man can take care of his own interests." This seems fair; and when two men meet on equal ground, it is fair. The manufacturer ought to be the best judge how many shillings a bale of cotton is worth to him. The cotton merchant ought to be the best judge how many shillings are worth his bale of cotton to him. The buyer may take it for granted that the seller will not take any sum but one which is, just then, of more value to him than the goods. The seller may take it for granted that the buyer will not give any sum but one which is, just then, of less value to him than the goods. The argument, then, seems complete: "I may buy as cheap as I can, and sell as dear as I can; for every one with whom I deal is the best judge of his own interests." It is not always that a piece of reasoning leads one to a conclusion so comfortable. But it is not to be wondered at, that many an honourable man should be perfectly satisfied with reasoning which seems so fair, when the conclusion is so inviting.

Admit two things; that the parties are equally solvent, that the parties are equally shrewd: and then, as a mere piece of dry mechanism, your principle may stand tolerably upright. But two men do not meet as two machines; they are two brothers. Each one is bound to look not only "on his own things, but also on the things of another." You cannot divest yourself of this duty. God has ordained it, and while God is love the law is unalterable. In your neighbour you are bound to see a brother whose feelings, whose reputation, whose property, whose family, are all as sacred as your own. "Let no man seek his own, but every man another's wealth," is a precept weightier than all the dicta of the exchange. It is highly convenient to evade this precept by assuring yourself that every man will look to his own interests, and that therefore you may just gripe all that others will let you gripe. But, in doing so, you let yourself down from the level of a Christian to the level of a scrambler. Even amongst men who meet on equal terms, commerce, on your principle, is not a system of mutual services, but a system of mutual supplanting. But among men who meet upon unequal terms, that principle will bear you out in cruel oppression. A clothmaker offers to a cloth merchant a parcel of cloth. His manner, or something else, tells the merchant that he is under the necessity of finding money. He asks a fair price. According to the best judgment of the merchant, that price would afford the maker a fair remuneration and would afford himself a fair profit. But he knows, or he guesses, that money happens to be, at that moment, of exorbitant value to his neighbour. On this conviction he refuses the fair price, and offers one that would double his own profit, but would leave the other without any profit, or with a loss. The other hesitates, reasons, entreats, but at last reluctantly yields. The merchant exults in a good bargain. A good bargain; is that what you call it? Why, the thing you have done is neither more nor less than taking advantage of your neighbour's necessity to deprive him of the just reward of his labour, and to put it in your own pocket. "But I am not bound to look after another man's interests." Yes, you are. God has bound you to it. He has bound all other men to do the same to you. "But, if my money were not of more value than his goods, why did he accept it? I did not force him." Yes, you did; as far as in you lay. You saw you had him in a position where he must either submit to the loss you imposed upon him or risk a heavier. You took advantage of him. You believed that the whole profits, fairly divided, would leave him a share and you a share. You saw a chance of getting his share for yourself, and you seized it. It was not fair. It was not brotherly. It was not after the will of God. All the mercantile maxims in the world will not consecrate it. You have deprived the labourer of his hire. You have denied your brother his equal rights. Had you done your duty, two hearts would have been the better. By foregoing this opportunity of excessive gain, your own heart would have gathered fresh strength to do justly and to love mercy; by seeing your consideration, your neighbour's heart would have gained fresh esteem for his fellow men and fresh courage for his struggle. But now, two hearts are worse. Yours is contracting around its ill-gotten profits; his is soured and distrustful. "Hearts," you say, "what have I to do with hearts? Hearts are neither pounds, shillings, nor pence." Very true; they are not: and if all your arguments lie within those three columns, I have no chance of convincing you. But you will soon be in a world where there are neither pounds, shillings, nor pence.

As a regular matter of business, it can never be your duty to purchase or to sell on terms which will not yield you "a living profit." This would be to prepare ruin for yourself and loss for others. It is certainly incumbent upon you to use all your tact and foresight to make each transaction pay. True, a case may arise wherein you would essentially serve a neighbour by making a purchase or a sale on terms that would be of no advantage to yourself. In such a case, you might save a man from all the social calamities and the moral dangers of bankruptcy, and thus perform a higher benevolence than by a mere gift. It may, therefore, happen that cases will arise wherein it is right to forego any advantage to yourself, in order to save, or even to serve, another. But it never can happen that a case should arise where you may wrong another to serve yourself. This you certainly do, whenever, *to the best of your judgment, you deprive another of his profits to double your own.* Such a transaction can never be justified by any force of circumstances, any traditional sanction of "the trade," or any galaxy of examples. "Live, and let live," is a good old maxim; with far more pith and sap in it than your dry hollow sophistry about "My money being of more value to him than his goods." To be sure it is, just then. But if that principle had justice in it, God would never have laid a curse upon usury.

A man engaged in business, who makes a profession of piety, is bound not only to maintain substantial integrity, but also to regard the impression his conduct will make upon men of the world. This is demanded of him by the honour of religion. He ought to aim at two things; first, at showing that his piety does not render him careless or incompetent; secondly, at showing that it does render him just and brotherly. The one and the other of these is absolutely necessary; the first as much as the second. Satan is perpetually preaching to men, that if they are to succeed, they must be on his side. Multitudes believe him. Multitudes abandon all hope of at the same time serving God and making their way. They take it for granted, that one of two alternatives must be chosen: an abortive career in this life, or a neglect of the life to come. Perhaps not without a pang, they choose the latter. Every servant of God, then, who stands up on that crowded field of commerce, and holds his ground, and goes forward and earns a good success, maintaining his steadfastness the while, and duly remembering things eternal, is a living discomfiture of Satan's boast, that men must serve him or go to wreck. Every such man is a proclamation to thousands that they may renounce the devil, renounce his works, renounce all unrighteousness, renounce the evil ways of the world, and yet succeed. But if you do renounce him, remember that his interest and his art will be to make you "slothful in business," that he may point you out as another proof that piety and success do not dwell together.

But while you outdo the worldling in tact, in diligence, and in knowledge of your business, remember that you are charged with the solemn responsibility of adorning the gospel. Let integrity and nobleness stamp your character. For the sake of Christ, cherish these, and manifest them. Do not give men the impression that you gripe, and snatch, and peel. Show them that they cannot overreach you; show them that you would not overreach them. Do not keep all your generosity for private life. Let not severe dealings be atoned for by liberal gifts. Do endeavour to render every man full justice; not only by paying him all you promise to pay, but also by offering him what, in your conscience, you believe allows to him a fair remuneration, and to you a fair chance. Strictly paying all you promise to pay, may arise from selfishness, from a pure regard to your own credit and standing, irrespective of one generous feeling as to the interests of those with whom you have to deal. Often you cannot help having a judgment as to whether or not a transaction will pay your neighbour. Whenever a case arises where you have a chance, to the best of your belief, of adding to your own profits by robbing another of his, surely then the

Christian course is both plain and imperative. You are bound to see that your transactions are safe; for in that your character, your usefulness, and the interests of all with whom you have to do are involved. You are bound to secure a fair profit; for it is God's law that labour shall have its reward, and that you should provide for your own. But you are not bound to make a fortune; you are not bound to gain money fast; and no intention as to the after use of money can justify you in urging your profits to a point which robs another of his just reward.

Commerce is a system of mutual services. The very structure of it protests against making self your centre. He receives the greatest reward who most successfully adapts his services to the general need. Herein, commerce bears the imprint of God's great law of brotherhood. Every man who enters into trade, proclaims, voluntarily or involuntarily, that he was not sent into this world to wait upon himself, but to find his own welfare in working for his neighbour. A man does not learn to make shoes because he means to display new shoes every day, but because he knows all people want shoes. A man does not learn to make hats because he has a fancy to mount a new hat every week, but because he knows all the world want hats. A man does not learn to spin cotton because he means to heap up mountains of yarn, but because he knows yarn is a general necessary. A man does not study law because he means to be perpetually in litigation, but because he is aware that some one is always in need of advice. A man does not learn to cure colic because he expects to be always in pain, but because he knows some one is always in need of cure. Thus, you go on; and you ever find that it is the general service which calls for and determines the individual proficiency. Thus God places on the very portal of life a plain declaration that we are all brethren; that none of us is here for his own pleasure; that the true path for any man to follow, is that whereto the necessities of his fellow men most loudly call him; that in pursuing the general service, we reap our highest good; that, in neglecting the general service, and regarding only our personal tastes, we sink into worthlessness and want; that, therefore, the man who, while ostensibly employed for the public, is only bent on his own promotion, is false to God's design, false to the brotherhood of man, false to his own calling and dignity; a poor and pitiful earthworm, seeking his God, his heritage, his reward, his heaven, in this vanishing world alone.

"But, I must look after myself; that is my first duty." Are you sure of that? Suppose that it is so. You are, say, a grocer. Then, taking it for granted that your first duty is to look after yourself, of course you will resolve to be the richest grocer in the town; and as to the public, the public is not a living thing, a number of your own brothers and sisters,—it is only the rude mass of ore from which you will extract the gold. You will strain every nerve to please the public, but not care a whit whether you advantage it or not so that you only nett a rich profit every week. You do not study of how much use you can be to the public, but of how much use you can make the public to you. Then, your place is filled up, your work is done, society is a gainer by your diligence and enterprise: but who has to thank you? Not God; you did it not for his sake. Not man; you did it not for his sake. God and man you put out of the question, and set up yourself as the power you would serve. Then, what shall your reward be? Of course, what you strove for,—pelf, pelf, pelf alone. That one thing you desired; that one thing you sought after. Take it, then, take it; eat it, drink it, wear it, sit upon it, ride upon it, build it in walls, display it in apartments, spread it out in lands, count it, lay it up, write it in large books, invest it in sure banks, engross it in solemn deeds, record it in legal testaments, clutch, carry, and cherish it right up to the door of death; then go forth and learn how poor a wretch is he, who, imagining that a man's life consisteth in the abundance of the things he possesseth, lays up treasure for *himself*, but is not rich toward God.

But, suppose that instead of taking it for granted that your first duty is to look after yourself, you should reason something after this manner:—"Here I am. I have not placed myself here. A little while ago and I was not. I have come forth from the hollow of the Creator's hand. He has not sent me here to sit still; even the stones are useful to mankind. He means me to be useful. I have something to do. What is it, and how should it be done? All circumstances say that I am to do the work of a grocer. I have been taught this; I can do it best. In this work, I join with the tea tree and the coffee tree, with the sweet cane, with the rice fields, with the wonderful plants that yield such pleasant fruits, such delicious spices, with the sun that warms them, with the clouds that water them, with the air that quickens them, with the earth that bears them, with the labourers of harvest-field and vintage, with the mariners that carry them over sea, with the winds whereby they are wafted, and the waves whereby they are borne. All this is but God's chain of agencies for providing these good things to regale and to nourish men; and into that chain of agencies I fall, the last link, directly conveying the creatures of God into the hand of those for whom they have been preparing by all my precursors. Welcome, then, welcome my task! Happy it is to labour where all nature around, set in motion direct by the Almighty's power, is constantly forwarding work to my hand. Did he that placed me here mean me to do my work loosely, negligently, slothfully? Surely not; see how these fruits are made, how perfectly, how wholesomely, how pleasantly. All *He* has done by his own hand in the process of provision is done *well*. What I do, must be done well. 'Be not slothful in business,' comes home to my ear from the double voices of revelation, and of its echo, nature. I must not be slothful; God has sent me to work, man needs to be served. Then, I am here to do all that I can do to promote the welfare of mankind, and so fulfil the appointment of my Maker."

If you take this view, then you have every motive to diligence and to proficiency which ought to be powerful with an immortal creature of the great Father. You cease to be a mere appetite,—craving, and craving, and consuming, and going on to crave. You become a helper to the happiness of the universe, a co-worker in the task of Providence, an agent of the benignant Lord above us, a finisher of the work of suns and showers. You become a servant of God and a servant of man; presenting yourself to the Father of all as a labourer in the great store where he lays up a provision for his family. Surely this position is more cheerful, more genial, more noble, more worthy to elicit all the energies of a rational being, than the grovelling destiny of just feeding your own desires.

"Then, I am to look after the interests of other people, and leave my own to look after themselves." If by this you mean that you are to neglect your duties, then, with all the authority of God's command, we answer, No! If you mean that, performing all your duties faithfully, you are to trust Providence with your interests, then we answer, Yes! Self cries, Mind your interests. Wisdom cries, Mind your duties. And believe that in fulfilling your duties you are really taking the best and surest way to true prosperity, which depends alone on the smile of God. Duty binds you to provide for your own. Duty binds you to make your transactions pay; for otherwise you do not fulfil your calling, but fail in it. Duty sanctions you in taking a fit reward for labour, for that is God's universal law. Duty supplies you with every motive for being a first-rate man of business. And the question is not whether you will be negligent or diligent, expert or useless; but, whether you will work as a mere self-seeking animal, neither caring to please God nor to profit man, or work as a Christian, as a child of God, taking an impulse from the Divine Father to lay out your abilities in promoting the universal weal.

"Ah! but I don't understand that. It is too transcendental for me. I do understand minding my own interests. That is a motive one feels. If I tried to live by the other motive, it would be only sham. I must be content to say, 'My business is to do what I can for myself.'" Yes, that is true. You must be content to say it; or, whether you say it or not, you must be content to live by it, so long as you have within you that heart which dictates such speeches. What do you know about being a child of God, and feeling like a child of God, and looking upon gains and duties with the eye of a child of God, and trusting your own interests to the heavenly Father with the faith of a child of God? You! Why, you live to buy and sell, and get gain. You desire nothing better. You dream of nothing nobler.

"The multiplication table is your creed,
Your paternoster, and your decalogue."

You do not cheat or steal; you know better. That would be the way to lose, not gain. It would not serve in the long run. That is your chief objection to it. It would be short-sighted selfishness. Then, yours is also short-sighted selfishness; it will not answer in the long run. It may serve your turn to-day, but look before you. You are not a machine constructed to catch money; you were made for something else. You have another life to live,—a life where wealth is not reckoned in coins, but in the commendation of God. You will not hold up your commercial countenance in that day, with a shiny leer upon it, and say you leave such deep points to others, but as for you, you go ahead. I tell you, you are not a money-making machine. You are a *man*, God's offspring, our brother. God's claims are upon you; man's claims are upon you; immortality is within you; judgment is before you; and every aspiration you waste upon self, is a step towards eternal poverty.

"But, I do not understand these high views of business life. I only understand business to be, doing the best I can for myself." Of course you do not understand them. That is just what I said. And you will never understand them, while you keep that same heart unchanged. If you profess to understand them with that heart, it will be a miserable mistake, or a more miserable hypocrisy. No, no! to understand God's ways, you must be God's child. To see the divine side of things, you must be born from above, born again, made another being; must pass through a change as great for your soul as the change is to an infant when it is ushered forth from dark existence into bright and breathing life. You must have a new heart, a heart created by the Holy Spirit in God's image; a heart that loves much, because much has been forgiven; a heart that burns to show its love; a heart that feels all men are its brothers; a heart that, like God and like his Christ, loves mankind deeply, and swells with fulness of good will. With such a heart, your views of life, of business, of duty, would undergo a right memorable change. Now, if you would rather be a conscious child of God than a pitiful grub, moiling amid pelf without one hope beyond it, you must stop where you are, and call upon God and ask him to open your eyes, and take his holy word and search out the way; and He will teach you. Your heart will grow soft, you will repent of the past, you will discover an escape through the merits of Christ, you will find in him an advocate, you will obtain mercy; and, hereafter, you will prove that a man may diligently ply his calling with the smile of God, the love of Christ, the law of charity, the hope of immortal joy, all present to illuminate his path and to dignify his toil.

We have been led into this digression by the mention of Mr. Budgett's habitual keenness in trade. As we have said, he justified to his own mind his habit in this respect on principles which appeared sound and fair. I do not mean to say that, in the heat of a negotiation, he *never* went beyond even what his own principles would sustain. It is probable that, yielding to his natural bent and eagerness, he sometimes did. But whenever he discovered such a case his self-condemnation was bitter. Whenever such a case was pointed out to him, his confession of the fault, his humbling of himself, were prompt and most instructive. His habitual, earnest aim was at unimpeachable integrity. That his rigid bargain-making did not arise from a love of money, from selfish ambition, from indifference to the interests of others, his whole life amply testifies. It arose solely from his natural passion for successful trade. It was in him, what the passion for shooting was in Buxton. It assorted ill with his entire being, but there it was. It prevented those who did not know the whole man from appreciating his extraordinary worth. It cost him, especially in his earlier career, much ill-will. It was *the* defect of his character; and I set it out broadly, preferring that his admirers should think I have said too much, rather than that general readers should suspect I was making up a man. It is for general readers I write; and they are far more likely to be profited by the study of a real man with a blemish, than of one all beautiful whom they suspect to be imaginary.

One would hardly have anticipated, as features of a mind

so essentially commercial, a strong love of poetry and of the beautiful in nature. But no element of his character was earlier or more permanently displayed than this. You will remember that the first indulgence wherewith he gratified himself, out of the fruits of his early trading, was a copy of Wesley's Hymns; and that, possessed of it, he felt himself "a rich and happy boy." At a yet earlier period, his passion for poetry had been developed. Before the family removed to Coleford, he had become possessed of a treasure which has awoke in the bosom of millions of children the first sympathy with sacred song, and which doubtless tended to form the taste which he afterwards gratified by the noble lyrics of Charles Wesley.

"About this time [shortly after they removed,] my father unpacked his large chest of books, and every search was made for my much loved and only canvass-covered book, Watts' Children's Hymns; but, alas! all in vain. And, strange as it may appear, it did not occur to my mind, for a year or two, that another could be obtained. My attachment to it was *indescribable;* and for weeks and months I would frequently be inquiring of my father, and getting him to search his chest to see if it could not be found. My peace seemed to depend upon it."

Andrew Fletcher, of Saltoun, tells of a wise man who said, that "if one were permitted to make all the *ballads* of a nation he did not care who made the laws." But since the days of Watts and Wesley, the ballad has lost much of its power. What James Montgomery calls the "invention" of the hymn has been fatal to the ballad. In the family, the congregation, the Sunday-school, and the infant school, the children of the country have been made acquainted with productions familiar as the ballad, and far loftier; so that the latter has insensibly fallen in esteem. In many districts of the country the children of the poor are now far more versed in hymns than in ballads. The moral, religious, and political effect of the substitution is of the most valuable kind. Would that the change were only complete, instead of being partial!

The relish for poetry which was first developed by the twin genius of Watts and Wesley, never abated. In after life, his special favorites were Young and Cowper. I have before me his own copy of these authors, and well are they pencilled over. Thomson, too, was one of his choice companions. But his range of authors was considerable. He delighted to store his mind with quotations; and sometimes, on a ramble, would challenge a companion to name any subject on which he could not produce a verse; a challenge he almost always made good. To love poetry and to love natural beauty are much the same thing. His love for spring is constantly appearing in his letters; and some of them also testify how he enjoyed a tour amid the lovelier paths of our own island. Busy as he was, he dearly loved a summer ramble.

It may well be supposed that he was not a voluminous letter writer. He had no leisure so to be. And so much did he desire higher qualifications than he had ever attained, that he underrated what he possessed, so as to make writing a considerable effort. To a very near friend he says, "the want of improvement, arising from the want of practice in writing, occasions so many defects in my every effort of this kind, that it is with reluctance I set about it." From such a man we are not to expect the letters of those who have elegant or learned leisure; but few men of his own order would be found writing to a young friend, then an inmate of his family, so copiously and so descriptively as in the following example. Though we do not find the hand practised in painting nature, we have the eye to see and to prize her charms.

"*Neath, September 14th*, 1840.

"My Dear Miss B——, I take this, the first conve nient opportunity, to thank you for your hasty but welcome note. It always gives us pleasure to hear from those we love, especially those of our own household. We wrote to sister Elizabeth from Pontypool, in which we endeavoured to give something like a description of our procedure. We left Pontypool on Thursday, the 10th instant, about half-past six o'clock—a beautiful morning,—and had one of the most charming drives for six miles, through a deep and beautiful valley, between high hills richly wooded with various shrubs and trees on either side, and a continuation of lakes at the foot. Sometimes we had these ponds on the left hand; and then, crossing, we had them on our right. The sun shining most magnificently through on the whole, produced an effect not easily described. All was still and calm, save now and then a foot passenger or a little girl from a neighbouring cottage picking blackberries, and the sweet warbling of the birds, which seemed to be vying with each other which should raise the highest notes of praise to their Creator in this beautiful valley. We drove slowly, admiring and adoring the wisdom, skill, and goodness of Him who gives us all things richly to enjoy, until we came to a little whitewashed house, called 'New Bridge Inn.' By this time we were, as you will suppose, quite ready for a good breakfast, which was very quickly provided,—nice coffee and cream, new-laid eggs and choice rashers, &c. My wife, whom I think I had never seen so charmed with the beauties of nature before, left the feasting her eyes and her intellect for the purpose of satisfying a more earthly appetite; and I assure you we both did justice to the breakfast. I suppose my wife had never so enjoyed a morning in her life. She thinks the scenery quite equal to the lakes of Westmoreland. After paying our bill, we proceeded about twelve miles further, to Tredegar,—quite a different road, but not without interest. We stopped there to feed our horse, and called at the bank, &c.; and then proceeded through a very thickly populated place, called Dowlais, to Merthyr,—as much the reverse of the morning's scenery as it is possible to imagine. In the morning, soon after five, we arose and commenced a journey of twelve miles to another New Bridge, in Glamorgan. On this side we had hills on both sides, beautifully wooded, but more open and more inhabited than the other, and the river Taff all the way on our right hand. This ride extended for twenty-four miles through the vale of Taff to Cardiff; but at New Bridge we stopped to feed our horse, nor did we forget ourselves. We took our little basket, and walked about ten minutes to one of the most beautiful waterfalls you can possibly imagine. There is first a semicircle, say not less than sixty yards, and then a straight fall of perhaps a hundred. The water of the Taff river here falls a distance of many yards, and produces considerable noise and foam. When we were there, the sun shone most beautifully, and my wife was again charmed,—not in a common way, but well nigh transported out of herself. She was, however, at length prevailed on to sit on a clean white stone, and spread the bounties of Providence on another stone or rock, just opposite the fall and under a large oak tree, which seemed placed there just to shelter us from the powerful rays of the sun, which just then shone with great strength.

"S. B."

A temper naturally tending to haste but never retaining displeasure, a heart singularly open, telling out to friends almost every thought with a freedom that scarcely any friend could return and beyond what more reserved natures could approve, and a warm genial affection, open to every claim but especially ardent in all family attachments, with a lively delight in giving pleasure, were the chief moral qualities that lay naturally at the basis of his character.

Next to the qualities with which a man is born, the influences which his parents and his family exert are powerful in shaping his after course. Mothers! your task in training your sons is often heavy, but your encouragements are great. How many of the good and the successful, of the wise and the happy, trace all that was bright in their character to influences lying as far back as their mother's knee! Samuel Budgett was born a merchant; but whether he would be happy and useful, or a pest, in proportion to his talents, depended wholly on the moral qualities with which his commercial powers were combined. Happily for him, truth and grace were valued in the home of his childhood. If his parents had not been remarkably successful in gaining this world's good, they had secured the pearl that was of far greater price to both them and their children. He was early taught to worship, and obey, and seek the God from whose hand his young being had come. What Lamartine so beautifully says of his own mother, might be said equally of his:—"We could not remember the day when she *first* spoke to us about God." An extract has already been given, showing that one of his earliest recollections was connected with attendance on the preaching of the celebrated Adam Clarke. He says also,—"we were in the habit of attending the Wesleyan Chapel, and the preachers were frequently entertained at our house." The following little incident shows the moral tone which was maintained in this Christian home:—

"While at Nailsea, the following circumstance occurred. Passing one day to school with my sisters, a neighbour's children were gathering in walnuts, and accosted us, presenting us with a hatful On our return home, we ran in with childish glee to exhibit our treasure; but we were sternly reprimanded by our father, who said it was dishonest, and that he would send for the owner, return the walnuts, and deliver us to him to do with us what he pleased. This made my poor little heart beat violently; and I could only think of living the rest of my life in jail, until the neighbour's kindness allayed all my fearful apprehensions."

His mother especially was eminently pious, and her influence on the character of her son was powerful and happy. His faithful friend, the Rev. Joseph Wood, who intimately knew his inner life, thus states one of those events which pass silently within the bosom of Christian families, but which reappear, in the life of their members, in blessed and memorable fruit:

"He was about nine years of age, when one day, in passing his mother's door, he heard her engaged in earnest prayer for her family, and for himself by name. He thought 'My mother is more earnest that I should be saved than I am for my own salvation.' In that hour he became decided to serve God, and the impression then made was never effaced."

Happy that son, whose heart is daily moved towards the ways of God by a mother's holy walk, and whose salvation is the daily burthen of a mother's fervent prayer! And happy that mother, whose son does not steal his heart against her solicitude! "It was early," many a mother would perhaps think, "to be concerned about the conversion of a good, well-conducted boy,—when he was only nine." Perhaps, had you been much concerned for the conversion of your boy when he was good and well-conducted, he might have been good and well-conducted still. "It is early," many a son will probably think, "to be anxious about a future life, when I am yet so young." Perhaps, if you defer now because it is too early, you will in a few years abandon the thought altogether because it is too late.

His religious feelings thus began at the door of his mother's chamber. They were soon strengthened by her recitals of the scenes that passed in the chamber of a dying neighbour. After they had removed to Coleford, he says:—

"The first thing I remember here was the death of a poor woman, named Betty Coles, who died very happy, in a small house just by the chapel. During her illness, my mother frequently visited her; and such was the effect of my mother's description, from time to time, of her happy experience and death, that I felt an ardent desire to lie down and die by her side. And I shall never forget the solemn delight I felt, on the calm summer evenings, walking in a field near the house, called Ashol, repeating the hymn, 'Ah, lovely appearance of death!' until my mind became so enraptured, that death, of all things, appeared the most desirable."

Doubtless, this good mother acquired far more moral power over the heart of her son, by the interest he saw her take in the dying woman, than she could have done by the most systematic teaching, alone. And doubtless, too, she drew his young heart towards the future with far greater effect, by telling him all that was passing in the happy soul of Betty Coles, than she could have done by any amount of dissertation on death and eternity. Living things teach the best lessons. It is singular, that when men are descending the graveward slope of life's hill, they are not near so alive to the closing scene as when they were on the sunny side, amid the morning beams and the morning flowers, pressing up to enjoy the summit. Death generally recedes from the thoughts as it comes nearer to the frame. Take care that you do not count upon being more alive to your latter end as it approaches. Young hearts are the most difficult to impress with earthly forecast, but the easiest to impress with care for eternity. By the statement just quoted, we see that young as Samuel was, his heart already warmed towards the joys that lie beyond the forbidding bourne of death. The faith with which his mother spoke of the better country, the peace wherewith Betty Coles approached its unseen shore, the rapt music in which Charles Wesley dwells on the Christian's release, all combined, as instruments in the holy Hand that was, even now, linking his life with immortality, to divest the grave of its fear by unfolding the bliss to which it admits the believer. It was hardly to be thought, that the little merchant, whom we saw in the last chapter buying, and selling, and getting gain with such precocious shrewdness, would be found, "on the calm summer evening, walking in the fields with solemn delight," and repeating these enchanting lines:—

"How blest is our brother, bereft
Of all that could burden his mind!
How easy the soul that has left
This wearisome body behind!
Of evil incapable, thou,
Whose relics with envy I see,
No longer in misery now,
No longer a sinner like me.

"The lids he so seldom could close,
By sorrow forbidden to sleep,
Seal'd up in their mortal repose,
Have strangely forgotten to weep:
The fountains can yield no supplies,
These hollows from water are free;
The tears are all wiped from these eyes,
And evil they never shall see."

This feeling, in which poetry and religion mingle, seems to have been familiar to him in those early days; for he speaks of being much affected by "the fall of the leaf, when his sisters would walk up and down, and repeat verses taught them by their mother." Around the memory of that mother all his early recollections of a sacred kind appear to centre. It is always a dreary day at home, when a mother's chamber is darkened, when the children may not enter, and those that go in and out tread lightly, and speak in under-tone. After such an anxious day, this boy, whose mother was so worthy to be loved, went to rest full of the dread that she was near her end. It was a dark winter's night; and most of us can imagine the feelings of such a child.

"On the following morning," he says, "between three and four o'clock, my mother was so much worse that she was supposed to be almost, if not quite, dying. The physician had been previously sent for, and he pronounced her to be in so precarious a state, that her friends thought that would be the last morning of her life. My father, in great distress, sent hastily for me, while he saddled old Bob, and catching up one of his own gaiters, and putting one on each of my legs, sent me off in the dark (for it was winter) to Mells, a distance of three miles—a most solitary ride—for Mr. Allens, the surgeon, to come immediately. On my way back, I shall never forget the impression made on my mind, (when a little bird commenced singing a cheerful note, as I rode by Mells Park), that, in answer to my prayers, God would restore my mother. My heart was filled with gratitude, and from that time I never doubted her recovery; and I went home exclaiming, 'Sister Betsey, mother will get well!' 'What makes you think so?' 'Oh! I know it, because God has heard our prayers, and will answer them; and I have not had a doubt of it since I came by Mells Park this morning.'"

He had gone to sleep full of the thought that his good mother was in danger. In the dark of the winter morning he is awoke: even then he must hasten away for the last available aid. How that little heart must have swelled and beat, as he set forth on his dark and solitary ride! And now the errand is done. He is on his way home. What news awaits him there? All his thoughts rise up to Him who alone can help in such dark and cloudy days. His mother's God is above him; his mother's God is tender; He hears prayer; and He can infallibly restore. He is passing by the Park at Mells, and praying as he goes. The silence, that has aided his sorrow and his abstraction, is broken. A little bird lifts up its voice, and sings. Sweet and welcome note! That music in the creation seems to testify of mercy in the Creator. His struggling prayer gains confidence. He trusts in the tender mercy of the Lord. Joy fills his young heart;—ay, joy, on that cold, weary, winter morning, with his mother at the point of death. It is no natural flush, no passing glow, but a strange and sacred joy that carries a message in it. The Comforter has come. God has heard his prayer: he is sure it is so. He is happy as to his mother's lot, and happy as to his own soul. He returns proclaiming his confidence. The issue establishes his faith.

That was a memorable morning to him. Throughout life, he *always* thought that then, for the first time, he tasted the joy of acceptance with God. After his mother's recovery, one day, in walking with her, he told her of his morning prayer by Mells Park, of the persuasion that she would recover, and the sense of peace with God, which then were given to him. She returned home full of a mother's hope, and said to some of the family, "My dear Samuel will, if spared, be made a great blessing. In conversing with him, I have been profited and humbled. Although young in years, he is a companion for age as well as youth."

"Slender ground," many mothers would say, "to found hopes of future character upon,—anything that passes in the mind of a child of nine or ten!" So *you* think, in the mind of whose children no such things are likely to pass. You whose little ones never overheard you pleading in your chamber that the God of love would lead their hearts to Him; never saw you frequenting the deathbed of poor neighbours; never stood by your knee to hear how one whose person they knew was going down to the grave, and rejoicing to go. Why, it is natural that *you* should think lightly of fruits which you take no pains to cultivate. But, however you may judge of religious feeling in the mind of so young a child, Samuel Budgett, when quite as experienced in the world as you—as shrewd, as clear-sighted, and as practical—looked back on his morning ride by the park at Mells, as a luminous point, which shed forward a stream of brightness on all his onward way.

"But how gloomy for a boy thus to have his thoughts filled with things eternal and infinite!" Gloomy, you say; ah! then, your own boyhood knew no such experience, or you would have cried, "It is not gloomy, but surpassingly glorious." Suppose that Mr. Paxton had a son at school, would it be gloomy for him to be taken from his tops and marbles, and introduced to the radiant microcosm where his father's genius gathers under its shining wings the assembled offspring of all the nations? As that scene opened on his eyes, would not tops and marbles be all forgotten, and the joys of his young heart gush again, to think, "And this was built by my father?" And they who think piety in youth is like sackcloth covering health and bloom, little know how gloriously the soul of a boy expands and soars, when he feels himself free of two worlds,—possessor of the present, heir of the eternal. When the eye of faith, newly opened within him, gazes on that better country, with its objects showing indistinctly amid depths of light, he feels himself launched upon a new life, as far exceeding his former life in joy and grandeur, as, to a warm-hearted son of the architect, the crystal palace would exceed his playground at school. Youth is the time for joy; but the joy of youth is only a pent-up, though pregnant, bud, till it has felt the beams of wonder and gladness which flow from the world-saving work of Christ, and from the Father's adopting love. Then, only then, it bursts into full and glowing flower. Ye that have let youth pass, and do not yet know the Saviour, you have slept too long. The sunrise is past; you will never see that glorious sight now. But the day is not over yet. The sun is not set. You cannot recall the morn, nor look upon the early light, amid morning flowers, and dew, and music of birds; but the sun is still in the heaven; up, and behold him, before he goes down. "The night cometh."

It was to be expected that with such a parentage as his, with such religious emotions, and with a heart naturally warm, Samuel would have family affections uncommonly ardent. In him, these affections acted on a practical and energetic nature. He was the eldest son of his mother. His father, much older than she, was well stricken in years. His brothers and sisters were numerous, and would require some one to open their way in life. He often saw his excellent parents struggling with severe care and difficulty. When Warren Hastings was seven years of age, as he lay, one bright day in June, on the banks of the rivulet that ran through the domains which his ancestors had owned, he resolved on recovering that lost inheritance; and he, poor and unlikely boy, "he would be Hastings of Daylesford."* When the first Sir Robert Peel was but a little boy, he confidently told that he would yet be rich, and great, and powerful; for in a country like ours diligence and talent might reach any position.† Both these boys were poor; but both had talent and perse

* Macaulay. † Gentleman's Magazine, 1830.

verance, and both reaped in the fall of life the harvest they had hoped for in its spring. Samuel Budgett, in circumstances about as humble and at an age equally tender, formed his own more modest scheme. He had no ancestral domain to win back. He thought not of personal power or station. But he had beloved parents, of whom he would fain be the stay; and brothers and sisters, of whom he would fain be the pioneer. His resolution was taken: he would provide for his family. He was not a boy to dream: he must work. He was not to make his fortune, as so many boys are, by some rich chance in the fair, fertile future; but he must make half-pence, pence, and perchance a shilling, even now, in the dull and sterile present. Accordingly, he betook him to such little merchandise as the neighbourhood offered and as his funds could command; fowls, eggs, and whatever else could be turned to profit. Doubtless, in all this traffic he was indulging a natural passion; but the pursuit was ennobled to his own mind because it was to be the pathway of his family to comfort. Full of this hope, he bought and sold, and attended the neighbouring markets of Shepton, Mallet and Bath; at every successful bargain gaining fresh confidence that he would yet achieve the desire of his heart. How far that desire may have sprung from pure affection, how far it may have been animated by family ambition, we can hardly trace. Both principles had probably a share in its origin and its intensity. That he had strongly the natural desire to rise, is unquestionable. That he had strongly, also, the sacred resolve to employ his gains, not in hoarding up wealth for himself, but in promoting the happiness, first of his family, then of his neighbours, is equally unquestionable. Without his family incitements, he had enough of natural ambition to urge him upwards. But with this natural ambition, the grace of God led him to decide, that instead of slipping the chain which bound him to the family burthen in order to rise unencumbered, he would bind that burthen on his own shoulders, and, seeking God's help, press on. On, then, he pressed; and in proportion to his burthen, so was his blessing. I do hope that some honest lad, who has set his own hand to the holy work of lessening the cares of parental age and smoothing the path of fraternal youth, will light upon these pages, and will take courage from the remembrance of how Samuel Budgett began, and how he went on and prospered.

One of his remarkable faculties was the clear discernment of *the relation which the little bears to the great*;—moments to years, drachms to tons, pence to thousands. We have seen how he multiplied five minutes, till a loss of years seemed to spring up as its inevitable fruit. So, in the waste or the overweight of a drachm, he would clearly point out to a man consequences so alarming that his hair would almost stand up; and in the neglect of odd pence upon an account, he would show you the spring of incalculable losses. In any sphere of life—in studies, in the delicacies of family relation, in guiding churches, in ruling a country, quite as much as in raising a business,—it is of the first importance that you clearly see the connexion between the little and the great. Our young merchant possessed that power almost in exaggeration, and therefore clearly traced a connexion between every little gain and his great ultimate design.

A remarkable illustration of his discerning the great in the little occurred not many years before his death. Walking in the neighbourhood of Clevedon, with his confidential servant Martha, he found a potatoe lying on the road. This he picked up, and giving it to Martha, told her to plant it and keep the produce, to plant that again next year, and so to go on year by year,—he promising to find her ground for her crop however extensive it might be, and assuring her that she might make a little fortune in the course of time. To this potatoe he added another, found also; and the first year the produce was sixteen, the second sixty-three, the third a sackful. And what may ultimately spring from that potatoe, I must leave to some other historian.

We now naturally ask, What part had the school in forming his habits and character? And it is really well that we happen to have some light on this point in his own words. In a few years more we shall hardly be willing to believe that the state of education in rural districts was, so recently, what the following passages will show it to have been. During the time that the family resided at Kingswood, he says:—

"At this time we went to school to a Mrs. Stone, at the Yew Tree, whose usual mode of punishment was to put us in the corner with her husband's long speckled worsted stocking drawn over our heads, either for a longer or shorter time, and with the foot hanging over our faces. This degradation I had twice to submit to; once for picking up an apple from under the tree, and the other time for washing my shoe in her pan of clean water."

This affords no light on the teaching practised by good Dame Stone; all we see is her method of discipline, and the glimpse is sufficiently picturesque for the pencil of Webster. But upon the actual instructions given by a successor of that worthy personage, the record is more explicit.

"I was then placed at school with an old woman who spun worsted, and the only good I ever remember receiving, was a tremendous belief in, and dread of, ghosts and hobgoblins. In order to keep the children quiet, she would tell us the most terrific stories of apparitions, as she walked to and fro by her spinning wheel; such as the following:—'A man once chopping wood at a place called Goodheavers, by accident, chopped his bowels out. The hatchet became so fixed in the block that it could never afterwards be removed; and this man's ghost ever afterwards haunted the place, and frequently when many persons were present would make his appearance, put his finger into the fire, and light his pipe with it. After annoying the people for some time, he would descend into the coalpit. He was twice laid, but still made his appearance and terrified those who attended the pit; when a number of good men met together, and laid him in the Red Sea, and she was not aware whether he had since made his appearance or not.' This is just to show the kind of tuition in that temple of literature."

"Temple of literature," indeed! And the priestess, too! It is positively a marvel that this giant English people have ever grown to the proportions wherein they stand before the world to-day, considering the mental aliment on which the bulk of them were reared. Poor children! handed over — by way of education, forsooth — to witness an old woman spinning two yarns, one of worsted, the other of hobgoblins. And the quality of her ghosts, too! They had not even the small profit of being poetical, to weigh against all the needless fears and pains they originated in the heart of a poor child. What an astonishment it would be for Mrs. Stone and her yarn-loving coadjutor, could they see the noble room that stands behind Kingswood chapel, fifty-one feet long, by thirty-four wide, and twenty-one high, with tidy forms, rising gallery, and garniture of plates and maps; and were then told that this was a school for poor children built by their own old pupil, who had washed his shoes in the pan of water, had worn on his naughty head Mister Stone's speckled stocking, and trembled to think of the fire-proof ghost who lit his pipe with his fingers! Certes, the spinning-wheel would stand still for very wonder. And how would the wonder grow, when the worthy woman heard the manner of knowledge there imparted; urchins just such as used to be in their own days—no older, no bigger, no less given to play, no more addicted to mischief, little urchins of five, six, seven, and other ages appropriate to hornbook or to pothooks, holding talk about parts of speech, mental arithmetic, and the vegetable kingdom, and planets, and Plantagenets; telling, before you could turn round, what would be the cost of thirty-nine pounds of butter at elevenpence three farthings per pound; and placing before you a map of England which their own fingers had drawn. The venerable priestesses in the ancient "temple of literature," would greatly wonder at all this; and also to see that instead of the salutary amusement of a ghost-story, the teacher should set the children to clap hands, and march, and sing, and now and then turn them out on a pleasant playground on purpose to have sport.

Have you ever spent a morning in a school conducted on Stow's training system? If not, go soon. It will be to you a pleasure and a gain. You will wonder at the amount of knowledge that can be given to children. You will be thankful to see the young so grounded in the habit of weighing and searching the letter of God's lively oracles. You will find your heart lightened to see how much of real enjoyment can be thrown into the exercises of a school. And, contrasting that scene with those of which Mr. Budgett has left us the record, you will be glad and grateful for the progress which has been made since the days of his childhood. Would that so much ignorance did not still remain to reproach the supineness of the churches!

Besides the two schools above alluded to, we find him naming another, at Kilmersdon, on the way from which he found the memorable horse-shoe. He also went for two years to a school at Midsomer Norton, where he and a younger brother were weekly boarders. This was doubtless of a higher order than either of the other three.

Life often turns on the result of some boyish struggle. Samuel's early piety had lighted up two kindred ambitions.

He would fain place his family in competence; he would fain bring the dark heathen to Christ. For the one he must trade; for the other, he must go far hence as a missionary, forsaking trade and kindred. How rapidly does a future race of gain, of glory, or of usefulness lie pictured before a boy of active mind, in colours that enchant for the time. Each course to which Samuel's heart pushed him had its own charm. Each charm was hallowed by a distinct sacredness. Filial love consecrated the one; love to souls, the other. It was a struggle which the heart of many a young Christian knows. How deeply it engaged the heart of Samuel, let his own recital tell.

"About this time, I was in a great strait between two courses of life; as to whether I had better direct my attention to obtaining a qualification for going out as a missionary, or to preparing for business. On the one hand I had a great desire to be useful in a spiritual point of view; on the other, I felt sensibly the strong claims which my family had on my efforts in a pecuniary way. One day, as I was riding along on my father's horse, so deeply was I engaged in the absorbing question that I fell into a reverie. I remember imagining, first, what advantages would be likely to accrue to the family by my diligently pursuing business; and again, I imagined myself transported to some clime as a missionary, engaged in preaching the gospel to the heathen, and almost fancied myself kneeling under the bushes and among the rocks, drawing down by faith and prayer blessings on my family; and so deeply was my mind absorbed at that instant that I entirely lost sight of where I was going, nor do I know how long I continued in that state. All I remember is, that when I awoke from the reverie I found the bridle loose from my hand on the horse's neck, and he standing under a large tree in a lane, eating grass; and it appeared to me that I had been for a considerable time surrounded by a large concourse of people, whom I had been entreating with feelings of the deepest interest to flee from the wrath to come, and to accept of present salvation through faith in Christ. One thing is certain,—I had been weeping a great deal, as the point of the saddle and the horse's shoulders were wet with my tears; and I rode home with feelings of conscious dignity and peace, such as I cannot describe; and I almost thought of giving up all idea of business, and devoting myself to a preparation for the work of the ministry. But from a fancied consciousness of my want of capacity, and my want of education or the means of obtaining it, I felt a fear of mentioning my impressions to any person who might have assisted me. I thought I must plod on as I could, and get my bread and help my family."

This simple narrative shows how deeply the love of souls had then penetrated his young heart. It brought him to a point at which nothing was wanting but a fair opportunity to make him sacrifice at once his natural pursuit of trade and his cherished design of family advancement. Even in the distant scene to which his young fancy bore him, his heart still clung to its home project. Even there, he pictures himself "kneeling down under the rocks and among the bushes, drawing down by faith and prayer blessings upon my family." Yes, and had he gone thither with such a heart, that "faith and prayer" exercised on behalf of his family would not have failed to "draw down" from the endless store above all blessings which they needed. Many a missionary has committed his kindred to the care of God, and afterwards proved that the promise to those who forsake father and mother, and houses and lands, for Christ's sake and the gospel's, is a good dowry for those who can trust it. But, to Samuel the door did not seem open. Had it been, probably the sacrifice would have been made; it was in his heart, and doubtless it was accepted.

His character, then, was based on an intellect of uncommon penetration, foresight, and power of systematising; on a temperament singularly active and persevering; on affections warm to domestic claims, eager to communicate happiness, and susceptible of intense emotion; on a natural love of trade, amounting to a passion; on a home where worth nurtured his affections, instruction guided him toward integrity and religion, and exigency called forth his efforts: on a childhood of which the great events were scenes of domestic anxiety that highly excited his feelings, or personal dangers that shook his system; on a school-training imperfect and unfavourable; on religious impressions early, deep. vivid, and influential; finally, on a conflict between two sacred desires—the one, to live for his family, the other, to live for souls,—a conflict in which not so much his will as his self-distrust cast the die and sent him forth to take the lot of an apprentice.

How did he fare on this stage of his journey?

CHAPTER IV.

EARLY TOILS AND TROUBLES.

> "There's not a man, from England's king
> To the peasant that delves the soil,
> Can share half the pleasure the seasons bring,
> If he have not his share of the toil."
>
> BERNARD BARTON.

It was on a day in spring (in April, 1809), that Samuel Budgett set forth on that seven years' journey which people call apprenticeship. He had already served an apprenticeship in his own way: for five years he had been saving, buying, selling, observing, and laying up stores of commercial wisdom. He had shown himself a tradesman of rare tact; and had he just gone on plying his own means and pushing his own opportunities, doubtless he would have shot up into some irregular eminence among the notabilities of the neighbourhood. It is hard to conjecture what sort of a business his would have been had he never been apprenticed; but certainly something unique, both in its grouping of wares and in its plan of management. However, it is not necessary to tell what he would have been if he had not been what he was. So many have written the history of things which would have been had not other things come instead of them,—for instance, what would have been the history of Europe had Napoleon died in Egypt or been victor at

Waterloo,—that it will suffice for me to write of the plain things that have been. True, one shows no depth or foresight in telling only what has come to pass; but that is a humiliation to which we may as well make up our mind. With his aptitude for trade, with the proof already attained that by following his own way he could prosper, and with his settled desire to acquire a competency (not for his own sake), the temptation to many a lad would have been strong to turn away from the tedious close-hedged road of apprenticeship, and to look for a shorter and freer way to wealth. But his haste was the haste of energy, not of impatience. He had gone to work just because he could not be idle; and he was perfectly content to forego his own little dealings in order to learn the regular habits of trade, which would prove a firmer base whereon to erect his future success. He started, then, rich in his parents' blessing, and entered on his new career under the roof of his brother, a good man and a thriving tradesman.

Trade is a university wherein every shop is a college, and every apprentice a graduate. And a very momentous matriculation it is, when a boy signs the deed which "binds" him for seven years. Three score years and ten seem a long term to the eye of childhood, though they seem but a fragment to the eye of age. Yet of that long term two tenths are already gone before the boy is fit to be bound, and then a third must pass away before he emerges into manhood;—three tenths of life's allotted time clean gone, before the art of gaining a livelihood has been mastered! Men do few more serious things in all the course of life than those boys do at life's threshold. That signing the indenture is the beginning of life's earnest work. Up to that day, it was to be seen in what ship the future man would sail, and what course he would steer; now his ship is chosen, his course decided; he is out to sea, and back he cannot put without loss and shame. Yet that solemn matter of handing himself over for seven long years to a dwelling, a master, and a calling from which he may not stir, sits more lightly on the unbroken spirits of the boy than a trivial movement of three days' importance on the man whose anxieties have become sensitive by the friction of many years.

I once witnessed the ceremony of signing indentures, and it impressed me greatly,—more than the first time I saw the signing of a will. It was a brave boy; a rough, strong, bold, well looking, hardy boy. His father, a staunch old man, was by his side, deeply serious,—his air strangely compounded of sternness and sensibility. His new master, too, was there—a bluff and not beautiful sailor, with a lip, a nose, an eye, and a voice which, to me, would not at all recommend an invitation to seven years' close company. The boy had by anticipation put on his chosen life; already gait, attire, and mien, were sailor-like. It was evidently a day of triumph with him: he had his way. Neither the physiognomy of his captain nor the cares of the future disturbed him. The father drew a sigh as he signed the indenture. Not so he; he signed it as though it had been the receipt for a good legacy, and he lightly raised his head. Ah, but, I thought, a great deal more lies on that head now than when you stooped it a moment ago! There you are, delivered up to the sovereign caprice, the wills, the words, the noonday and the midnight mandates of that uncomely skipper; no small matter, depend upon it.

Apprenticeship is a great improvement upon caste. A perpetual succession from father to son of jewellers or tailors, of joiners or blacksmiths, dooming every boy that is born in the line to follow the calling his fathers followed, is a most dreary sameness; a dead level sweeping away age after age till it is lost in the future; a turning of the social world into strata, resting one upon the other, each with its appropriate deposit of men, as the successive strata of rocks have their deposit of fossils, no one of which can ever change its position in the scale. It is very well for trilobites and saurians to be fixed in strata for ever; they suffer nothing from want of sympathy, and have no impulse to better themselves: but it is not the way for those who live and move, and have a being. It is no plan for a world of brothers; no plan for a world of sinners; no plan for a world over which a Providence watches. It was natural, as a first thought for securing proficiency in the various branches of trade, scholarship, and arms; but it was not a contrivance to last for ever. Yet something must be found to secure for men a concentration of mind and habit which would fit each to do some one thing well for the general good. Apprenticeship, in one form or other, is the resort of all who want to accomplish anything upon the earth. Each of the professions has its curriculum: the future ambassador apprentices patiently as an attaché; the embryo statesman "binds" himself to his leader, and "serves" his party; the soldier has his drill; and in all lines of art, a man must either make up his mind to lay out a long time in learning, or else to be a blank and an abortion. Men enter the highway of life by ten thousand portals; but over each one of them is written the injunction, Learn, learn, learn! And he that attempts to go forward without having waited to learn, soon trips and is lying in the way of others.

Rejecting, then, the succession from father to son, we secure a succession in lineage of craft. One man adopts the son of another to all intents and purposes of trade. The son of one man takes another for his father to all intents and purposes of trade. A very solemn parentage and a very solemn affiliation it is. The boy has elsewhere the parentage of his affections; here he is most likely to find the parentage of his principles and habits. The man has in others the children of his blood, the heirs of his money; here he is likely to find the offspring of his conscience, the heir and the propagator of his practices. It is astonishing how strikingly the conscience of men bears the image of those by whom they have been trained. If we could make all the consciences in this wide London march out before us in one great array, you might easily classify them by the family likeness. You would soon select a group of the soldier conscience, another of the lawyer conscience, another of the shopkeeper conscience, another of the innkeeper conscience, another of the pawnbroker conscience, another of the publican conscience, and so on. Men talk of conscience as if it were a determined something, like the colour of a man's hair, which depended altogether on interior causes, and was not modified by things from without. It is far otherwise. The maxims which men hear passing from hand to hand, the proverbs and the usages of their comrades, the sanctions which are conferred upon actions, the gloss given to dealings, all form a style of thought whereby the moral appearance of acts is wonderfully modified. The soldier has a morality of sack and duel, clear enough to himself; the slave-owner has a theory of servitude, according to which he is an excellent person; the loaf-and-fish parson has a syllogism upon simony, whereby it is shown to be exceedingly proper; the diplomatist is copious in proofs of the utility of "mystifications," which, in a nursery, would be downright fibs; the lawyer can plead for equivocal morals till conscience declares them not guilty; the doctor can gild ill-tasted morals till conscience swallows them without disgust; the grocer can spice unsavoury morals till conscience declares them fragrant; the draper can dress misshapen morals till conscience sees no deformity. Men always love to find a good reason and a good name for a bad act. They do not like to go on in a steady course, and confess that it is wrong they are doing; they like to stand well with themselves; and it is really wonderful with what ingenuity they will father a whole brood of illegitimate acts on some most irreproachable principle. Never fail to suspect yourself, when you find that you are getting up a great array of reasons to prove that what you are about to do is right.

Yes, ye masters, it is an adoption, a right serious and responsible adoption, when you take a boy out of the hands of his parents, receive him under your roof, and place him under your eye for seven years; to provide him a chamber by night, a board by day, a place to labour, work to do, and lessons to form his future manhood. The seven years he is to pass in your hands are the spring and the seed-time of his life; the future crop for this world and for the other is chiefly dependent on the present sowing. His whole constitution is now flexible, his principles are just evolving, his manhood is taking mould; and, according to the care and example he may have during those seven years of seed-time, he will hereafter pass a life of uprightness and worth, or a life of shuffle and mischief. He will go forth your son in trade. He will bear your image and likeness. He will be a credit to you, or a reproach. In him others will read you; and happy for you if their conclusion be, "O! I should like my son to be apprenticed to the master he served."

There is a peculiar closeness in this adoption. When your pastor does not see you, when your fellow-communicants do not see you, when your friends and visiting circle do not see you, your adopted boy has his eye on your works and way. Ay! tests of principle, traits of character, proofs of your real estimate of truth and honour, to which even your wife is a stranger, come by degrees before his eye. That which brother or wife may have only chance opportunities of seeing, he is ever finding out. Yes, while your own children are far away under the training of others, your son in trade is ever there under your own hand, up to the day when you must send him forth to tell, by his walk, how you have discharged your duty. Your character acts upon his with a tremendous directness and continuity; it meets him at every turn, it penetrates into his mind through every inlet. All things around him convey it into his soul; the house he lives in, by its arrangement or confusion, its taste or vulgarity; the family of which he is a member, by their order or their negligence, their mutual love or their bickerings; the shop in which he spends his day, by its system or its disarray; the account books to which he has access, by their regularity or their confusion; the companions with whom he labours, by their discipline or their demoralisation; the board at which he eats, by its plenty, economy, and cleanliness, or by its stinginess, waste, or slovenliness; the chamber he sleeps in, by its comfort or its cheerlessness. In fact, through his work, his food, his week-day, his Sunday, his bed, his home, his companions—through all objects that encircle him, you, you are day after day, month after month, year after year, flowing into his soul as silently as the air flows into his breast. You, you are modifying his thoughts silently as the air modifies the blood. You form the atmosphere which his mind breathes, and if the mind is to be healthy the atmosphere must not be unwholesome.

And, ye masters who make a profession of religion, what tongue is to tell the responsibility that lies on you! A solicitous pair have decided at last that their boy is to follow your trade. They have inquired for a place where his comfort would be thought of, and his soul not forgotten. They have heard that you are a member of such a church, therefore to you they confide their lad. They tell him that under your roof he will be protected from many temptations, and encouraged in everything good. They leave him with you. For a slight mistake he receives a savage rebuke. Or, he is soberly instructed in some method of dealing which is plainly unfair. Or, at family prayer he sees that his master is evidently under the excitement of the glass. Or, on Saturday night he is kept at work till the Sabbath has set in. Or, on Sabbath morning he finds that it is expected he will go out for that day, to save the trouble and expense of a table at home. Ah! far better for a boy to be thrown among those who name not the name of religion, but sin on consistently, than among those who blend religion and sin in a most poisonous combination. A poor boy doomed to be five or seven years under the hands of an unworthy professor of religion, is in the highroad to all evil; and, if he escapes that goal, surely both he and his may bless God. The man who was to be his pattern teaches him to coquette with truth, to tarnish honour, to be an adroit money-catcher at all hazards, to make integrity a convenience and gain a necessary, to invent quirks, to mask unfair doings, to reconcile fraud and family worship, fibs and the Lord's table, selfishness and devotion. The man that was to be his pattern becomes his tempter; the years of his youth, which were to fortify the principles imbibed in his childhood, sap and undermine them; and his training, which was to strengthen him against the temptations of life, has been one perpetual education to sin. Ah! ye faithless masters, who mislead and undo the youth committed to you by honest parents, your repentance had need be swift, it had need be bitter; for one human life blighted is a vast and woeful evil—an evil, whereupon the great Father of the young soul you have injured looks down with a displeasure as deep as it is holy.

Alas! for that man under whose malign or negligent guardianship the sons of worthy fathers are formed into worthless men! But joy, and honour, and blessing be upon the head of him who, walking before his house in a perfect way, invests all uprightness with an authority and an attraction which invite young affections; who removes everything that could enfeeble the hold of truth and righteousness on the heart; who ever represents integrity and not finesse as the way to prosperity; who endeavours to shed upon apprenticeship the feeling of home; who, by sacred Sabbath rest, by winning Sabbath comfort, by constant example of devout habits, and by an occasional word of warm, friendly, fatherly heartening toward piety, succeeds in leading the youth under his care to the knowledge of God, and in sending him forth to pursue his calling a good and a happy man. Many a successful and faithful tradesman, in reviewing the mercies of his life, has ever to pause with especial gratitude when he comes to the moment that placed his training in the hands of a wise and worthy master. Many such masters there are, upon whose head and upon whose children meet the blessings of a family of former apprentices, who are now in their turn imparting the good they received. O that such masters were a thousand times more in number than they are!

When Samuel Budgett set forth on his apprenticeship, he turned toward a brother's door. But that brother was fifteen years his senior, was master of a house and a business, and to Samuel appeared immensely his own superior,—far above him and formidable. Although Kingswood seems backward now, it was then greatly behind what it is at present. Of the modern houses which bespeak progress and comfort, not one had yet appeared. The house occupied by Mr. H. H. Budgett was very humble; yet it was the most considerable in the place, "the great shop on the *cassy*." This house has now disappeared, but the same site is occupied by a shop which is the lineal descendant of the former. All around were the rude and humble cots of the collier population. In the immediate neighbourhood were nests of organised robbers, who preyed with terrible effect on the surrounding country. Samuel, then, began his regular trade life in a little shop, replenished with all things which the matrons of such homesteads as abounded at Kingswood might want for person or for board. His duties were heavy and his hours were long. It was the wont in those days to work on, on, as if men inside a shop were made of other material than all out-door labourers, for whom the fall of evening proclaimed a rest. By six o'clock in the morning they were at their weary counter; and nine, ten, or eleven at night, found them there still. He worked in the shop, he worked in the house, he went upon errands to Bristol; he was ever at it, "work, work, work;" and often, when in the height of his career, has he told of the toil and weariness of those apprentice days. If he often relieved a foot passenger by giving him a lift in his own vehicle, it was not without citing times when such a kindness would have made his own heart grateful. Sometimes, when in haste, he has driven past a woman or a man with a burthen; but his heart smote him—he could not proceed; he has returned and eased his own feelings by easing the weary. He was very little of his age; he was not strong; he failed to give satisfaction to his brother; so that in the middle of his time, namely, in June, 1812, the latter gave him notice to leave, assigning as the reason, to use the words of a memorandum of his own now before me, "want of ability." To his self-despising and sensitive heart this was a terrible blow. A month was allowed him to look for a situation. He heard of a Mr. B——, in Bristol, who had a vacancy. With a trembling heart he entered his shop. He felt as it his size, his looks, his dress, everything was against him. Timidly, but eagerly, he addressed himself to Mr. B——.

"I fear, you are not strong enough for my situation"

"O, do try me, sir, I am sure I can do."

"Will you write your address?"

He was not quite certain what the word "address" might mean, so he replied, "I can write an invoice, sir."

"Very well; write 86lbs. of bacon at 9½d. per lb."

He wrote, but the reckoning was wrong. He tried a second time, but again failed. His heart sank. Then in came a young man looking for the situation, taller, better dressed, and in every way far more eligible in appearance than he. At him he looked with despair; against such a rival he could have no hope. Mrs. B—— was by, and observing the excitement of the poor boy, said a word in his favour.

"But he is not strong enough; you could never carry those heavy cheeses," pointing to some high on the shelves.

"Do let me try, sir; I am sure I can do it."

In a second he was up to the cheeses, and triumphantly displayed his strength. His feelings were always highly excitable, and on an occasion so urgent rose to nervous intensity. This, with his whole spirit, quite won Mrs. B——. She pleaded for him; her husband consented; and he left the shop happy in the knowledge that when his month was ended he had a place awaiting him.

He obtained permission to leave Kingswood two or three days before the expiration of the month, that he might visit his good parents at Coleford. A younger brother was now apprenticed in Bristol, and desirous that he too should have the pleasure of visiting home, he applied for permission for him, and succeeded. The last morning came, when he had to leave the scene of his three years' toil, a dismissed apprentice. His heart was sore—how sore you may judge, when up to the last he could tell every minute incident of that morning,—all the little kindnesses shown to him, what was given him to breakfast, and what to eat upon the way. He had asked for a character; but no sooner was it in his hand, than he trembled lest it should be unfavourable. In his excitement he turned into a gate close by, opened it, and read; and to his comfort found that want of strength was all that was alleged against him. On the spot where he made that palpitating pause, afterwards stood his own house and grounds.

Joined by his brother, he set out for Coleford. To most lads, the failure to cast up correctly the price of 86 lbs. of bacon, at 9½d. per lb., would scarcely have recurred, except to make them congratulate themselves on having got over it so easily. Not so Samuel Budgett. He saw that would never do; he should not get on if he could not tell the price of pounds, half-pounds, quarter-pounds, of bacon, butter, and all things. His brother had enjoyed greater advantages of education than he, and the walk with him to Coleford was a chance he was not likely to let run to waste. So as they walked he practised addition and multiplication on all the changes of bacon, butter, cheese, and such practical matters. "One hundred pounds, at a penny a pound, eight and fourpence;" and so on, on he went, mercilessly forcing out of his brother all his arithmetical lore. His brother soon grew tired of these peripatetics; but Samuel was not to be tired where an object was in view, so he kept repeating what he had learned, varying it, getting into difficulty again, asking, and extracting all the information he could get; thus making great head in the art of ready reckoning. As they trudged and studied, night fell, and they were yet far from Coleford. Still they pressed toward home,—the one brother eagerly pursuing knowledge, the other wearied both of travel and tuition. They found that they had lost their way. Presently they were by the fire of a coke kiln at Newton, near to Bath. Their strength was worn out, so down they sat, overpowered by fatigue, to pass the night by the kiln. Sleep came pressing heavily; but oh, those hobgoblins whose feats had been impressed on the susceptible mind of Samuel by his worsted-spinning schoolmistress! they kept rising in his imagination, and every noise was the harbinger of some coming horror. Doubtless that special ghost who had been addicted to haunting the coalpit, would be vividly present to his recollection. What with the ache in his heart, the fatigue in his limbs, the loss of his way, the sleep on his eyes, and the sprites in his brain, even that June night was long and dreary—a night of discomfort, that would return to the memory when a thousand nights of sweet repose were all forgotten. It passed, however, without any worse evil than a great alarm from a footstep, a figure, and a voice, which, nevertheless, belonged neither to a ghost nor an enemy, but only to a man connected with the pits. At length the summer morn dawned on the weary boys, and a good carter happening to pass, indulged them with a ride to Coleford.

It would seem that things at home had not prospered during Samuel's absence. The family was large, and trial seemed to be the allotted portion of his admirable mother. When they arrived, she was preparing breakfast for the children. The fare was hard: it told Samuel of straits and pinches. It went through his heart. It woke again all his purposes to lift the family up. Had his impulse to rise and prosper for their sakes been in danger of failing, that day's visit would have roused it afresh.

He started for his new situation; but his early taste for bye-trading seems to have been rekindled. On the road he met a man who had a jay; and fixing his attention on the bird, concluded a purchase for threepence. On he went to Bristol, and having a good part of a day to spare, he hoped to make a profit of his jay. Therefore he proceeded to the bridge, and taking his stand there with the jay on his hand, offered it publicly for sale. The day was passing away and he had found no purchaser. Fearful of losing his chance altogether, he forsook his exposed but unsuccessful position on the bridge, and set off to some private houses where he had an idea that they were fanciers of birds. At length he "effected a sale" for a shilling; thus realising ninepence for the labour of the day.

That spectacle of the lad standing in the thoroughfare with his jay on his hand, is one we cannot help looking at. He was now about eighteen years of age. He had been frequently in Bristol, and therefore knew something of a great town. The simplicity of his childish village dealings could not now exist. He must feel the peculiarity of his position as he placed himself there. But he had seen his mother preparing poor, hard fare for the children. He had, years ago, devoted himself to the work of making for her a happy home. It had seemed to him a call and a commission; and that so sacred, that it balanced his desire to become an evangelist of the heathen. He had an edifice to build, and he cared not into what uninviting quarry he went to find even one stone to lay at its foundation. Perhaps there was not in England another lad of his age and circumstances who would not have been ashamed to place himself on that bridge to make a few pence by selling a bird, even though urged by the most sacred family claims. Yet our potentates of the press would be more apt to dwell upon a brilliant pirouette of a ballet dancer, a successful quaver of a cantatrice, a happy couplet, a brilliant metaphor, a glowing peroration, or a flashy jest! Any bright trait of talent—albeit disjoined from every worthy purpose and every sacred application, any sparkling of genius—albeit the man who sparkles wallows at the same time and is foul, any blaze of the wonderful—albeit he who astounds never ennobles his own life or ameliorates the lot of others, is welcomed with devotion by the literati, and proclaimed in chimes of eulogy. But a boy whose purpose to do good for his father's house pushes on his heart till he forgets youthful pride and braves the eye of all, is just acknowledged to do a feat, but a feat in which the comical would, in their sight, overlay the noble. Well, so be it. Yet we would rather be writing here of that lad and his jay, than of all the Siddonses, Malibrans, and such like comets of your fashionable hemisphere. Ay, and in his exposure of himself to personal fatigue and shame that he might begin the good work whereon he had set his heart, we would see a worthier theme of commendation than in the play of gorgeous genius linked only with objects useless or unwise.

The jay sold, he next morning repaired to the house of Mr. B——. Here he was very successful. His master soon knew his value, and his mistress treated him with the greatest kindness. Of these worthy people (the latter of whom still lives), he always spoke with gratitude. When he had spent about six months with them, his brother became desirous to recall him to his service. To this Mr. B—— strongly objected, alleging that as his brother dismissed him he could not possibly have any claim. He was very warm upon the point, and offered Samuel an "advancing salary" if he would only stay. But his brother told him that it was his *duty* to serve out his time. This decided him. He gave up his salary in Bristol and returned to Kingswood to complete the three years and more of the apprenticeship which remained.

I do not know whether it was in this second apprenticeship or in the first, that, by some means, he became possessed of fifteen shillings. Two of his sisters had come into Bristol and begun business, and he went to a coalpit, and laid out all his fifteen shillings in coals for them: thus a second time, when he had saved a little, he "gave it all away." In fact his two passions for gathering and giving followed him in all things, both great and small. He soon became a favourite with the customers of the shop. He put so much heart into his attentions, and had, withal, such address in his mode of serving them, that many imagined they got better weight from him than from any one else. Many of the good women would wait long till he was at liberty to execute their orders; and as many of the cottages have gardens attached to them, it was not uncommon for his friends to bring him presents of apples. Here, again, his economy and his generosity came in. He would not eat the apples; they were too valuable, he thought, to waste upon himself, so they were all carefully stored, and regularly sent to a pious widowed aunt residing in Bristol. When she died, he did not appoint himself her heir in respect of the apples, but voted another friend into that privilege.

During this time his Sundays were welcome days. The first dawn of improvement on Kingswood had come with Whitefield and Wesley. Their words had been wonderful to the rude, bad men of the neighbourhood; and on not a few the effect had been wonderful too. Many an evil life had been fashioned anew, and many a wretched home lighted up with the charities and the joys of pure religion. Whitefield had built a tabernacle; Wesley had founded a school. Each had been a light to the place. Adjoining the school, was a chapel; and there it was the wont of Samuel Budgett, in his apprentice days, to repair each Sunday morning, with a mind eager for every beam of intellectual light, with a heart hungry for every crumb of spiritual food. For the week his intellect had been doomed to dearth; and no week ever passes but it brings the soul temptations. On the Sabbath morning, his intellect gasped for knowledge, his soul gasped for grace. To him, a sermon was indeed a repast, a banquet, a festival. Oh, ye preachers, did ye only know what hungry minds and hungry souls go to you each Lord's-day and look up to be fed, it would both stir you to search for wholesome bread, and encourage you in dispensing what you bring! Often, often when Samuel had heard a sermon, he would put his fingers in his ears to exclude every sound that might drive away one thought from his memory, and hurrying from the chapel, would not stop till he had reached an old quarry that lay behind their house. Here were scattered about some pieces of "slag," from abandoned "spelter" or zinc works. On one of these pieces of slag he would seat himself, and with eager joy lay up for future recollection every important point of the discourse. He would then turn to his hymn-book, and to a volume of the Methodist Magazine; and from one or other of these would commit to memory some passage every Sunday without exception,—something that might serve both to yield him good thoughts during the week, and to relieve the hunger he continually felt for mental food. Sometimes, as he sat on the piece of slag and looked around on the old waste quarry, he wondered if any of those places would ever belong to him. Afterwards his own shrubbery flourished over the site of the quarry, and some blocks of the slag garnished the edge of a piece of water in his grounds.

On a fragment of paper which has survived his destruction of his memoranda, I find a few sentences evidently belonging to a date about the close of his apprenticeship, in which his eagerness for improvement breaks out strongly: "My time is flown, and I am what I *am*, instead of being what I might have been. My object, now, is to regain as far as possible what I have lost, and to obtain all that is attainable. My question now is, how shall I become what I *may* be? Shall I not do better, as I am single, to remain so for the present, and to keep my eye singly directed to the attainment of religious and useful knowledge? O wisdom! O knowledge! The very expressions convey ideas so delightful to my mind that I am ready to leap out *and fly;* for why should my ideas always be confined within the narrow compass of our shop walls."

Yes, why indeed? In whatever department of labour Providence may assign to man his task, he has within him the mind which is open to the infinite and destined to the eternal. It is ever there, capable of expansion, growth, and fruit, although it may be benumbed and frozen by the cares and toils of earth. All minds should have food; for the soul to be without knowledge is not good; and they whose calling places them amid the bustle of commerce in its lower and more hurrying walks, require, as much as any class of men on earth, the refreshment and the elevation which knowledge, fitly sought and judiciously selected, is calculated to bestow. But, in the aspirations of Samuel Budgett quoted above, we certainly have not the mawkish longing of a would-be intellectual for amusing books instead of fatiguing business. We have there the honest outcry of a mind which by innate energy must work, for material to work upon.

There are two things which, to look upon, are very uncomely. The one, a man who has risen in the world, and as he rose has improved his attire, improved his abode, improved his fare, improved his furniture, improved his children, improved his servants, improved his circle of friends, but has never improved his mind. There it is, the same mind precisely in fine broadcloth and "velvet hat," that it was in fustian and paper cap; the same mind with a carriage and pair that it was with heavy clogs; the same mind with silver services and champagne and venison, that it was with pewter and cheese and ale; the same mind with daughters that can play Handel and read Racine, that it would have been with daughters who never touched a key or opened a grammar; the same mind with circles of educated friends, who value his sense and worth despite the remnants of the outlandish, as it was with friends whose talk was a dialect of other days and all on themes intimate to the village.

Now, that kind of spectacle is beyond doubt most particularly uncomely. You never see it without feeling your temper a little tried. In the name of common sense and common propriety, why did not the man, when he saw that Providence was lifting him up in society, take a little pains to fit himself for his new position, as he did to fit everything about him for it? He would not furnish his fine house with the same articles which sufficed for his original dwelling. The house must needs have seemly furniture; and it should also have a seemly master. Three-legged stools and plain deal tables would look quaint beside damasks and mirrors and chandeliers; but do not queer rough accents and vulgar phrases look quite as odd there? Do then, if rising in life, take a little pains; not to make yourself an accomplished man in letters or in etiquette, that is out of the question now, and it is not the thing for you to run after even if hope of overtaking it remained; but, take a little pains to rub off all offensive roughnesses which have been left by early neglect, and which abridge your influence and usefulness in your new sphere. But remember, young lady at the grand piano, you are not to blush for the ill-ordered grammar of papa. He is of a great deal more consideration in the world than you will ever be. You will never rise above the level to which his brave arm carries you, and had it not been for his talent and worth you would not have been at that piano, but mayhap at a spinning jenny. Honour him as he deserves, and all sensible men will honour you. See that you use well the valuable fruits which his labours have obtained for you.

But uncomely as is the spectacle of a man whose mind is behind his circumstances, there is another spectacle quite as uncomely and far more provoking. A young man whom Providence has plainly designed to serve his generation by following some useful business, has taken it into his head to be a man of parts and a hero hunter. He has some notion of the new books and of the great men who are just now a going. He is deep in Warren, thinks well of Macaulay, patronizes Carlyle, has an opinion on Chateaubriand and Alexander Dumas, knows that Tennyson is poet laureate, and kneels down to Dickens. He is versed in the Parliamentary orators, balances Disraeli and Derby most nicely, is at home on the merits of the great preachers, and, above all things, his talk smells of science. He often hears Professor Polysmatter, Professor Panprattle, and Professor Poluphloisbos, who lecture on æsthetics, megalosauri, metempsychosis, and several other things with brave names; he, therefore, talks of elements, strata, developments, oxygen, carbonic acid, and the vital principle. He is very "intellectual," and, in business, very good for nothing. He makes a great figure in discussion, but a poor figure in work. He sneers at his neighbour, who has not "two ideas;" but his neighbour has a quiet consciousness that with his one idea, he manages to get on better than Polysmatter with his profusion of ideas. He wonders how his neighbour has so little taste; his neighbour wonders how he has so little sense. He is surprised that his neighbour does not buy more books and hear more professors; his neighbour wonders how he can be constantly running after everything but his business. He thinks his neighbour not at all fit to converse with men of education; his neighbour sees that men of education never laugh at him, while they always laugh at Polysmatter.

Now, this Polysmatter is ridiculous even beside the good man who is untutored amid glittering affluence. You may regret that the latter has not been awake to the duty of self-improvement; but you cannot despise him. He has not missed his way. He is no abortion. He has done his work. He has elevated a family. He has set an example of energy. He has filled up in the movement of society the full place of a workman. As he stands there in his homeliness, even though you were as fastidious as Beau Nash, you prefer him ten thousand times to an imposture of a man, who, being called to labour at an honest trade, betakes himself to dandifying his intellect. "But," cries Polysmatter, "a man ought to improve his mind." To be sure he ought; but do you call that kind of work improving the mind—turning it away from the task God has set before it, giving it a disrelish for plain and serviceable duty, habituating it to sips and scents and whiffs and glimpses and passing tones of every sort of glossy, pretty, jingling smatter, and thus unfitting it for all sober thought and real knowledge, all deep search after truth, all earnest application to duty. Improve your mind, indeed! You are leading it, poor mind, a most ruinous course; you are spoiling its taste, spoiling its digestion, relaxing its muscles, enfeebling its joints and sinews, and making it fit neither for books nor business—a sheer wreck of dissipation. You are just doing with your mind what a man would do with his body, if, under pretext of improving it, he set to and learned the names of all the most celebrated pastry-cooks, made acquaintance with all the tastiest dishes, all the richest wines, all the best spicery, and fed himself with scraps of dainty confectionery and scents of perfumery. He might be a great connoisseur, might have a deal to say, and might enjoy the thing for a while; but his poor body would soon be unfit for any purpose for which God ever sent a man into the world. This is quite the case with the mind of a man who, having little time to read, sets up for a *savant*, and runs about tasting literary confectionery, instead of taking some substantial food, eating it, digesting it, absorbing it into his own frame, and deriving from it both vivacity and force.

Many who pretend to be improving their mind are not

only dissipating it, but debasing it. Improving it! what do they introduce to it by way of improving it, forsooth? Fiction, nonsense, trifle, trash, intrigue, the vices in court dress. If their mind is to be improved by that, it must be bad indeed. No, no; it is idle to say that the things which many read are read from any view to improvement. Such things are read from sheer badness of heart, from the love of evil excitement, from the impulse of the great tempter. For one man who reads novels from anything like a literary aim, there are a thousand who read them just because they stimulate low passions.

Yes, you ought to improve your mind; but then, take care you do not set up for a man of parts. From that day your mind is in a lost case—as lost as a garden plot in which you attempted to grow cereals, vegetables, flowers, shrubs, and forest trees all in one crop. If you want to improve your mind, do what Samuel Budgett did. Feel that you know little; be content that others should see that; ask questions which show your ignorance; set about reading something solid,—something which will enable you better to understand man, the earth, the sky, the Bible. Learn your own tongue. Learn your own world. Know not only its continents, but its nooks; not only its nations, but its tribes; not only its great systems, but its sects. Learn history, ancient, modern, ecclesiastical,—any branch of it; for all tell of man and of Providence. Learn poetry; fix some of it, however little, in your memory. A few good pieces made thoroughly your own, will insensibly refine your taste, elevate your conceptions, and improve your mode of expression. Learn, in fact, anything that is real, solid, useful; but *learn* it. Do not taste and smell; eat. Do not perfume your raiment with the scent of knowledge; what you know, know it, and be the better. Be content to know little. Be content to add to your knowledge slowly. Be content to be unnoticed when Polysmatter is passing for a prodigy, and to hold your peace when Poluphloisbos is rolling forth cataracts of erudition.

In our day, the race of business men who pass through life in stolid ignorance of all outside their trade, is rapidly passing away. But then arises the danger of a race of Polysmatters. Men of sense will, of course, avoid both extremes; and instances abound on all hands, where the most useful habits of business are admirably combined with an extensive and a modest intelligence. The scholar must ever respect the man who well understands his own calling, even though, to all beyond it, his opportunities or his abilities have left him a stranger. But no man can respect one who spoils himself for his own calling by affecting anything else. But it is specially pleasant to see a man combining with the punctuality, the order, the self-reliance, the promptitude, the knowledge of men, the common sense, which belong to your thorough-made man of business, a sympathy with all higher pursuits, and a becoming acquaintance with the history of man and the handiwork of God.

It is not necessary to say that ardent as was Mr. Budgett's desire for knowledge, he never permitted it to trench on his proper engagements. He would as much have blamed him who permitted a love of reading to seduce him from his clear path of duty, as he would have pitied him who had no relish for anything above bargains and profits. What he wanted was not to be a scholar; much less to put on the air and talk of a scholar; but to have some actual knowledge and some ennobling sentiment laid up within him, that his mind might feed and grow stronger. The annexed letter, written about the close of his apprenticeship, will show precisely in what spirit he coveted knowledge.

"*Kingswood Hill, August 29th*, 1816.

"My very dear Friend,—Your affectionate letter I received last week. After I had dismissed the business of the day, I retired to my room, sat down, and began to think, how long is it since I received Mr. M.'s book of extracts?—How long since he requested me to send him a plan for keeping a common-place book?—turning to my little library, Why did I place so many books on those shelves? &c., &c. The feelings of my mind on that occasion I cannot describe to you; I believe it was something like one awakening from a dream who ought to have been on an important journey some hours before. I saw that all my powers had been in a state of dormancy. I began to reflect on your past kindness, and considered that I had not even read all your book, though I intended copying a great deal of it. How plainly did I see, and to my sorrow feel, the truth of your observation, that the mind when once enlightened, having lost the love of God, is in a more inactive state than ever. I saw that my whole mind had been swallowed up in business, to the great neglect of my spiritual and mental concerns. I considered that I had been but little different for seven years; and from your letter I discovered that you appeared to be sinking into the same state. After pausing some time (for I had no supper that night, but continued in my room reasoning and endeavouring to think on what had passed until bed time), I thought, What a deplorable state are we in! what can be done? I determined however to do something. I took up my pen and wrote down a few little things that I had neglected, and resolved to execute them in order, and as fast as possible, praying for the blessing of God on my weak endeavours. One was to comply with your request in getting Locke's method of keeping a common-place book; secondly, to write to you and Mr. T——; thirdly, to finish reading your book of extracts and copy what part I intended. Another was to get a little book arranged after Locke's method, to enter all the pieces I commit to memory, that I may have a kind of index to my mind; with several little things relative to the improvement of my own mind. Join with me, my dear friend, join with me in praying that the Lord may add his blessing to my resolutions, and I believe we shall soon see better days. Let us look to that God who has promised 'I will instruct thee and teach thee in the way which thou shalt go, I will guide thee with mine eye;' 'I am the light of the world; he that follows me shall not walk in darkness, but shall have the light of life.' Surely we err in not following him more closely; perhaps we have not thought highly enough of our calling. Let us begin to double our diligence, and henceforward walk as children of the light. Inclosed you have a small book with the index to Locke's common-place book ruled in it, of which I must beg your acceptance as a small token of my love and affection for you; for an explanation of which, I must refer you to the third volume of his works, as the limit of my room will not allow me to give it sufficiently clear to be understood. I have not written a list of my books yet, but hope to do it soon, and will send it you in my next. As it respects my coming to Frome, I thank you for your kind invitation. I have intended going; but I assure you, when it comes to the point, I have no inclination to go anywhere; for if I cannot find happiness at home, it is in vain to seek it anywhere else. I think if I were to come with the determination to enjoy the company of my friends by going to any places of recreation or amusement, though I am very fond of such kind of engagements, particularly where religion and real happiness is the subject of conversation, yet it may tend rather to divert my mind from God as the source of my happiness, than unite it to him. But for one thing I have long felt an earnest though secret desire; which is, to spend a little time with you and Mr. T—— alone, where no object but God could attract our attention; that we may, by devout conversation, by humble, fervent, faithful prayer, get our souls united to each other and to God, our living Head, by the strongest ties of love and affection. Pray for me, my dear friend. I have only one more request to make; that is that you will write soon, and believe me your most affectionate friend, "S. B."

But many who have some relish for reading while youth is warm, lose it all as cares or riches multiply. Then they have no leisure for a book, and no heart if they had the leisure. The morning paper is their Bible, their Milton, their Rollin, their Bacon, their Humboldt, their Burke, their Scott, their intellectual all. And, perhaps, that is prized, not exactly because it deals with knowledge, but because some items of the knowledge affect the pocket. A Kafir raid and a Parisian revolution are interesting, not because they display the condition and affect the happiness of mankind, but because they tell upon stocks. Ah! how some of your "hundred-thousanders" would be stunned by a sentence condemning them to read Josephus or the Diversions of Purley from end to end. Would not some of them prefer a three days' panic upon 'Change? Would not some of them almost as soon "promise to pay" the Spanish bonds as promise to read through the Wellington Dispatches? But, up to the last, Mr. Budgett evinced a vivacious zest for knowledge. As he began to withdraw from the more active duties of business, he plunged into his library, and there, day by day, spent happy hours in studying geography, studying history, studying God's holy word. In all these pursuits his interest was intense, and proved that had his lot been cast otherwise than in business, his literary tastes would have been not less ardent than his mercantile. Hereafter it will be my duty to furnish a specimen of his time table, showing what he read and how many hours he spent daily in his study.

His knowledge was not jewellery, worn as ornament, but capital turned to account. In his apprenticeship he became an active Sunday-school teacher, and in that avocation then spent many Sabbaths which he always counted among the happiest days of his life. When he rose in influence and wealth, he did not, as so many do, forsake the toilsome and humble school; but, as we shall hereafter see, laboured in that sphere with heart and success to the last.

He was about twenty-two years of age when his apprenticeship expired. He then made an engagement with his brother for three years, at a salary of forty, fifty, and sixty pounds respectively. Thus at last, twelve full years from the time when he began his trading, he was fairly started in the way of earning a livelihood and laying the foundation of success. As of wont, his economy was strict; not one farthing that human art could bind, escaped on any errand for his personal purposes. For those he loved they were free enough to go; but as to himself, his attire was the humblest that care could make it, and of luxuries all he indulged in was a few modest books. At the end of the three years, he had full one hundred pounds saved out of his salary. Here, then, he was once more in wealth; and that to threefold the extent of his first fortune at Coleford. That had been procured by trade; this by the more adhesive process of saving. What men gather by little and little, by shutting up every outlet of self-indulgence, by watching a penny and weighing it, they are prone to value and to hold. Samuel Budgett, habituated as he was rapidly to discern the great in the little, would see in his hundred pounds the germ of large possessions. But his thirty pounds had gone; his fifteen shillings had gone; and now his greater hoard was menaced. His brother had embarked in a banking speculation. It had gone wrong; and though the regular business was thriving, Samuel saw him in jeopardy. He at once begged him to accept his store. And thus, the third time, after having laid up the foundation of a fortune, he, at the call of family affection, "gave it all away."

He had now been fifteen years in trade; five as an amateur, seven as an apprentice, and three as a salaried assistant. Yet he was no richer than when the blacksmith gave into his hand his first penny. The most successful do not succeed at once. But if he had no store of money, he had gained and permanently secured the habit of making, the habit of saving, and the habit of giving. These three habits accorded with all his own purposes, and expressed the sense of a motto which he early adopted and resolutely held. John Wesley, in his powerful sermon on the use of money, lays down these three rules—Make all you can; save all you can; give all you can. Samuel Budgett's natural dispositions, early habits, and intentions for life, all prepared him to accept these principles. To make, to save, to give, he set himself. To make without saving, is useless and absurd. To save without giving, is covetousness and idolatry. To make and then save, is wise. To save and then give, is Christian. Samuel had now well habituated himself to all these three habits. He maintained them to the last. Their acquisition in his youth was more to him than if he had started with ten thousand pounds.

We have already said that the business was prospering; and Mr. H. H. Budgett, who had founded it, now rewarded Samuel's industry by taking him into partnership. Soon after he took a little cottage in a lane opposite the shop. He had very early formed an attachment to Miss Smith, a young lady of respectable family, at Midsomer Norton. But he waited for the time when Providence should place him in circumstances to offer a home to a wife. Up to that day he would say no word of what had long been in his heart. That day came at last. He believed that the good hand of Providence had marked the moment when he might properly make himself a home. After the struggles of his youth he found himself blessed with a happy fireside and a cheerful prospect in trade.

CHAPTER V.

RISE AND PROGRESS.

"Business is what it is made to be."

OF the many proverbs which Mr. Budgett familiarly used, none was firmer set in his convictions than that which stands above. He would have it that a business was limited only by the energy of its conductors. Obstacles of time, situation, poverty, and competition were, he insisted, all capable of being overcome. He would contend that every first-rate man of business could create a first-rate business. This may be perfectly true; and yet it does not follow that every man can create a first-rate business, just because every man is not a first-rate man. It is not to be inferred that because a man has failed of rising to *wealth* therefore he has not done his best. He may or he may not. But if he be only a man of limited resources, great achievements are not to be expected from him. Men who have an energy before which obstacles appear to vanish, and an address to which no embarrassment is inextricable, are often in danger of forgetting that feebler men cannot effect what they have effected. It is perfectly true that business is what it is made to be; but that very thing, so far from proving that every man may have a flourishing business, only proves that every incompetent man is sure to be always low. A book, as well as a business, is what it is made to be ; but some of us know full well that when we have diligently done our endeavour, we cannot make a first-rate book. Even so, in business, many there are who cannot rise, many who cannot help descending, many who of necessity fall, many who may earn their bread while others direct, but who only waste it when once the direction is in their own hands. "Every man in his own order." He that made us has not made us equal. Some have powers that will accomplish anything: let them be thankful; they must give account. Some have powers before which difficulties enlarge, and opportunities vanish: let them recognise their weakness, be humble, take advice, and find a sphere suitable to their actual capabilities. But, though all cannot gain eminence, every honest, frugal, and hard working man will make his way.

Mr. Budgett was naturally fitted for an enlarged commerce. The same impulse which in childhood had set him upon trading, urged him in manhood to extend and rise. While still in his brother's employment, he suggested new plans of conducting the purchases, and took that department, to a considerable extent, into his own hands. The markets were well watched, every advantage of time or change turned to account, and his singular power of cheap buying exerted with all vigour. The trade steadily grew; every now and then those in their own line were surprised at the sales they were able to make, and the neighbourhood resounded with the news of the great bargains to be had at Budgett's. As custom increased, so did envy and accusation. Many scrupled not to declare that they sold cheaper than they bought, and therefore must soon come to an end. Yet they went on, year by year, in steady and rapid increase. I am not, however, prepared to say, that the expedient called in trade "leading articles," was not sometimes resorted to. Leading articles in commerce, like leading articles in journalism, are articles set forth in a more prominent manner than others, and meant to make a character for the whole. A man takes a certain article, and sells it at cost price, or below cost price, to give the public an impression that his goods are surpassingly cheap; meaning to make up what he loses on that article by the sale of others. In the retail grocery trade, almost every man sells sugar in this way, without profit, or even sometimes at a slender loss. It is impossible to say that a man is bound to charge a profit on every particular article in his shop. And Mr. Budgett, being persuaded that he could on the whole "do better" for his customers than others, thought it was perfectly fair to gain their attention to that which would be to their benefit by means which did not involve any wrong. This would be perfectly satisfactory if the only parties concerned were the individual trader and the customer. It is altogether a different case from that of the unquestionable sharper, who offers a few articles at tempting prices, that he may catch unwary folks, and fleece them by sales of poor goods at great profits. This man cheats even his customer, and deceives him too; for he makes the impression that he is going to sell cheaper than others, whereas, in fact, he means to charge more. When a man really means to serve the customer better than he believes him to be served elsewhere, it is easy to see how he might be strong in a conviction of his own integrity, while he offered one article at an inviting price; but he ought to bethink him that he and the customer are not the only parties affected by the transaction. There is some other dealer from whom that customer is turned. If a man feels that he can serve the public with a certain article better than they are usually served, he is right to do so. But he ought only to take such modes of attracting the attention of the public as arise out of the actual advantages he has to offer. He is not bound to withhold a general advantage because it may cause an individual loss,—quite the contrary: but he ought not to parade any advantage that is not real, to create any impression that is not correct; to hold out the bait of one kind of service, while he means to perform another. The Messrs. Budgett, I fully believe, were convinced that in this point they allowed only what was quite defensible; and, so far as their customers were concerned, I am persuaded that to them no wrong was done; but as a mode of competition, the system of leading articles is decidedly to be condemned in itself, and especially so as it offers to dishonest men a bait whereby to entrap prey. Your duty as a tradesman is so to frame your method of business that it shall serve the interests of the public in the highest possible degree; and then, as to gaining the public eye, why, trust to sterling industry, to the intrinsic excellence of your system, and above all to the blessing of Providence, for as much "custom" as will suffice for your legitimate ends. In competing with others for public favour, no expedient should be permitted that will not bear close examination. Better fail of success, than fall into improper rivalry. Many of the rumours which were circulated about the Messrs. Budgett with regard to the practice of selling under cost, were absurd, and contradicted themselves. If people dealt constantly on that scale, they must some time show the effect.

As the business grew, the views of the younger brother began to stretch beyond their actual sphere. He already seemed to descry in the distance the possibility of a great wholesale establishment; but this must be reached by little and little. He would not attempt what he could not accomplish. Any sudden bound, therefore, by which he was at once to pass the gulf now separating him from his object, was not to be thought of. A little at a time; secure what you have, work it well, make it fruitful, and then push on a little farther; but never stretch out to anything new till all the old is perfectly cultivated. Such were the maxims he laid down for himself; such the maxims which he enforced upon his travellers. Under the guidance of these rules, his progress from the retail shop up to the great establishment, was not to be made by brilliant strokes, and venturesome speculations, and heavy credits, and reliance on the exchequer of others. He was willing to begin humbly, and to proceed slowly, that he might proceed in surety.

Among the customers of the shop were numbers of good women who came from villages at a few miles distance, mounted on donkeys. As the flow of purchasers was great, a crowd of these patient steeds would often be for a long time about the door, while their respective mistresses were obtaining goods. In this concourse from a distance, the quick eye of Samuel discovered the germ of an extended trade. Why should he not go into their neighbourhood regularly, and obtain their orders; so securing their custom always, and affording them accommodation, while he obtained new chances of extension? His brother was much more inclined to pursue the regular course than to branch into anything new; and the caution of the one probably acted as a useful counterbalance to the energy of the other. But Samuel was not to be held within the shop walls; he had his plans for erecting a great business, and no power could restrain him. He soon set forth to the villages of Doynton and Pucklechurch, and arranged to meet the good folks at fixed times, in one house or another convenient for them, and there to receive their orders. He made himself their friend; he was hearty, familiar, and in earnest; he noticed their children; he knew their ways, and he rapidly gained their favour and effected considerable sales.

This point gained, he began to talk of supplying the smaller shops. "Why should not we supply them, as well as other people?" His brother shrank from anything that seemed to approach the wholesale. He feared that they would get beyond their means, and wished to pursue only the old course. Samuel could wait, but he could not surrender. Supply the smaller shops he would, and by degrees he managed to accomplish it. Very gradually the range of this quasi-wholesale trade extended. Firmly keeping to his purpose of working all he had got, and going on little by little, he made no abrupt enterprise, no great dash; but on, on he plodded in the humblest way, caring nothing for show, but careful that every foot of ground under him was solid. He gradually began to make a modest sort of commercial journey; and among tradesmen to whom he would not venture to offer the higher articles of grocery, raised a considerable trade in such descriptions of goods as he might supply without seeming to push into too important a sphere.

Well would it be for our modern tradesmen did they generally seek advancement only on such sure grounds. But, instead of patiently waiting to work their way up from an inconsiderable to a respectable position, they are eager to start on a large scale, to make a show, and to rival their neighbours. The consequence is, an untold amount of unhappiness, ill health and sin. Many a man who is gasping for life in trade, might have been pressing on at his ease; many a one who is trying to keep his head above water by seizing any friend within reach, might have been swimming cheerily; many a one who is quailing before his creditors, might have had them bowing attendance upon him; many a one who is breaking the hearts of his family, might have been their delight,—had he only been content to adjust his scale of business to his amount of capital. But when a man is too proud to suit his establishment to his means, he must take the consequence. If you build half of your house on your neighbour's ground, it is no great wonder if it should be pulled down. I know one eminently successful trades-

6*

man who ascribes all his prosperity to the fact that when, at an early stage of his course, he found that he had taken on hand more business than he could manage with his capital, and embarrassment was imminent merely from the rapid extension of his trade, he had the courage to curtail, and decline all business which he could not safely manage. This appeared to throw him back for the time, but from that day his feet were firm under him, and his future progress was solid.

Half of the heavy hearts, and broken spirits, and sleepless eyes among London tradesmen might be spared, were they only willing to conform their appearances to their substance. But to many that simple advice would sound as the perfection of severity. As men of fashion enlarge their establishments in rivalry with wealthier neighbours, and thus make themselves miserable for the sake of show; so men of business enlarge their establishments to rival older and wealthier neighbours, and they too purchase show at the price of misery. Be admonished of one thing,—among all articles upon earth show is the most costly. You think the public will pay for your show; but be assured if you keep up a show you will pay for it yourself, and that with sighs, broken sleep, indigestion, bile, headache, irritability, with blushes before your friends when you ask for "a little help," with confusion before your creditors when you ask for "a little time;" ay, probably you will pay for it with the loss of respect before those in your employment, with the loss of credit, the loss of domestic comfort, the loss of principle, with the crash and shattering of all your hopes in the noontide of life. Do then fit yourself into the niche which Providence has prepared for you. Adapt your show to your substance, your surface to your groundwork. Have a small business and a calm breast, rather than a great business and weariness of heart. Begin lowly, rise slowly, lay out nothing for show, be honest, and fear God, you will not fail. Perhaps, when the man who started at the same time, and quite eclipsed you, is coming down with a crash, you will be emerging from your obscurity. But should you never emerge, better ten thousand times to be all your life on good terms with your circumstances, than to be perpetually at strife with them. Of all quarrels, the most senseless, the most bootless, the most worrying, is a quarrel with your circumstances. You may as well be wise at once and make peace with them. Poor circumstances are like poor relations; if you try to deny them they will humble you; if you take to them kindly you will raise them. "Circumstances" is but a name for the lot which Providence has assigned you; and if your heart is right with God, you will cheerfully believe that you are rightly and wisely placed, and will be content that the allotment of the Divine hand should be known.

"But so much depends upon a respectable commencement." Ah, the thousands of burthened minds which are wearying and groaning under the loads first imposed by that fair pretence! Among the gods of the world, Respectability is a great favourite. He competes with Mammon. He is not so coarse: his worship has more of grace to win the eye. His worshippers abound on every hand; yes, and he even sits proudly in the temple of God, receiving for his sole honour the obeisance of many a brilliant plume, of many a perfumed head, which bow there at another name it is true, but which come there at no call but his, and which seek there no blessing but his approval. He is a fair-faced, well robed, goodly idol, with winning mien and imposing adornments; his presence is graced with all that is ancient, all that is brilliant, all that kings bestow and princes covet; with beauty and wealth, with valour and genius. Prosperity seems to dwell in his temple and peace to dwell at her side. But he is a cruel, greedy idol, like all other idols. Those brilliant devotees worship in chains; and, day by day, broken fortunes, broken families, broken promises, broken characters, broken hearts, are heaped in hecatombs upon his altar, albeit the blind idolaters say that these offerings are welcomed only by his ill-favoured neighbour Misfortune.

Tradesmen, as a class, are as desperately addicted to the worship of respectability as young ladies. To place themselves under his tutelage, they will depart from that humility and honesty without which they cannot hope for the care of God. But, as to the care of God, they think it very good indeed if it could be had upon their own terms; but to come down to their circumstances and only attempt such an amount of trade as their capital can match—that would be humiliating, and they want to be respectable. Very well, then, be respectable, and be in torment. But rely upon it, that if, with a capital of five hundred pounds, you undertake a trade requiring a thousand, you are not to expect that a Providence who is wise and just, who loves candour, humility, and straightforwardness, who hates pride, show, and every deceit, will ease you of the load which you take upon yourself despite of his counsel. Your respectable commencement, indeed! That is respectable which is honest and sensible. The reason why so many are no better after years of toil is that they begin too high Had Samuel Budgett resolved that he would not compromise his respectability, but would at once sally into Bath and Bristol as a wholesale merchant, instead of going to Doynton and Pucklechurch, and humbly working on, going just a step at a time and guarding it well when gained, in that case he would never have looked upon the results he lived to see. He began where he ought to begin, he ended where he hoped to end. He went first to Doynton and Pucklechurch, and in due time to Bath and Bristol. But many of you are resolved to begin at Bath and Bristol; then most probably you will end at Doynton and Pucklechurch. The same good advice has been given by so many that one has little heart in repeating it; but be assured, my young friend, that it is not from indifference to your feelings, but from real interest in your happiness, that we advise you to begin at Doynton and Pucklechurch.

In process of time success invited bolder efforts. They resolved to venture on offering sugars and teas to the respectable grocers in the important towns. About this time they had succeeded in making a large purchase of butter remarkably cheap, and immediately after, it rose. Samuel therefore felt that in this article they had an advantage, and he determined to try his fortune in a higher sphere. He rode to Frome and applied for orders at the chief shops of the town. His reception would have daunted an ordinary man. They were much affronted that a shopkeeper from an out-of-the-way village like Kingswood should offer to supply them wholesale, indeed! They said very uncivil things. They told him very plainly that they could buy quite as well as he could. One man, after hearing him open his commission, said, "Well, young man, and where do you come from?"

"Kingswood."

"Kingswood! I dare say you are very zealous, but you had better go back to Kingswood and mind your shop. I dare say you can earn bread and cheese there, but you had better not try to sell us goods at Frome."

Another gave him a less courteous welcome still, and almost ordered him out of the shop. Before facing these grocery magnates, his heart had sunk and sunk again; and in entering their shops he was almost overcome with trepidation. But he only wanted this rough usage to bring all his energies into play. His spirit gradually rose; at last he said, "Well, I am come here to do business and I will do it. If I cannot do it with you, I will with others. I have tried the respectable shops, and you won't look at me; I will see what they will say in the little shops which you supply, and you shall see whether I can serve them to advantage or not." This was not without its effect. The good man, who probably, in spite of his dignity, had been struck with the prices at which some of the goods were offered, said: "Well, let me see, what are you doing those butters at?" And then he ordered ten casks. The traveller took out his order book, placed it on the counter with great importance, entered the order, restored the book to his pocket, buttoned his coat over the record of his victory, and marched out of the door triumphant as a plenipotentiary who has obtained the cession of a province. He had scarcely gone when his new friend called him back.

"I think I will have five more casks of those butters."

"No, I have taken the order and crossed your threshold, and I do not alter the order after it is taken." Thus showing his independence he marched forth again.

That day the battle for a real wholesale trade was begun and one advantage gained. But he saw that he must yet hope for his chief customers among the small dealers, who were overlooked by the wholesale houses and obtained supplies from their neighbours, who, though retail dealers, were so on an extensive scale. Accordingly, whenever the larger shops refused him, he addressed himself to the minor ones, and would take any order, however small. A regular monthly journey was organised. On his next return to Frome he did not pass one of the men who had handled him so roughly. He did not try to coax and jest them into dealing with him; but in a straightforward independent way told them his prices and showed how it would be to their advantage. By degrees he made his way. When he had got one customer in a place he would pay comparatively little attention to others. Sometimes he would just call, quote his prices, leave a sample, and pass on as if his time was too valuable to spend among them. In other cases he would not call at all; and I have been told of one case in Trowbridge where a respectable tradesman, seeing the attention he paid to his sole customer in the town, told him to ask Mr. Budgett to call upon him. In other cases, again, his heart would be set upon a certain shop, and there he would resolve to make an entrance however long he might persevere. But once he had gained a customer in a place, that man had his first attention. He was not near so anxious to gain new customers as to serve the one gained, so that he would really find it to his interest to deal with them constantly. His travellers, in training whom he took great pains, always had this impressed upon them as their prime lesson, "Gain a little at a time, and take care of what you have got." Every new customer he represented as a cottage. What was the use, he would say, of running away after something new and neglecting the cottage you had? Attend to it, see that it is not neglected, that it does not go to decay; and when you have it in a thoroughly good condition you may get another cottage if you can. "O, Mr.——, you say you have some new customers this journey."

"Yes, Sir."

"How many?"

"Four."

"Four; ah! very well, very well; but are you sure you don't neglect the old? Take care of that, you must mind what you have got."

It soon proved that not a few of his customers who had been small and inconsiderable rose swiftly. The energy of the new house at Kingswood seemed to some extent to pervade its connexion. In many places, the respectable shopkeepers, who at first rejected their overtures, saw humbler neighbours prospering and followed in their train. Some of the very men who had shown the least civility were afterwards valuable and faithful customers. The tide of prosperity set in fairly; and Bristol merchants, who had looked at the little shop on Kingswood Hill a few years before without one anticipation but that of a moderate custom from its owners, now saw it expand to dimensions that threatened to dwarf themselves.

Such an unheard-of success would naturally awaken much wonder and much enmity. To old wholesale houses it was offensive to see a shopkeeper from Kingswood, of all places, enter their walks and attempt to measure himself with them. That violent opposition, that rancours and rumours assailed the new firm, no one will wonder. It is not to be doubted that the rancours were rendered fiercer, and the injurious rumours more credible, by the exceeding keenness in trade referred to at length in a former chapter. But in spite of opposition, in spite of rumours, in spite of combinations to destroy their credit, in spite of predicted failure and lavished accusations, in spite of the unfavourable locality, of the utter want of prestige, in spite of the active rivalry of old wealthy houses in a great city, this new, anomalous establishment gathered and grew; the retail business absorbing the trade of Kingswood, the wholesale business gaining clients from all the neighbouring districts. Mr. Budgett soon ceased to make regular journeys. First one traveller took his place, and then another was added. The connexion rapidly extended: purchases which had been in parcels soon rose to cargoes; sales which had been in trifles swelled to tons; traveller was added to traveller, journey to journey, till the connexion covered the country from Penzance to Birmingham, from Haverfordwest to Wiltshire. The aspect of things at "the Hill" changed; men multiplied, horses multiplied, the premises grew. From the port at Bristol waggons were constantly rolling with goods for the warehouse; from the warehouse waggons were constantly rolling with goods to the port at Bristol. Neat houses for the clerks sprang up, and an air of prosperous activity overspread the neighbourhood.

This rise was probably as rapid as any that ever occurred under analogous circumstances. There was no new invention, no introduction of a strange article, no caoutchouc, no Morison's pills, no gutta percha, no rails. It was a plain homely business expanded; and that not in a great city, where a commanding centre was offered, but in a village noted for its rudeness, and so situated that nearly all the goods had to be carried four miles from the market to the store, and carried back again four miles from the store to the wharf or the carrier. In fact they had no one advantage, no one facility, and had against them every possible obstacle. Yet they went on.

But this progress was not unaccompanied by struggles. They had not at the first a large capital. Notwithstanding all their caution to secure their ground under them, the business had grown almost more rapidly than they could manage. Many of the men from whom they purchased were jealous of their progress. Not a few efforts were made to bring them to a stand. Sometimes it went hard with them. On one occasion an account from Bristol was sent in before the usual time. It was at once paid. Then another, then another, and so on with rapidity; every account came in as if by concert. Mr. Budgett saw that something was the matter, and resolved that, although irregular, all should be met. He made those prompt exertions among his friends which only men of his energy can make. When the last account was presented he knew there were no effects in the bank, but he knew that he had means to put in a deposit; he therefore gave a cheque, and soon afterwards mounted his horse and rode hard. As he entered the bank at one door the bearer of the cheque entered at another, for he too had evidently been in haste as if under the impression that payment was doubtful. The battle was won; the terrible answer, "no effects," had not been returned; and, now they were free to bless that Providence which had enabled them to turn this sudden attack to a victory.

But now that the danger was past, it became necessary to ask how it had arisen. It was evident that some common impulse must have led to this run upon them. Mr. Budgett was resolved to reach the source of the assault. Going to a respectable firm which had sent in an account before the regular time, he demanded the reason, and would have his reply. They acknowledged that a man who had lately belonged to his own establishment, had warned them to look after their account, for things were going wrong. It proved that the same individual had carried this statement round all the houses from which they were in the habit of making purchases. He had just been discharged, and this was his remedy. They compelled him to make a public apology. This was not the only time a similar plot was directed against them, and at least a second time they required a public apology from one who had thus attempted to undermine them. You must not forget the case detailed above, as that man will appear in our pages again.

The day of embarrassment is the tradesman's day of proof. Then, what is in a man shows itself. It is the day of temptation too; a thousand new impulses to do wrong arise and push with giant power. Directly above the great cataract of insolvency lie most dangerous rapids. Once there, the tide hurrying him toward ruin, and the fall close by,—resounding as with the powers of destruction in his ears,—the tradesman's conscience runs imminent risk of bewilderment. Many who have not lied before, begin to lie then. Many who have not cheated before, begin to cheat then. Many who have never preyed on any man, begin then to look around for a victim. Some strange, confused, irrational hope of staving off the evil day, of postponing the shame, beguiles the poor debtor into fraud after fraud, into folly after folly, till, at the day of exposure, inevitable after all, his father has to mourn over a son not only unhappy, but disreputable; his wife to mourn over a husband not only ruined, but disgraced; his children to mourn over not only blighted prospects, but a tarnished name; his religious connexions, if such he had, to mourn not only the disaster of a brother, but the dishonour of the Christian name.

Ay, the day when ruin impends *is* the tradesman's testing day. To be suddenly lifted up is a keen test; one under which thousands fail. But oh, it is also a keen test to be dragged down, down, down; to feel ruin, shame, and reproaches coming; to feel Hope, driven wild, suggesting a thousand idle plans of rescue; and all nature within rising in convulsive protest against disgrace. Take care, young man, take care that you do not precipitate yourself into that danger. It is easy, very easy for you to say, that if you found things going wrong, you would soon see whether there was a possibility of working them right, and if not, you would submit to misfortune while your character stood clear, rather than protract a heartbreaking struggle. Ah! we are all wise for difficulties that have never crossed us, and strong for temptations that have never come. But you are just as liable as another to be gradually seduced from integrity to shuffling. There are three things which most wonderfully reduce a man's moral strength,—hunger, dependence, and debt. He on whose principles one of these is pressing, is like a man of strong limb whose heart is diseased; he carries weakness within him; you know not the moment when he will fall down. I tell you again, that if you run deep into debt, you are just like a man in the rapids above a waterfall; you are drifting and struggling, now hoping to gain a foot-length, now going downward ten; drifting and struggling, with ruin below and rocks around; drifting and struggling, till quite bewildered; and casting about hither and thither, scarce knowing what you do, you at last grasp a friend or a brother, who is hurried down with you, sharing your disaster, and doubling your remorse.

Bankruptcy is a woe which no man should wantonly provoke. He that has once descended that fall, has enough to weigh upon his heart for years. True, he may have done all which vigilance could do to avert the evil; and all that honesty could do to lighten its stroke upon others. Yet others have suffered by confiding in him, and his head may well be held downward. It is no credit to any man to treat a failure by which others have lost severely, as if it were only a chance of trade, about which he need not trouble himself. "It is no sin to be unfortunate." Certainly not; but mark the man whose failure comes by misfortune alone, and not at all by fault. Does he not feel his miscarriage? Is not his heart bowed down? Does he not bleed at the core, to think that he has been the occasion of loss to any? He who, after a failure, is brisk and consequential, does make one imagine that his conscience is not very lively, or his sense of honour high. Some men seem to take a failure quite comfortably; they stop, and go on again; stop, and go on again, without changing their style of living, or lowering their heads. That is a feat which no honest man can admire. He by whom others suffer ought to show that he suffers too. And then to see these men who are apt to break down in the counting-house, come forth into the corporation, the election committee, the vestry meeting, the Mechanics' Institute, or the assemblies of some religious society, and prate with brave brow as if wisdom and strength were with them! Well, the man may have been honest, perhaps, but he is not humble; he may have had no fraud in him, but he has no sense. He who is habitually unsuccessful should be habitually retiring. This is especially the case with men who profess to be religious. None such can fail, however free from rightful blame, without causing many to speak evil of religion. Whoever, therefore, has been overtaken by bankruptcy, ought thenceforth to deport himself meekly, as one through whose suffering (if not through his errors) religion has suffered. He ought to set his heart upon proving, even though many years should be necessary to prove it, that no man lost by any fault of his. True, the law has absolved him from his debts. The law is just and good. It is well that when a man has nothing to pay, an escape should be afforded to him. But no law can alter the fact that men have trusted him, and been disappointed; have placed property in his hand, and lost it; that he has promised, and never performed; has borrowed, and never paid. It is, certainly, right to have laws which free the helpless from the relentless; but no law can annul the obligation of him who has promised, to perform (when in his power), of him who has borrowed, to pay. An honest tradesman is trudging on foot from his little house at Dalston into the city; another passes him in a sober, respectable carriage and pair. The pedestrian remembers that this flourishing merchant once failed, and he lost five hundred pounds. It is twenty years ago: the other has prospered, and he has not. Yet it is very natural for him to think that it would have been more honourable to pay him his money than to set up a carriage; he might have had an honest carriage of his own, had it not been for the check that loss gave him.

One thing which materially aided the Messrs. Budgett in their upward struggle was their system of selling for cash. That system was begun at the outset, and maintained throughout. Customers in the neighbourhood paid for all purchases immediately. This could not be carried out in the same form with customers at a distance. When they ordered goods they could not, of course, pay for them till they had been received; and that, in many cases, would be days after the order was given, when no representative of the firm was on the spot. But a plan was adopted which came as near to prompt payment as possible. Each customer was waited upon by a traveller once in four weeks. Each customer knew what day and what hour to expect the visit. If Mr. S—— had called on a tradesman in Hereford on Monday at ten o'clock, that tradesman would expect Mr. S—— four weeks after on Monday at ten o'clock. If he had given Mr. S—— an order on his former visit, the cash would be expected now; if he had ordered any goods in the meantime the cash for them also would be expected now; so that up to this moment, Monday at ten o'clock, the account would stand perfectly clear. If the tradesman was not at home, or had not prepared himself with his cash, the traveller did not call again; and no order was taken from one who had not discharged his account. Mr. Budgett regarded the maintenance of these rules as of the first importance. He would at any time lose customers, and sacrifice much prospective advantage, rather than diverge from them. His case was not that of a house which waits till it has attained a commanding name for one particular article, and then imposes stricter terms of payment for that article. He began with his principle when he had everything to gain. He fought his way up with it, even though he found it continually blocking up his path, making him enemies, and abridging his sales. He was persuaded of its excellence, and by it he would stand. Every new customer was clearly told what were the principles of the house; every man who bought did so with the clear understanding that he was not to pay in bills, but in cash. This being the case, any one who endeavoured to evade the rule showed that he had not been honest in the previous understanding. It was not like a case of long credit, where one may be utterly deceived in his expectations from one term to another. Mr. Budgett, therefore, felt that he could not do a customer a more serious injury than to permit him to trifle with his engagements. He had known precisely on what terms he received the goods, and if it proved that he had not been candid, then it seemed to him as if indulgence were a bounty on fraud and an encouragement in a course of loose dealing which must terminate ruinously. He would not tolerate any man in imposition; and he considered it a clear case of foul play when a man concluded a bargain on certain well-understood terms, intending to evade those terms. He was willing to give away money to any amount, willing to lend to any amount, willing to sacrifice custom to any amount; but he would not be imposed upon; he would not trade with any man who met him under false pretences; he would not for any plea relax those rules of business which he knew to be right, wise and good—good even for the man who in his short-sightedness would rail at them or trifle with them; and he knew that if these rules were to be maintained at all they must be maintained invariably. Many thought it was hard of him not to give longer credit. He would have thought it as great an unkindness as to indulge a spoiled child with dainties which had already injured his health and were likely to destroy it. Many who bought, and had imagined they could do as they pleased with his rules, thought it was abominably hard to hold them to their promises. He would have looked upon indulgence as a licensing of foul play, and as destroying their only chance of getting upon a solid foundation where they might succeed and be comfortable.

The Rev. B. Carvosso, who knew him well, and saw

clearly the originality and worth of his character, has furnished me with many valuable glimpses of his life, both inward and outward. On the point now in hand, he says :—

" While he would so readily give away thousands of gold and silver *out* of the sale-room and counting-house, *in* business he was rigid about pence and days. A man in small business, his neighbour, had dealt with him contrary to rule. He ordered flour at the end of the twenty-eight days—the period of credit—but did not bring the amount of the former order. The flour was in the waggon, the carter on the way with it. The mistake was discovered; a messenger was dispatched with orders *to give the poor man one sack of flour*, *bring back the rest*, and henceforth cease to do business with him! To maintain a small business principle he would readily submit to an astonishing pecuniary loss."

Had his poor neighbour gone to him and told him he was in difficulties, doubtless he would have found a ready friend. But, instead of taking that honest course, he tries by a trick to obtain goods. That must be stopped, and is stopped at once; yet stopped in a way which shows that the fear of the little pecuniary loss which might be involved in this case was not the motive for decision, but the principle of adhering to the rules of the establishment and of checking unfair dealing in their customers. To him none of his business principles were "small," nor were they to any who had learned from him their real bearing on the course of trade. Respecting a cash commerce instead of a credit commerce his views were large and his convictions deep. He saw many a family wrecked under his eye, who had been tempted by credit into a trade to which their means were inadequate. He saw men suddenly reduced from prosperous ease to struggling embarrassment, just by a few return bills. They had industry, tact, and a growing connexion; yet, because a few large customers have deceived them, their lawful profit for years of toil is swept away. He saw, when one such house fell, a whole circle of families shattered by the stroke; another circle of families, linked with the former shattered too; then another circle and another, of families which had known wealth and honour, dashed down to want and shame, till the whole country was startled with the noise of ruin. Witnessing scenes like this, no wonder that he wrote it on his heart, that the system of credit was a system of curses; no wonder that in every establishment erected on a foundation of cash payments, he saw a conquest from chaos and a step towards puplic repose; no wonder that in every facility to incur debts, he saw a decoy and a pitfall; no wonder that the ambition to set an example of success on a system of cash payments was strong within him, that he viewed it as a deed of right serviceable patriotism,—a thankless, but most substantial offering to mankind.

The modern history of Europe, apart from all other branches of experience, abundantly testifies to the value of Mr. Budgett's favourite principle. All nations have not been so reckless as our own and our American cousins; and well for them in the days of their trial that they have not. An able writer on commerce states:—

"If we begin with Holland, we find that bargains in that country were, in its better days, almost always made for ready money, or for so short a date as six weeks or two months. Profits were small in their ratio, but the quickness of returns made them eventually large. Failures were rare, even in so distressing an era as the occupation of their country by the French, which began in 1795, and involved from the outset a stoppage of maritime intercourse with all their possessions in India and America. The consequence of this stoppage was a decay of trade, a suspension of various undertakings, a scarcity of work, a miserable dulness in the 'sale of goods,'—all leading, in the first instance to diminish income, and eventually to encroachment on capital. But amidst this distress the failures were surprisingly few,—fewer, indeed, than occur in Britain in any ordinary season. Another example, equally replete with instruction, was the state of France after the double invasion of 1814 and 1815. There prevailed at that time a general discouragement among the upper ranks, and a great deal of wretchedness among the lower, trade being at a stand, and stocks of goods lying unsold in shops or warehouses for years; still bankruptcy was exceedingly rare. All this shows what a satisfactory prospect we may anticipate, when we adopt the plan of transacting the greater part of our business for ready money."

When we contrast these instances of comparative security amid the most frightful national convulsions, with what we have all seen of the terrible panic-times which overtake us every now and then in the midst of national tranquillity, it is quite enough to drive every man who hates all things which breed wretchedness, to rise against the debtor and creditor system with downright animosity. Were we to be invaded, were we to have a revolution, were any such disaster to befall our nation as has befallen others, who can placidly contemplate the ruin which would accrue in every town throughout the country?

One of your great men of the city, one who has figured in some of the most famous of its financial feats, one who lived and died worth his thousands and tens of thousands, was at the fireside of a friend when a cheerful little girl was bidding good night; "Ah!" exclaimed the man of stores and cares, "she has got no return bills to think upon." He did not expect to go to sleep so blithely; there was a load upon his heart—return bills to be sure. And of those well dressed, well-looking, intelligent, energetic men, who teem towards all the metropolitan termini between four and five o'clock every afternoon, in hot haste from the city, not a few are carrying upon their hearts that same dull load, return bills. Many when they come home, instead of enjoying their leisure hour, are smarting under the harass of return bills; many a one, when he asks his daughter to play and sing, is only seeking relief from the necessity of talking that he may muse at leisure on his return bills. Many a one who goes out to spend the evening, wishes the party was at Nova Zembla, for his head is pestered with return bills. Many a one, when a friend calls to spend an hour, wishes he was at the antipodes, for he has enough to think about with his return bills. Many a one who dances because he has promised to be at the ball, seems at every step to awake a rustling of return bills. Many a man who has his eye seemingly upon a book, is studying the unloveable literature of return bills. Many a one who is wont to go to the week-evening service, and there to find one hour of spiritual quiet amid a week of worldly din, can hardly bring himself to go, his thoughts are so harassed by those return bills. Many a man who is in his pew on Sunday, hears neither prayer, nor hymn, nor sermon; his poor lorn mind is chased round dingy counting-houses haunted by return bills. Of old times, ghosts, fairies, brownies, witches, and such tribulations were familiar to all men in their struggles. These have disappeared; but our counting-houses have a new race of *revenants*,—bills, which were seen out of the world and were counted as dead, suddenly reappear and must be laid before there can be peace. Not a day passes over us but these modern goblins strike a deadly chill to some hearts, sour tempers, spoil appetites, render husbands unwilling to tell all at home, fathers pensive as their children laugh, masters irritable; make the peevish scold, the wicked swear, and the good man lift up his heart to God with the prayer men pray in time of trouble. What a leak is at sea, what a mine is under a fort, what a heart disease is in the frame,—that is the system of bill-bubble in trade. And yet sensible, solvent men, with homes to cheer and a country to serve, will go on encouraging and prastising that preposterous torment.

One has seen children build up a little fabric of card board and call it a house, and keep it up as long as they could; but down it came soon, and they did not take it to heart. But it is quite another sight to see men, not children, build up a structure of paper and then call it "a house;" not a plaything house, but a serious house for people to buy and sell in, and to trust to for a shelter from the tempests of misfortune; to see them rear a whole row of these paper "houses," build one on the end of another, so that if one fall all fall, and seriously persuading themselves, and their wives and children, that these make-believe sheds are "houses" to spend their lives in. It is a quaint, half lunatic sort of exhibition; but it mingles the sad with the comical, when some jolt capsises one of the paper piles, and down rustles the whole row; while the builders, unlike the children who counted on the tumbling of their structure, take it mightily to heart and are in anguish.

John Bull and Jonathan between them have a very mischievous propensity to set up these paper "houses" and delude people into trusting them. They have over and over again seen what a shocking sort of game it is, and how misery and wretchedness come out of it; but all in vain,—they go on, and are likely to do so, in spite of any little sorrow we may utter here upon the subject. Which of the two is worse it is hard to say, though John lays great blame on Jonathan and says he builds his houses far higher, putting on six or even nine stories, which John thinks quite too much. But it is no business of ours to arbitrate between them; they are both foolish and mischievous; which is the more so is little matter. But they had better, both of them, take warning in time and cease to play at hazard, laying the happiness of families and the equanimity of nations as the stake.

The new merchants who rose so rapidly, and to their neighbours so unaccountably, at Kingswood Hill, were never haunted with return bills. They were never travelling in the dark, liable suddenly to meet an apparition that would block up their way. They always knew where they were and whither they were going. They had not looked upon a hundred pounds as paid, when it turned out that they had it to pay. They had not to sacrifice the profits made by fifty honest men to cover the loss made by one rogue. They had not to look to fifty sensible men to pay a loss occasioned by one fool. They had not to ponder which were safe bills and which were risky ones; they had no bills at all. They had not to study what were good debts and what bad debts; they had no debts at all. Vast as their transactions were, a petty loss of forty or fifty pounds was quite an event, a crisis which set the whole staff in motion as if their honour were tarnished.

It is one distinctive beauty of the credit system that honest men have to pay for the articles bought by rogues, and wise men for the articles bought by fools. The merchant, of course, must make a profit on the whole, and he has no alternative but to charge John and Thomas for the coat which Horatio bought and did not pay for. I confess it seems to me, that John and Thomas had better not be taxed thus. If Horatio needs a coat provided by other people, he had better say so and come by it honestly, rather than steal a piece by aid of the merchant from one neighbour and another, and so make up a fine garment at their expense. John and Thomas are very much wronged, and I defy the merchant to prove that he is not the accomplice of Horatio in defrauding them.

The advantage of a trade based on cash instead of on credit to the comfort and morality of the nation is incalculable. Credit does occasionally enable a man of energy to take a position he could not else have taken; but for one to whom it proves a substantial benefit, it allures thousands to uninterrupted trouble, and a whole spawn of unfair practices owe their existence to it alone. The credit system ought to be exploded. Men ought to be trained to place themselves in accord with their circumstances, to overcome difficulties not by artifice but by labour. Families ought not to be exposed to live in uncertainty as to whether the bread they eat is their own. The honest and the apt should not be mulcted to the amount of the frauds and waste of those who reject principle or lack sense. The commerce of the nation ought not to rest on a hollow foundation, exposed at every pressure or collapse. It was one of Mr. Budgett's leading desires that the example of their firm might induce many to place their trade on a firm footing, and thus the national stability and happiness would be advanced. This was his work of patriotism, and a more valuable service he could not have done to the state; much better than if he had been a great speaker at corporation meetings, and a great man among the legislators of his own circle. A more conclusive proof that success is possible on a system virtually of cash payment, could not be afforded than that found in his own case. You may talk of impossibility as you please, but no impossibility can confront you which did not confront them. Yet, without making friends by giving "liberal terms," constantly losing friends by enforcing cash, often turning a customer into an enemy, often sending away large offers of trade; by fidelity to a sound principle and to the advantages which it offered equally to merchant and to customer, a little village trade in the hands of men without influence or wealth, was raised against most powerful opposition to great extent and profit. The thing has been done: therefore it can be done again.

To a tradesman, stock-taking is always an exciting time. According to the state of his heart, he receives the favourable or unfavourable result; the sorrow of the world which worketh death, the bitter pining over money lost and toil ill spent, the impatience of life and the distaste for action, the meek submission to a Father's chastising hand, the close searching of heart to see where the rod has been provoked, the tranquil joy in acknowledging a fruitful blessing, the godly fear lest growing wealth should bring with it pride, the turbulent delight at plenty of gain, the boastful self-laudation on talent and power, the malign triumph over rival houses,—all these feelings, and a thousand more, are raised yearly in the breasts of our busy neighbours when they learn how much they have lost or won. One of the oldest servants in the establishment of the Messrs. Budgett, one who saw it rise and grow, told me that, as his station lay immediately above the private counting house, he found that year by year, as soon as the brothers had struck the balance, they retired into an inner office, and there kneeling down before the Lord of all, acknowledged His allotment of success or of failure, giving thanks or presenting humiliation as the case might dictate.

As they advanced Samuel bought the ground in which lay the old quarry, wherewith you are already familiar. Here he built a substantial house, which, with alterations, was his abode to the end. His friend the Rev. Joseph Wood was standing with him in his new home, the monument of past success and of expected abundance. On looking out in front, the eye caught sight of the parish workhouse beyond the garden; on looking out behind, it rested on the tombstones of a cemetery. Mr. Wood said to his prosperous friend, "You have something here to admonish you. In front you have the workhouse to which you *may* come; behind is the graveyard to which you *must* come." Ah! it were well for all of you who are growing rich fast, had you at hand some honest friend to tell you now and then a useful truth; but would *you* receive such homely words in a spirit of cordiality and gratitude? Samuel Budgett did. And you, ministers, would you all, with an acquaintance so rapidly acquiring wealth and importance, venture to go so close? If you have some of that class in your flock, do give them now and then a faithful word; they need it, poor men, if any upon earth do.

We have just, once more, named the old quarry which had been the scene of his boyish meditations. This recalls a circumstance of which it was also the scene during the progress of the rise. Grocers have never enjoyed an immaculate reputation in the matter of adulterating goods. Not a few of their most costly wares are capable of easy mixture. Conscience is generally trained to the posture habitual to the trade. Of course the grocer has exceedingly good reasons for his apprentices, why they should adulterate. Yet if he went to the draper and found that for linen he had bought a mixture of cotton and flax, he would call the draper a cheat. Or if he found that the silversmith had sold him plated spoons for silver spoons, he would call him a cheat. It is only, you see, in his own line of business that such strong reasons exist for doing a little deception. In Mr. Budgett's early days, pepper was under a heavy tax; and in the trade, universal tradition said that out of the trade everybody expected pepper to be mixed. In the shop stood a cask labelled P. D., containing something very like pepper dust, wherewith it was usual to mix the pepper before sending it forth to serve the public. The trade tradition had obtained for the apocryphal P. D. a place amongst the standard articles of the shop, and on the strength of that tradition it was vended for pepper by men who thought they were honest. But as Samuel went forward in life his ideas on trade-morality grew clearer. This P. D. began to give him much discomfort. He thought upon it till he was satisfied that, when all that could be said was weighed, the thing was wrong. Arrived at this conclusion, he felt that no blessing could be upon the place while it was there. He instantly decreed that P. D. should perish. It was night; but back he went to the shop, took the hypocritical cask, carried it forth to the quarry, then staved it and scattered P. D. among the clods and slag and stones. He returned with a light heart. But he recollected that he had left the staves of the cask in the quarry; and as there was no need to let them go to waste, his first act in the morning was to return and gather them up.

Now, ye busy shopmen, and ye, more lordly merchants, say, before the only witness who beheld that act under the night heaven, have you no P. D. which ought to be scattered before you go to sleep? Your thought turns towards something; you were taught it; men worthy in their way justify it; you are able to laugh others out of their scruples about it; you argue with yourself till it appears "fair enough;" but do for once just go to your private room, and sit down and think. Be rational for a moment or two; do not refuse to converse alone with your conscience and your God; ay, go down upon your knees and pray for light, for it is no small matter to be doing wrong. You may smile at it, you may gloss it over, you may "pooh-pooh" warning; but wrong is wrong, and there is a Judge above us; wrong is wrong, and it will find you out. Be sure this world is not a lawless common, where all who can may plunder and go harmless: it is a kingdom with a strong, just King, whose laws cannot be broken without bringing punishment on the offender.

This world of ours contains a great deal of P. D. The

ship-owner has a ship which has become too old to carry sugar from the West Indies without damaging it; so he fits her out as a passenger ship, and advertises her for Sydney as the "well-known, favourite, fast-sailing ship;" and that is P. D. The corn merchant has a cargo damaged in a gale at sea; but as the underwriters will not pay unless the captain can swear that the vessel struck, the merchant, who was snug in his bed when the gale blew, tries to show the captain that, just off Flamborough Head, the keel did actually touch the ground, and that therefore he may safely take the requisite oath; and that is P. D. The private banker who feels that he is sinking, takes a finer house, starts an additional carriage, and sets up for a member of Parliament, that people may think he scarcely knows what to do with his money; and that is P. D. The director of a joint-stock bank who sees that the concern is hollow, sells out his own shares, but retains his place till the three years during which he is liable are past, that no one else may take fright; and that is P. D. The shareholder gets up a rumour that the Petty-borough railway is going to be amalgamated with the Great Central line; and that is P. D. The warehouseman is standing by a parcel of goods which have been on his hands for some weeks; a customer enters and is received with smiles. "Are these new?" "The latest things we have—just out; in fact I almost thought you would look in to-day, and have this moment had the parcel opened for you;" and that is P. D. The glove seller is asked for Dent's gloves, and produces you an article which never passed through Dent's hands, or cost Dent's price. "These are not Dent's." "I beg your pardon, they are Dent's best; I bought them there myself;" and that is P. D. The provision merchant finds that Cork butters of No. II. brand "open" well, and changes the brand to No. I.; and that is P. D. A dealer selling to a man he knows to be "shakey," *makes a mistake on purpose*, so that the debt seems larger than it really is; if, therefore, he must take a dividend, he will have it on more pounds than are due to him; and that is P. D. If you go on you will be astonished how P. D. is in most places. In fact, if some just power were to-night to take all the P. D. casks in this great shop we call the world, and stave them in, scattering the deceitful contents to the wind, there would be such a confusion to-morrow morning that the whole shop would have to be re-arranged.

Your business, just now, is to search out P. D. under your own roof, and be sure you do not let it pass the night there. Out with it, a curse is in it. Stave the cask in pieces. Scatter the cheat to the night winds. Let the eye of heaven which is looking down behold its dispersion. Then go and crave pardon for all the acts in the past wherein you have touched, tasted, or handled the unclean thing. Do not mock the Almighty by asking pardon for the sin of to-day, when you are holding the same sin in your right hand for repetition to-morrow. Pardon for the past is freely offered; but think not that God will forgive sins you will not forsake. What would you think of a father who would forgive a son for cheating his neighbour when he was continuing to cheat, and who would not immoveably refuse his favour unless the cheat were discontinued and as far as possible repaired? And do you imagine that the great holy Father above will own for a child of his any man that tricks, defrauds, or lies? If with a penitent heart you turn from your evil ways, He is merciful to forgive you; but woe to you and woe to all of us were He so cruel a ruler as to be at peace with the unjust. No, no; the righteous God loveth righteousness. As you are guilty, you feel it is terrible to believe this. But it shuts the door of hope only on the path of transgression; it leaves the path of repentance open, and into that, God manifest in the flesh invites you, with a tender effusion of love and a royal promise of mercy.

This fact respecting P. D. reminds me of another. A few years before Mr. Budgett's death, a person came to him stating himself to be a Wesleyan and a local preacher, and offering to disclose an invention which would be an immense saving to Mr. Budgett in his extensive business. He received him and heard his explanations. It proved that he had a plan for making mock vinegar which cost hardly anything, and might be sold for real. Mr. Budgett led him to disclose his scheme fully, and when he had the plot open before him, he broke out upon the tempting rogue with an astounding burst of indignation:—"What! you want to lead me into dealing like this. If you are resolved to go to hell yourself, why should you try to drag me with you? And you profess to be a Wesleyan and a local preacher!!" And with words of stinging rebuke he dismissed this emissary of evil, who, wishing to bribe him to sin, had used religion as a card of introduction. When men coming on business do that, one is apt to suspect them. With a good man, religion is the pathway to the favour of God; with the hypocrite it is the pathway to the favour of man. And as to this swindler, just reflect on the errand whereupon he had set out. He had discovered a clever way of cheating, a way that would pay; he knew that men of business have their weak side; so he set forth to seek a partner in fraud and gain—set forth, as he was so unexpectedly told, on a direct journey to hell, seeking whom he might lead with him. Whosoever you are that dare to sell yourself for silver and gold, if you are determined to sin, do, for mercy's sake, sin alone. Do not tempt others; they are weak, as weak as you were. Do not tempt them, or they will sin with you, and together you will taste the bitter pains of eternal death.

Gold well gotten is bright and fair; but there is gold

which rusts and cankers. The stores of the man who walks according to the will of God are under a special blessing; but the stores which have been unjustly gathered are accursed. "Your gold and your silver is cankered, and the rust of them shall be a witness against you, and shall eat up your flesh as fire." Far better have no gold at all, than gold with that curse upon it. Far better let cold pinch this frame, or hunger gnaw it, than that the rust of ill-gotten gold should eat it up as fire.

Perhaps you may once or twice in your life have passed a person whose countenance struck you with a painful amazement. It was the face of a man, with features as of flesh and blood, but all hue of flesh and blood was gone, and the whole visage was overspread with a dull silver grey, and a mysterious metallic gloss. You felt wonder, you felt curiosity, but a deep impression of the unnatural made pain the strongest feeling of all which the spectacle excited. You found it was a poor man who, in disease, had taken mercury till it transfused itself through his skin and glistened in his face. Now go where he will, he exhibits the proof of his disorder, and of the large quantity of metal he has consumed. If you had an eye to see the souls that are about you, many would you see—alas, too many,—who are just like that; they have swallowed doses of metal, — ill-gotten, cankered, rusted metal, — till all purity and beauty are destroyed. The metal is in them, throughout them, turning their complexion, attesting their disorder, rendering them shocking to look upon for all eyes that can see souls. If you have unjust gains, they do not disfigure the countenance on which we shortsighted creatures look; but they do make your soul a pitiful sight to the great open Eye that *does* see. Of all poisons and plagues, the deadliest you can admit to your heart is gain which fraud has won. The curse of the Judge is in it; the curse of the Judge will never leave it;

it is woe, and withering, and death to you; it will eat you up as fire; it will witness against you; ay, were that poor soul of yours, at this precise moment, to pass into the presence of its Judge, the proof of its money-worship would be as clear on its visage as the proof that the man we have described has taken mercury is plain upon his.

"But if I don't, others will; and a man must live." To be sure, if you do not others will; and what reason is there in that? According to that you may resort to piracy and pocket picking. "A man must live!" Yes, but a man must not live on all conditions; there are some things worse than death; and though the world is slow to own it, be assured that it is better to die than sin, better to want than defraud, better to hunger than lie. "A man must live!" Do you mean that a man can live only upon the fruits of sin? If so, what great use is there in living at all? But perhaps all you mean is, that if you are to keep up your present show, if you are to be above your circumstances, you cannot do it by fair means. You do not mean that by fair means you could not find food and raiment, but that you could not take the stand you do. Well, I do not see that Providence ever meant to furnish you with facilities for keeping up a pleasing imposture; and if His government does not harmonise with such a design, surely we cannot complain. But if you really mean that the way to find food and raiment is to sin against God and against your neighbour, then I protest you utter wickedness and unbelief. Do you mean to tell your Maker that, did you perform his will, He would not give you daily bread?—that you can only subsist under His heaven by yielding to Satan? Dare not to imagine such vain things; put them very far from your heart. The Father above is Father to body and soul. "The Lord is for the body;" He set every one of its strings; He has kept it from its birth till now; the breath thereof is in His hand. His own Son took upon him such a body, and with such a body went up on high, where he is seated now at the right hand of God. He has chosen the body for his living temple; He has chosen its members as his instruments of righteousness; He has destined the body to outlive the everlasting hills, and rise above the unapproachable stars, incorruptible and glorious, with his sons for ever. Do you then dare to think that the thing to be done for the welfare of such a body is to place it at the service of sin, to let its members work wickedness? He does not promise to feed your pride, to feed your imposture, to feed your idleness, to feed your fancies; but He does, in covenant grace, promise to care for your body if its members are devoted to him. "Must live!" And is it living to be doing wrong for the sake of a hundred a year more than you could gain by doing right? "Man shall not live by bread alone; but by every word that proceedeth out of the mouth of God." This is the answer to all Satan's cry about "you *must live.*" He is ever showing you some method "to make bread," but I warn you, never make bread at his bidding. You have another life than that which bread nourishes; you have another store than that which holds bread you can weigh and measure;—"every word that proceedeth out of the mouth of God." That is your store; a promise is better than a fraud; and he is more certain to live who trusts in the word out of the mouth of the Lord, than he who, distrusting that, proceeds under the pressure of want to make bread in the way suggested by Satan.

After the brothers had been in partnership for about twenty years, the elder retired, leaving the business to the sole direction of our merchant. About this time he made his first and last essay in speculation. The Chinese war suddenly threw the tea-market into agitation. He came to London, and though his intention had been but slightly directed to the tea department of their business, he bought with great advantage, and, I think, on the transactions of one week cleared some two thousand pounds. But in the course of a year it proved that he lost almost as much. He frequently cited this as a fair example of what was to be got by speculation; and though so energetic in the legitimate prosecution of trade, he always condemned every hazard for the chance of rapid profits. A little at a time was his principle; and he preferred the slow and laborious progress made by secure trading, to the risky adventures which in a single day might bring a fortune or a failure. His hatred of speculation did not arise from want of enterprise or want of nerve; he had both, but he had enough of healthy energy not to require articifial excitement. When the railway rage arose, he firm. No man naturally would feel a stronger attraction stood towards a commercial arena where acuteness and push seemed certain of golden fruits; no man could have entered that arena with a clearer probability of coming off a winner; but he was convinced that the thing was wrong and foolish—a form of money-madness into which no religious man should allow himself to be seduced; and that sums gained by such bargains were not the wages of honest labour, but the winnings of questionable play. Ah, what sighs would have been spared, what hearts left unbroken, what families saved from ruin, what consciences from defilement, had all religious men been equally wise and virtuous in that time of fiery testing for the Christians of this country!

Mr. Budgett had not been long at the head of the establishment when a calamity befell it which seemed at the moment ruinous. A Bristol paper gave the following account at the time:—

"Alarming Fire.—At about half-past seven on Tuesday evening, considerable alarm was felt throughout this city by the appearance upon the horizon of a conflagration, evidently of immense extent, the heavens being completely lit up with it at about five or six miles distance. Large crowds of people, in consequence, congregated upon Kingsdown and the various hills, and conjecture was rife as to the place where the fire was raging. The arrival of an express messenger on horseback for the attendance of the engines and firemen soon brought the intelligence that the conflagration had taken place upon the premises of the Messrs. H. H. and S. Budgett, at Kingswood Hill. The Messrs. Budgett are among the most extensive flour, sugar, tea, and general merchants in this part of the kingdom, and are well known throughout England for their extensive mercantile transactions. They have several establishments in Bristol, but, from some motives which are unknown to us, have always held their central establishment at Kingswood Hill. The fire was discovered by one of the men in their employment, at about a quarter-past seven o'clock, in a room called the titler-room, in which refined sugars are kept; and, it is supposed, originated in one of the flues communicating with that room. A messenger, as we have already said, was instantly dispatched to Bristol; and, in the mean time, the alarm spread rapidly through the village and neighbourhood, all the inhabitants of which immediately went to assist in subduing the fire. Their efforts, it was hoped at first, would have been successful; but, in a few minutes, the fire spread in a most alarming manner, and speedily communicated with the entire range of warehouses. At this period the Norwich Union engine arrived, and played on the fire; the engines of the other offices also speedily arrived. The fire in the warehouses had, however, now reached so great a height that it was evident, the more especially considering the combustible materials with which they were filled, that their total destruction was inevitable; and the efforts of all therefore were directed to the preservation of the adjoining dwelling-houses, upon which the engines played, with a view to cut off the communication with the burning warehouses. These efforts were happily successful, and both the dwelling-houses and stables of the establishment, in which were forty-seven valuable draught horses, were saved. The fire in the warehouses continued raging until four o'clock in the morning, when it was got under; but not until all the warehouses, the counting-houses, and the retail shop had been completly destroyed. The books were, however, fortunately saved. This was most fortunate, as their loss to a house of such transactions as the Messrs. Budgett, would have been irretrievable. The stock consumed consisted of refined sugars, cheese, coffee, teas, flour, &c.," and must have amounted to several thousand pounds. They had just imported two large cargoes of fruit and a heavy stock of sugars; which were, however, fortunately in their Bristol warehouses. The Messrs. Budgett are insured to a large amount; £8,000 in the Phœnix, and other sums in various offices."

Beyond the sums insured the pecuniary loss did not much exceed three thousand pounds. The next morning, while the ruin was still reeking, a circular went forth to all the customers who were expecting goods, stating that a fire in the premises had delayed the execution of their orders, but that on the following day the goods should be dispatched. It had for some time been necessary to have a warehouse in Bristol; but this was of inconsiderable size compared with the demands of such a business as they had to carry on. Thither Mr. Budgett hastened; he at once concluded an engagement for the house adjoining the one already in possession; all energies were worked; the goods ordered were all dispatched the next day; the two houses were soon made one; the business was rapidly organised in the new premises; and these grew and grew till they assumed the dimensions with which we found them at the time of Mr. Budgett's death. The fire, instead of a disaster, proved eventually to be a great boon. It had transferred the establishment to Bristol, a change involving a number of conspicuous advantages. From this time the progress was amazingly rapid; the internal arrangements were gradually perfected, the system of business began to be better understood, early prejudices and animosities considerably abated, and the flow of prosperity rose higher year by year.

While so rapidly extending his business, Mr. Budgett had much improved his residence. He had filled up the quarry, the scene of his meditations on the happy Sabbath days of boyhood, and turned the surface into gardens; he had surrounded his house with extensive grounds; and he had some forty or fifty acres of land, in farming which he took great delight, and upon which he contrived to find employment for large numbers of his neighbours. An old and tottering man, who had been "in the employ" from the time of Mr. Budgett's youth, and who gloried in the growth of the establishment as if it had been his own, said to me, in alluding to the large numbers occasionally employed on the farm, "Yes; I remember when there were five men and three horses, and I have lived to see three hundred men and one hundred horses."

Mr. Budgett had now a comfortable mansion, spacious grounds, a business working regularly as a chronometer, paying richly as a miser could desire, and a family all that was fitted to make a Christian father glad. He stood on the very scene of his apprentice toils, of his early mercantile endeavours, in the eyes of the very people who had known him then, and who, in his position, now beheld a most notable example of the Successful Merchant.

CHAPTER VI.

MASTER AND MEN.

"For there are reciprocities of right which no creature can gainsay."
TUPPER.

THE feudal time is gone; the feudal tie is broken. Some may mourn for it; but they will never bring it back. Baronial castle will never more be the centre of activity and protection; baronial pennant will never more lead out the neighbouring hinds at will. The sons of the ancient barons are still the princes of the people, but they are no longer their leaders. Of old, the noble was to the people what the commodore was "during the war" to the merchant fleet he convoyed—the defence around which they clung, the director to whom they looked, the leader whom they followed. Now, the noble is to the people what the star is to the fleet—a bright exalted spectator of their low and distant progress, who, in a sphere inaccessible to them, has a share in marking out their destiny. Direct personal intercourse with active masses of the people, the noble has none. Doubtless many of the order retain a hold on the population of their ancestral districts; but that population is scattered and politically inert, not the population on which the future career of the nation depends. The hordes which dwell in our great towns, whose passions play under constant stimulus, and whose movements tell as a combination of levers, they are the people now; they are the hosts of England with whom our national character is identified, and by whom our national course is mainly determined. Between these and the aristocracy there is neither intercourse nor sympathy.

But new barons have arisen, ruling in new castles, and leading new bands. The baron of our day is the manufacturer; the castle, the mill; and the retainers, the factory troop. Many of these barons are lofty enough for any rank wherewith either Mammon or imagination may invest them. If some barons of old could reckon a thousand spears, they can reckon a thousand spindles. If the one was fain to watch his stalwart yeomen shooting the feathered arrow, the other is fain to watch his troop shooting the nimble shuttle. The mansions of the new lords are far more luxuriously adorned than were those of the old; and if their tables are less spacious, they are abundantly more superb. You may think of these new barons as you please, but there they are, and well awake to their importance; quite as stately as the sons of the ancient barons, though not quite so courtly; quite as high, though not quite so graceful; quite as sumptuous, though not quite so polished; quite as lordly, though not quite so gentlemanly; altogether a redoubtable array of purse-girded potentates, the real lords of this real *golden* age. They *are* the English barons of the nineteenth century. It is around their castles the people cluster; it is from their hand the people take their bread; it is with their fortunes the people thrive or pine; it is at their bidding the people sit down amid plenty, or go out to struggle with the world for food. The great manufacturers and the great merchants are now our only feudal powers. They have real interests involved with the people, close relations with them, personal contact, and personal influence over their temper and condition. In their persons the workman meets the ranks above him. Their influence on the legislature is rapidly outstripping that of their more noble precursors, and their influence on the people is far more direct, continuous, and fruitful.

Our peace in the future little depends on the dispersed population of those districts wherein the personal influence of the aristocracy is yet considerable; but it does most closely depend on those aggregations of stirring men over whom our commercial magnates preside. From these we have to dread the hurricanes, the earthquakes, and the eruptions. It is important in this day that the English lords should be wise and magnanimous; but, perhaps, it is still more important, that English masters should be considerate and winning. We are not much in danger of cruelty: we are greatly in danger of indifference. Few would do their men harm, would tamper with their rights, would enforce anything manifestly injurious. All would pay the men regularly, punctually, and in full—of course they would, just as they would oil the machinery, because if they did not, all would soon be at a stand. But the cases are many wherein the machinery is regularly oiled, the men regularly paid, and the master has just as much communication with the one as the other. He knows what the one does, and what the other does. If the one breaks a wheel, he sends for an engineer; if the other breaks a bone, he sends for a doctor. If the one is worn out, it is dismissed; if the other is worn out, it is dismissed. Both are very useful, and, perhaps, the master can tell you the name of both—of the machinery, always; of the man, sometimes.

Ah! ye lords of cotton, wool, and silk, of linen, lace, and hose, ye smile, well pleased, when one alludes to the large number of men in your employment. You like us to know that you have "more hands than any one in the town."

Well, we must not chide you much for that smile; we all look pleasantly on our own importance; it is ever comely. But of all those men in your employment, how many receive a friendly word from you in the course of a year? How many ever see you within their door? How many could tell how kindly you inquired for their wives or children when un well, how you called to see themselves when laid up at home, how your wife or daughter brought them something nice? How many of them have ever heard from you a hearty word of good advice, urging them to be thrifty and push on? With how many have you kindly reasoned when they have been foolish and unfaithful? How many have you put on their guard as to the stuff they read, the way they spend their idle hours, the company they keep, or the habits they form? How many have you helped out of difficulties of their own making, pointing out to them their folly, and endeavouring to train them to do better? To how many have you personally given a present of some wholesome book? How many have you asked how they spend their Sabbath, or counselled as to the ever-living soul that is in them?

Some of you never thought of sustaining any personal relation to your men. Your relation is merely commercial; all you have thought of is, to obtain their proper quota of labour, and to give your proper equivalent of pay; there your relation terminates. As to cultivating any sympathies with them, it has not entered your head. You "do justly by them," and what more can be looked for? Yet, after being in your establishment for years and you all the time "doing justly by them," they do not feel either affection or respect, and you know it. You know that if they saw you in a difficulty they would hardly move to assist you, and would make no scruple of going off and leaving you to sink if they could improve themselves ever so little. You and they are eating of the same loaf; that which constitutes your provision constitutes theirs; yet no fellow feeling exists between you. They and you stand in a relation exceedingly close, and have mutual interests very important. They are hands to you; you are head to them. Without them, you are helpless as a head without hands; without you they are helpless as hands without a head. You plan, they perform; both are served. Surely, then, those who are so connected ought not to be strangers; between them some cordiality should exist. Their relation should not be merely mechanical; there should be heart in it, warm heart and fellowship.

To cultivate affection is the duty of the stronger. The inferior finds it hard to make approaches; from the superior they come with grace and effect. It is often most chilling to find how carelessly a master will speak of the total want of attachment his men display; and how unsuspectingly he sets it all down to their unsympathetic nature. But what pains has he taken to gain their hearts; that is, what pains has he taken to make them happy? Be assured that human nature is human nature though in fustian or in frieze; and patient kindness, if it fail on some, will win the majority. He who declaims on the unloving and reckless character of his men, tells two tales—one of the men, another of the master. There are some workmen whose master could not honestly charge them with being indifferent to his interests; but that master is one whom the men could not charge with being indifferent to theirs. Be assured that it is the superior who is to seek affection; every master should hold himself bound to watch for the happiness of his men, and in seeking their happiness he will gain their hearts. Every man in his establishment is a partaker of his efforts and is fed of his gains, he ought to be part of his care. But you say you have no time to attend to them. What does that mean? Why precisely that if you devote all your time to your own interests, you cannot devote a part of it to theirs; that if you spend every available hour to make yourself rich, you have no hour to spend to make your men happy. That is plain enough. "But, business must be done." Yes, it must be done; but no duty binds you to undertake so much business that you can do no office of Christian kindness. Far better that part of the business should be done by some one else, than that all the charity should be neglected by you.

As at present existing, the relation of master and men is loose, changeable, material. The man works for a certain firm just as he rides in a certain train, because it happens to suit him; but he feels no more affection for the masters and no more interest in their prosperity than he does in the directors of the railway and their dividend. The firm takes up men just as a train takes up passengers. The concern needs them; but whence they came, and whither they go, or at what point of the journey they part, are matters of no interest. It is full time that masters as a class did begin in earnest, to do what some have long been doing—attempt to create between themselves and their men a close and permanent connection and a moral tie. It is high time that masters learned that business has two sides,—duty as well as interest. They are ready enough to tell landlords that property has its duties as well as its rights; and they have just cause to do so, for the thing is true. But, it is not true of landed property alone, not of the relation of landlord and tenant alone, but of all kinds of property and all kinds of lordship. The master has his duties as well as his rights, and they are not done when the wages are paid. That is just oiling the machinery, no more. It is a purely material act; without it you would have all in a blaze. It is done to keep the concern going, not to elevate or bless the men. Now, undoubtedly the master ought to consider it part of his business to make his men happy, ought to spend hours and energies and sums for this one end, ought to labour at it, and sustain disappointments in it, and brave discouragements, and feel how hard it is to do good, and persist in doing it till at last he saw that he had not laboured in vain. It is a proud thing for a master to show his beautiful engine-room, clean as a parlour, his bright machinery, his admirable textures, his vast production. He has a right to take an interest in all these; and, if conscious that other things were right, we should take a most lively interest in them also, share his pleasure, rejoice in his success, and pour our honest blessing on the labour of his hands. But it is not always one can do so. True, great care has been taken about the engines;—what has been done for the mind, heart, and life of the engineers? The "mules" and "jennies," the rollers and looms, are all in perfect trim, the gear runs smoothly, the produce is unblameable; a world of diligent application has been spent to bring the work to this perfection; but what has been done for the mind, heart, and life, of the workers? Some masters there are, who have learned the lesson of their duty, and follow it with a cheerful heart. As I write some rise up to my memory. I think of their schools, the plans of improvement, the care for the comfort of their men's houses, the training of the children, the effort to spread good feeling and good living, the attention to the soul's welfare; and, as I think of these men, my heart within me blesses them. Go on, my friend, go on and be hearty; your work is often thankless, as are all good works in this bad world, but keep to it, nevertheless. Doing good is no idle enterprise; its difficulties abound, but its fruits are not doubtful.

The French revolution of 1848 has proved an abortion; but the parent of that abortion lives, and still threatens society with pains and travail. Socialism, whence it sprang, and by which it sank, is capable of assuming a thousand forms and following a thousand banners. It is abroad in

England now, wearing innocent veils and using creditable names. It has won over honest, forcible men, who fight its battles with heart and valour. It is raising, under English forms, the same feelings it raised in France. It is baptising with Christian names dogmas which elsewhere seek no such consecration. It is spreading further, deeper, swifter than most of your masters imagine. It is reaching our workmen, enlisting and combining its soldiers, laying up its ammunition for another day. Some of its agents dream of new eras of brotherhood and equality; while, in good truth, it is preparing a time when the distinction between men shall not lie in richer and poorer, master and servant, but in assailant and defender, in victor and vanquished. You masters have no fear of Socialism in England, and most certainly you have abundant guarantees against it, if duly improved; but many of you are too busy to read, too careless about your men to know what they read, too much strangers to their habits and their haunts to know what they discuss and what they hear. I tell you it is quite time for you to be alert. Sleep a few years longer and you may be awoke by thunder. Thoughts are spreading, things are doing, well calculated to gain the ear of the workman, and well calculated to throw society into agonies. Were it only to save a class it would not be worth while to raise an alarm. No good man would seek to protect a few in absorbing that which might properly be distributed among the many. Did I see in Socialism unquestionable benefits for the men, as all see unquestionable ruin for the masters, why then, for me, the masters might repose till they found the irruption begun. But that system, though potent to impoverish the affluent, is powerless to enrich the poor, and must reduce all classes to destitution; cripple, hamper, bewilder, and chafe, till society perishes in confusion, or finds escape in a return to the laws of free commerce. While some imagine they are seeking the welfare of the workman by framing new schemes and shapes of society, others who see in those schemes and shapes an earnest of hunger, and battle, and military tyranny, ought to urge on those attainable and Christian ameliorations of the relations between men and their masters whereby a healthy state of feeling would be induced, which would be unfavourable to political epidemics. How much of the country's peace depends on the bearing of masters no one can tell. If men see themselves used but not valued, employed but not improved, necessary but not noticed, they will inevitably become sour and ready to embrace any theory about the hostility of capital to labour and the community of goods. Duty cannot be neglected without harm to those who practise and those who suffer the neglect. Masters ought to take pains—patient, costly, systematic pains for the happiness of their men. If they will neglect this staring duty, and perform for their men only the one unavoidable service of payment when pay-day comes, how can they expect the men to feel towards them anything but disregard inspired by their indifference, and envy inspired by their wealth?

In Mr. Budgett's conduct towards his men, nothing was more prominent than a rigid enforcement of discipline. Both he and his brother were fond of system, and had taken much pains to bring the whole business under a code of laws, and to instruct each man precisely in the duty pertaining to his department. The laws were ever undergoing improvement, but they were never suffered to be broken. A rule in force was sacred; no excuse would be accepted. A breach of law was a fault to be confessed, and whoever repeatedly disobeyed any rule whatever was inexorably dismissed. With those who gave evidence of talent Mr. Budgett would take considerable pains—training a young buyer by his own side in the market, accompanying a young traveller on his journey, or giving a warehouseman or clerk frequent lessons in the system they were expected to pursue. When he had thus educated a man up to his satisfaction, he would place him in a post of considerable responsibility, and take great pleasure in his success.

To many, especially to young men, a master whose discipline is lax seems a much kinder master than one who holds them to rule and duty. Whatever may be the intentention of such a master, his influence is cruel. A more serious injury cannot be inflicted on a young man than is inflicted by the indulgences and negligences of a master who does not maintain discipline. Rules should be reasonable, duties moderate, hours considerate; but if the master would do his duty, he must train every man who passes under his hands to unflinching habits of order, punctuality, and obedience. He ought not to let any man dilly-dally, or go forth from his instructions incapable of making his way among able and well taught men. Of all who have been in Mr. Budgett's employment, I do not suppose that one could charge a failure in life on the habits acquired there; while some, who are now in circumstances of comfort and respect, have told me, with a gush of feeling, what pains he had taken to train them up to the habits which have made them what they are.

A disciplinarian who wants to form men to a standard existing in his own mind is ever on the watch for men after his model. This was Mr. Budgett's case; he ever wanted men capable of seizing and accomplishing his purposes. "He has no head," would be his rapid sentence on a man with some good points. A man who would waste or dilly-dally was to him intolerable. His favourite formula of qualification was, "Tact, push, and principle;"—the three things, indubitably, which form your proper man of mark in trade. For them he was constantly on the look out, and when a man came under his eye in whom he discerned them, he would be most anxious to add him to his staff. Without tact and push a man of principle may be very good for many things, but not for business; and without principle tact and push are only powers to do evil. Speaking of a sharp, stirring man who would lie or play tricks, he would say, "What is the use of a tub that is tight all round but has a hole in the bottom." One often hears of masters, honourable men, who would not do an unhandsome thing in their proper persons, who yet look very kindly on men of tact and push who show a lack of principle only at the expense of customers. Mr. Budgett would see that no man wasted his goods or time, that none gave overweight, or sold carelessly, or in any way damaged his interests; but he would insist that they should do justice to all. Masters, be assured that no blessing will come with the smart salesman who can cozen the public and tell fibs with facility: he is a "tub with a hole in the bottom," and you had better be without him. Employers may be quite assured that it is not enough for them to abstain from telling a man to lie or cheat; they may lay tasks upon him which can hardly be discharged by fair dealing; they may show an avidity for results and an indifference as to means, which act upon all but men of stiff integrity as a certain lure to foul play. Gentlemen of honour, who would blush to be accused of an unfairness, have dozens of ill-complexioned doings in their warehouses every day, and that perforce of their haste to do an immense amount of business, and of their lauding success in their men without any attention to principle. If you have a conscience, if you would really rather be without money than have money stained with dishonour, then, I can assure you of what you might know very well yourself, if you were much awake,—that you have something to do to keep soiled money out of your store. You must not leave to your men to deceive or not just as they like; you must, in very great earnest, and very often too, tell them that no man in your employment shall practise anything which you would not defend before God and man.

While Mr. Budgett was constantly on the alert for men after his own heart, he had, as we stated long ago, a remarkable discernment of character. One instance I may give, out of many. A friend of his, a grocer, told me that on many occasions when he passed through his shop, he would make remarks upon the young men whom he had seen behind the counter, saying that one was not worth his salt, and that another would do well; and scarcely ever was the estimate thus formed at a glance erroneous. Once he said, after just passing through the shop, "Where did you get that young man?" The answer was given.

"I would not keep him for a day."

"Why? He is a very clever young man."

"Yes, he is clever enough; but he is a rogue."

"Well, certainly I have seen nothing wrong about him, and I never yet saw his equal behind the counter."

"Very well; I tell you I would not keep him an hour, and you will find it out yet."

"But I can't dismiss him without cause, and he has given me no cause."

He insisted to the last on his view of the young man, and, after leaving, told a mutual friend that a very improper young man was in such a one's shop—he was sure of it. His discernment was so well known, that the young shopman had now his master's eye upon him with restless vigilance. It was not long before he was detected stealing money. He was lodged in the jail at Shepton-Mallet. On the day when the trial was to come on, the master was there. A solicitor came to tell him that a sister of Mr. Smith had come down from London, a very respectable married woman, near her confinement and in great agony at her brother's disgrace,—in fact, so excited that he quite feared the consequences if the trial went on; moreover she was a Wesleyan, to which denomination the prosecutor belonged, and she begged an interview. They met: she was respectable, prepossessing, and well spoken; her condition was touching, and she talked touchingly of her poor unhappy brother. The heart of the prosecutor was almost won; but something aroused his suspicion. He put a question or two as to her brother and the family: the tale did not precisely fit. He put one or two questions more: the interesting Wesleyan sister of Mr. Smith, appeared simply as a clever partner in a fraud. Mr. Smith was sentenced to a term of imprisonment. On the very week of his release he obtained two situations in Plymouth and lost both through dishonesty. Then his old employer heard no more of him till he was summoned to Coventry to identify a Mr. Smith who was there awaiting trial. He had been in the service of a grocer there, and had managed daily, for a long time, to send off a hamper of goods to London by railway; and when the police traced his store it amounted to two waggon loads.

What he did not see at a glance he would soon find out in conversation. His power of eliciting from a person all that enabled him to tell precisely what they were and what their history, was very remarkable. A young man is now in the employment of one of his friends whom Mr. Budgett was requested to see before he was engaged. He perceived that Mr. Budgett was aware of the reason why he had left his former situation, and as he had obtained from his late employers a promise that they would not state anything on the point, he was displeased, and wrote to reproach them with a breach of agreement. The fact was that Mr. Budgett had discovered the matter in conversation, without the other being conscious of it.

He would not be imposed upon. If a man was in fault and frankly confessed, nothing could be more cheerful than his forgiveness; but when once he saw the least disposition to equivocate, all his powers were called forth to reach the truth, and the truth he would reach. He was as persevering as he was quick; as careless of wounding a man's pride as he would be prompt to heal any worthy sorrow. Into the man's heart he would get, no matter how long it took him, by questions directed this way or that way, near the point or away from it. In proportion to the dissimulation manifested his displeasure would rise, and if the case were really bad his rebuke would be tremendous. But the man who showed an open heart always found a generous consideration above what he would have thought possible.

This determination not to be imposed upon he carried out everywhere, with men, neighbours, and customers. Ever indulgent to an acknowledged fault, he was ever most inexorable against an attempt at imposture. Men who will not be imposed upon always make themselves enemies. Many will not forgive him who defeats them in an attempt to play foul; they will represent him in all bad lights,—as hard, heartless, and so on. It is one thing to forgive a wrong when it is done to you; it is another to permit a man to do a wrong with your eyes open. It is a Christian duty to repay the man who has done you evil with good; but it is no duty at all when you see a man intending to do wrong to shut your eyes and let him do it: by stopping him there you may save him thereafter. No kind of imposture so roused the ire of Mr. Budgett as when a man put on a profession of religion with any left-handed design. His well known character exposed him to attempts of this kind; but woe to the caitiff whom he caught at it;—his ears heard plain words, and words of fire. In the case of the vinegar maker we have already seen with what force he would stamp on that reptile,—the stealthiest, the slimiest, the most poisonous, the most loathsome of all the reptile race,—who would make merchandise of religion. Easy, undiscerning Christians who can be quickly practised upon, are great favourites with people who require such subjects; but while we suspect no man without cause, and pardon all men without reserve, we should not invite deception, but exert ourselves to bind every one by the rule of right. Every religious man should endeavour to drive fraud and deceit out of the world, first in his own dealings, secondly in the dealings of those who act in his name, then in the dealings of all mankind; but let him see that he begins at home.

On this point of discipline many young men are apt to mistake masters, and to think that religious character is not prized, because they see a man indifferent to religion often advanced before one who consistently professes it. But, in business, men must be estimated by their business attainments. If two bootmakers serve you, and the one gives you a better boot than the other, you cannot help saying he is the better bootmaker, even though the other may be the better man. So in two salesmen; if one is apt, adroit, and successful, and the other less so, the master cannot help seeing that the successful one is the better salesman, even though the other must be considered the better man. Young men ought not to expect that piety alone should improve their position in a house, except as it forms them to better habits, and ought to concede to others all the superiority they may happen to possess. But, on the other hand, masters should take good care that the honest and conscientious man does not see another raised above him just because he uses unfair arts and thereby secures sales which could not be effected by truth-telling. Masters should make up their minds to lose all that sharp subordinates might gain by unjustifiable means, and to set their faces against all such practices; and we may assure them again, that if they are not to pocket money got by such means, they must be careful to mark a man who will lie or cheat in order to effect sales, as they are careful to mark one who fails to sell pentifully. No blessing is with the unscrupulous though clever servant, and every honest master ought to make him feel that he believes it, and that he values principle and uprightness more than mere tact. The man of tact and push without principle is a cask of P. D., and ought not to be suffered.

One or two cases show his determination to detect and get rid of men he could not trust, and at the same time show his benevolence in a light almost amusing. There was a tree whereof the fruit was very fugitive. The man he suspected "never touched," no one touched; yet away and away went the fruit. He made a present of the fruit on the tree to the party suspected, and thenceforth it staid quite safely. His point was gained; he "had found it." Another man and his wife were suspected of petty pilfering about the farm. Proof was long impossible: at length a discovery of potatoes secreted set suspicion on foot anew. Neither man nor wife would confess. Another woman was somehow connected with the matter: he took the two women, placed them in different rooms, interrogated them separately, passed from the one to the other, compared their statements, and elicited a confession from the second woman. But the principal one was proof against all his tact: she and her husband received orders to leave the premises immediately. But he wished them to have means of living honestly if they would; and, in Kingswood, any one who has a horse may do so by carting, or, as the phrase is, "hauling" coals to Bristol. In dismissing them, therefore, he gave the man a horse. The wife, little moved by this generosity, raised an outcry about the hardships of being turned away, and demanded, "What is the use of a horse without a cart?" Mr. Budgett reasoned with her, told her how another master might have prosecuted them; but her mood was unchangeable. "It is very hard to be turned away; and what is a poor man to do with a horse without a cart?" He reproved her again; but he gave them a cart. The ingratitude of the poor is constantly urged as a reason for neglecting them. The dishonest and the idle are ungrateful; but as for the honest industrious poor, it will be found that real service always meets from them a hearty and a long continued thankfulness. Some are astonished how their great kindness begets so little gratitude; others have been astonished that little kindness begot so much.

A person in Mr. Budgett's employment gave him dissatisfaction. He felt he could no longer confide in him, and when that was the case with any man about him he could not be happy; he dismissed him. The man took his revenge by going to the houses with which Mr. Budgett had accounts and causing a run for payment, as we saw in the last chapter. Some time after he heard that ——— and his family were in great destitution; they had been away from the neighbourhood for a time, but had returned. Mr. Budgett went to see them accompanied by a friend; the house was in a miserable state, the garden was desolate, neither meat nor bread seemed within the door, and two fine boys were lying in bed because they had no clothes. Mr. Budgett at once ordered meat from the butcher, bread from the baker, sent groceries, sent a tailor to clothe the children hired a man to till the garden, and gave them an allowance of twelve shillings per week till the father of the family should find employment. But he had no "push," and found no employment. He soon applied to be taken back; Mr. Budgett refused. He applied again; then Mr. Budgett consented, but only with a salary far below what he had enjoyed before, and on condition that he should look out for another situation. Every week he set down to the credit of the man, in a private ledger, some twelve shillings, which he thought was about the difference between what he was paying him and what his services would be worth should he prove worthy of confidence. He did all he could to make him trustworthy, and even became a teetotaller to induce him to follow his example. At length, however, both his confidence and his patience had gone; he called ——— into his private office, and told him they must part; "But Mr. ——— I will give your family fifty pounds in weekly pay while you are seeking employment, *and I am assured of it.*"

"Give, Sir, I do not regard it as a gift, my remuneration has not been just."

The merchant just looked up from his desk, pointed to the door and said, "O, very well, Mr. ———, that is enough."

"Sir, I did not mean to offend, I hope you will forgive what I said."

It was long before he found any employment, and for a very lengthened period Mr. Budgett regularly allowed his family twelve shillings a week.

As a matter of course, where strict discipline is concerned, punctuality was a prime virtue. He was himself punctual as a chronometer, even out of business. If he had made an engagement with his neighbour the Rev. J. Glanville, and was a minute late, he would apologise and account for it. So his men must be at work at the given moment, and his travellers must so arrange their journey that every customer shall know at what hour to expect them. But as discipline and punctuality are not meant to abridge but to defend happiness, he contrived to place the arrangements enforcing these in a light which commended them to the men. The hour to begin work was six o'clock. By the gate hung a black board divided into squares, each square was numbered and contained a nail, on the nail hung a little copper plate. Each man had his number, and as he went out he took a plate with him, leaving his number exposed on the board. As he entered he placed the plate on the nail, so covering his number. The moment the bell ceased ringing, the board was removed, and all whose numbers were not covered were at once set down as defaulters. He who did not appear once on that list during a year received at its end a sovereign as his reward. But in the early days of the establishment it was usual to give porters beer. This custom Mr. Budgett disapproved, and to it he would not submit; but close by the number board, he placed another board laden with pennypieces; each man as he entered in the morning took a penny, on returning from breakfast a penny, and on returning from dinner a penny; thus making three in the day, which Mr. Budget considered a full equivalent for beer and of far greater value. If, however, the poor wight was late, he lost his penny; thus paying a fine out of what was considered his due, as well as forfeiting the reward which punctuality would secure at the year's end. At first even a single lapse occasioned the loss of the whole sovereign; but afterwards that rule was relaxed, five shillings being deducted for one, and proportionate sums for additional faults. In the course of years, the beer-pence were commuted for eighteenpence per week additional wages; and then every defaulter was fined,—if a porter, a penny—and so on, in proportion to rank, with every one in the house, up to the partners. The post hour was a quarter-past seven: at that hour the clerks must be in their places, and one of the principals present to open the letters; if he was late, his fine was half-a-crown. With such spirit was this discipline maintained, that though many of the men chose to live in Kingswood after the business was removed to Bristol, they made their four miles journey and many never were late. Some who have been years in the establishment have not once been reported absent.

The system of fining might easily make the discipline appear harsh to the men; but besides the corrective to that provided in the reward for punctuality, the fines are so applied as to take away all idea of severity. A sick fund exists for "the business," to which all are required to pay one penny weekly. Into this fund go all the sums accruing from fines. In cases of sickness, allowances are made on something like the following scale:—

One who has been in the establishment		
less than 5 years	5s.	per week.
Above 5 and less than 10 years	6s.	"
Above 10 and less than 15 years	7s.	"
Above 15 and less than 20 years	8s.	"
Above 20 and less than 25 years	9s.	"
Above 25 years	10s.	"

This fund did not hinder the men from belonging to any other benefit society, and provided them a real help in time of need at a cost they could never feel. Of course, it is apparent that such a scale of allowances could not be kept up by a subscription of a penny a week, eked out by petty fines. The deficit came out of Mr. Budgett's pocket, costing him from thirty to fifty pounds a year.

With punctuality comes dispatch; both are apples of the same branch—both springing from a sense of the rapidity wherewith time flies, joined with a determination to accomplish all that has been undertaken. Men who are not punctual can never be abreast of their business; they talk superbly about not being slaves of time, while time is laughing at them, for they never mastered it yet—never made one week of their lives serve the purposes they meant it to serve. Time has always beaten them, always left them discomfited, amid heaps of work undone and work ill-done. And they are the masters of time, while the man who holds his hours with a firm hand, and makes each one serve his purpose, is its slave! Very well; he can comfortably hear his high-spirited neighbour vaunt his liberty, and exhibit his confusion.

At the outset, we noticed the incredible celerity wherewith Mr. Budgett transacted business; but it was not enough that his own deeds should be swiftly done. Everything must speed around him. He could not bear to see any move as if time were plentiful. But he never sought velocity by haste; it must ever be gained by order and cool energy. Plan after plan, arrangement after arrangement were put in force to bring the establishment into the condition of a machine, wherein every part worked with equable and yet amazing speed. The success was great. Every morning the waggons start with what is called the "first load," at eight o'clock,—that is, with the first instalment of goods to be sent out that day; which goods have been bought in the sale-room on the preceding afternoon, or ordered by an evening post. The morning post, as has been stated, arrives at a quarter-past seven. The "second load" consists of goods ordered by the letters then arriving, and that leaves the premises at from nine to half-past nine o'clock. Thus the work of opening letters, entering orders, transferring to the different departments, weighing, measuring, packing, and lading, has been done in two hours or so. At different periods of the day, load after load is dispatched, till every order which arrived by that morning's post is executed. This is the day's work, and within the day it must be done. When the immense number of the orders is considered, and the endless variety of articles which they embrace,—everything, in fact, that a retail grocer can want,—it really is astonishing how all can be accomplished on the same day; at least so it seems to those who are not "business men." Without discipline, without punctuality, without dispatch, such a feat could never be accomplished; but all these are made to subserve the good end of affording the men rational leisure, for they are at liberty the moment the day's work is done.

One of the oldest servants of the firm related to me their progress from the old hours to those now established. When he entered the "business," it was small; all resided in the house. The hours were nominally from six in the morning to nine at night; but it was generally ten, and sometimes eleven o'clock, before they could retire; and these hours continued even after some of them lived away from the premises. As "Mr. Samuel" began to take a lead in the business, he would often express dissatisfaction with this state of things. "It is not rational," he would cry; "you ought to be at home with your families; we might just as well get done sooner." As the wholesale trade sprang up, of course, there was an increasing press of work; and every now and then he would say, "I do not like to see you here; I want to see you at home: we *must* get done sooner." He made efforts, and presently the bell was regularly rung every night at half-past eight. This was a wonderful relief, and the men were well content. "Mr. Samuel" was of course pleased with the improvement for a time, but he soon began to feel that they had not gone far enough in the right direction. Presently he was again expressing his dislike to see them working so late, and saying, "I don't see why we should not get done by seven, yes, by six o'clock." They thought this very kind of him, but quite impossible. Before long, however, they all found themselves starting for home at seven o'clock. Still he was not content: he aimed at six o'clock, and gained it; and then came the change whereby the work was done within the day, and the present result secured. By bad arrangements, or by employing an insufficient number of hands, the plan of clearing off the orders of each day within the day might have been the very cause of endless detentions; but Mr. Budgett so adjusted his methods, that the effect was a clear and considerable gain to all. Among other arrangements tending to shorten the day, one very efficient one was that none of the men left till all were ready; if, therefore, the men in one department were behind, all the others were kept waiting. Of course, they did not like the hindrance, and those who caused it had abundant admonition; in this way the interest and the influence of the whole staff acted on each particular branch, and without any hint from the master about speed, the men were sufficiently prompted by their comrades. Thus, with an increasing rush of business, the hours of labour were abridged, and every man in that great establishment could daily turn homeward at five or half-past five o'clock, with a full evening at leisure.

And why upon earth should men in a shop or warehouse be condemned to toil in the hours which other men give to rest? Is it not enough, if from morn till eve they are pent up, and on the stretch? When the bricklayer lays down his trowel, and the weaver quits his loom, when the reaper puts up his sickle, and the ploughman drives home his team, why should the shopman and warehouseman kindle artificial light to witness further drudgery? True, the bricklayer or the ploughman has heavier muscular fatigue; but he has also the bright sun and the fresh air. His limbs are more taxed, but his vitals are more refreshed. It is one thing to spend twelve hours on a Bedfordshire farm, and another to spend twelve hours in a close shop or store. Within the last few years public feeling has much improved on this point. The oppressed class have taken up their own cause, and a cry for early closing has reached the ears of all. In the higher circles of trade something has been done; noble and valuable examples have been set by some important houses. Many have reaped the benefit in better health, in mental feasts, in spiritual privileges. I have joined men in a house of business, both before and after their hours of work, in noble and profitable exercises; in meetings for prayer, for Christian philanthropy, and for self-improvement; and one has felt moved to say, Peace be on the house where men can spend such hours, instead of submerging all their waking life under the one turbid, headlong tide of London commerce.

Some have heard so much of the early closing movement, that they imagine the thing is accomplished. Why, just start for a walk in the streets of London some night at half-past ten o'clock, and open your eyes. Take especially the lower and less airy neighbourhoods. See how the windows glare, and the shop doors gape, as if Mammon were sitting within all greedy and unsatisfied yet; and master and men, pale by the gas-light, were his slaves, waiting to bear to him any morsel of prey that may pass. See that close-smelling, lumbered oil shop, with boxes and bundles, firkins and jars, chips, matches, candles, ill-odoured paints, and all sorts of unloveliness. See the youth with red hair and white cheeks attentively waiting on that lady who asks for night-lights. That youth opened the door this morning as it was striking seven; the shop clock now stands at a quarter to eleven, and during those sixteen hours he has been there behind that dirty counter, among oils and ochres, white leads, black leads, red leads, shoe-blacking, lamp-black and glue, indigo, rosin and grease,—among sights and smells that never yet made eyes bright or olfactories happy. When he leaves this beauty of a shop, he will go up into the attic, and *share a small room with three or four comrades.* Then to-morrow morning he will be there again behind the counter by seven o'clock; and because to-morrow is the "preparation for the Sabbath," he will be immersed among his unloveable commodities just up to the moment when midnight is passing into morn. Now, should you wonder if those white cheeks grew whiter?—if his poor mother, who thought that when her son "had got a place in London," he was in the way of well-doing, should see him come home next autumn with death upon his lungs?

You ask the lady who has bought the night-lights, if she thinks it right to come to a shop at this hour. She tells you, "No, she really does not like to be seen in a shop at such an hour, but she and her husband were just returning home from a friend's, and remembering that she had no night-lights in the house, she procured them." But when you speak of the poor youth who served her—of his sixteen hours daily work, of his cheerless life and imperilled health,—"O really that never struck her. The clear, soft, gentle tone, the good, kindly, honest look, tell you conclusively that the farthest thing from her heart was harshness to any mortal; yet, had she gone into such a shop at that hour and seen a son of her own there, it would probably have struck her.

Even yet the state of things in London is very bad. The most protracted hours are still persisted in by the greater part of the grocers, chemists, oilmen, and tobacconists, by the lower class of drapers, and by the shops of every description in the closer and more unhealthy neighbourhoods The greatest improvement has taken place in the highest class of shops, where, though urgently needed, it was not so urgently as in those which remain as bad as ever. At eleven o'clock on a Saturday night, you may see young men in that grocer's shop over there, where they have been from seven in the morning. The summer air is oppressive, the gas lights are warm, their work is unceasing. They will not be at rest before the morn of Sunday; and one of those young men, I know, is a Christian brother,—a thoughtful, reading, upright, useful man—one who loves God and keeps his commandments,—and to-morrow he will teach the children of others for love of their souls. I do declare it makes me indignant to see him shut up there at this hour.

Even in the wholesale houses, where the ordinary hours are tolerable, the protraction of labour in the busy season is really horrible. It is a fact, that just during the rush of the spring or autumn trade, young men are often at work till midnight, and sometimes till one or two o'clock in the morning. After a man has been labouring for a whole day in the city, with its depressing air, with its haste, wear, and tax, that he is to go on labouring by gas-light from sunset to midnight, and then to pass into morning, is intolerable; it is a pressure on human life and happiness which no plea of commerce, which no mass of lucre can justify. "Business must be done," is with some men the whole moral law of the warehouse; the ten commandments with all the words of charity flee before it. But no business must be done which mars happiness, risks life, presses and wears out your fellow-creatures for no higher end than to avoid "losing an account," or forfeiting an order. Perish your orders and your accounts, rather than one of my fellow-creatures should be made consumptive, or should be rendered sickly for life; ay, rather than he should go on toiling with a heavy heart, feeling that man was cruel to him, and tempted to think that Providence was indifferent. If you cannot do all your business without grinding men, abridge it; better do less than commit cruelty. Better that fewer invoices should be written under your roof, than that hearts should be broken under it. No power can compel you to undertake more work than can be performed without oppression. How can you drive home and dine and go to bed, knowing that in the murky city men are labouring by gas-light for your wealth alone? If "business must be done" at those hours, do it yourself; break up your own evenings, wear down your own health, make your own mother sorrow, make your own wife droop; but do not inflict all that on others. Not long ago a young man, who had been out on an errand from his warehouse, went into a room not far from it, and sat down for a while to rest; he was overcome with fatigue; he said to a friend, "I am worn out; and to-night I shall probably be at work till one or two o'clock; we *have* been for the last two nights. Messrs. ——— may be very good Christians, but their religion is of no use to me."

The difficulty of employers, both wholesale and retail, is great. They cannot do justice to their men without a sacrifice; but the sacrifice should be made. The extensive merchant ought to provide such help as would bring the labour within a reasonable time. Now and then men who have always easy hours, may work for a night without serious mischief; but not in London air, and not often. No man is justified in leaving such a disproportion between the work and the hands as will force the latter every now and then to murderous hours. You cannot press men to a point that stings their feelings and endangers their health without sin. You should take care that no man is cursing you in his heart at the hour when your wife and children are going to rest. You may be liberal, you may be munificent, may have fine points of character and an attached circle of friends; but it is a canker in your gold and a blot on your name that men who call you master feel the iron go into their soul. To them your virtues are all lost if you do not show consideration to themselves; and perhaps the very gifts of your liberality may be followed by a malign look from those who think it would be better that you paid more, even though you gave less.

The case of Mr. Budgett shows that when a master is awake to the duty of bringing business within reasonable hours, he may effect much. In few establishments could the variety or the number of orders be greater; yet from that house the father can go forth to spend a long evening with his children, the man who loves a book can find time to read, he who delights in a ramble may enjoy the fields on a summer evening (some I have seen take share in hay-making after their day's work was done), and he who loves the house of God can enjoy the evening service and close the day in leisure at home. If masters cannot secure all this without sacrificing income, and lowering their style, let them count the cost and choose deliberately whether they will benefit their dependants at their own expense, or benefit themselves at the expense of their dependants. Human nature has its decision on such an alternative quite ready; the charity which comes from God has its decision ready too. You may adopt the one or the other, and according to your choice, so verily shall be your reward.

That attention to the comfort of his men which was manifested in abridging the hours of labour, was not the only token of his interest in their welfare. Every sign of industry and of sincere interest in the establishment gave him pleasure; and he was never slow to meet it with a reward. One, very long in his employment, told me that but a short period before his death he mentioned to him some improvement which had occurred to him for one part of the business; and he immediately thanked him, putting a sovereign into his hand. When a year wound up well, the pleasure was not all with the principals; several of those whose diligence and talent had a share in gaining the result found also that they had a share in the reward. Stock-taking became to them a matter of personal interest, and they would often enquire, "Hope you find things satisfactory, Sir?" Surely it must be far more cheerful for a master to feel that those around him have some pleasure in his success, than to know that it is indifferent to them, because they are aware that however large the cake may be he will eat it all alone. One, after describing the pains Mr. Budgett had taken to make him master of his own branch of the business, and how, when satisfied with his fitness, he had devolved upon him important responsibilities, said, with a fine feeling which I should love to see masters generally kindle among those in their employment, " And he never had a good year, but I was the better for it when stock-taking came! Indeed I may say he was a father to me in body and soul." Another who gave a similar report of the pains taken to train him said, " At stock-taking he has sometimes given me a hundred pounds at a time." He also mentioned to me that on one occasion he called at his house, and seeing his three children, said he would like to make them a present, and when he went home gave him a ten-pound note for each of them.

His ambition was to make all about him feel the same interest in the business he did himself; and by means such as these he succeeded to no common degree in inspiring that feeling.

A trembling old man who had spent the chief part of life on the premises at Kingswood, spoke with great zest of the rise of the business " from little to more." He had seen the little shop swell into warehouses, he had seen the new dwelling house rise and enlarge, he had seen the quarry filled up and turned into a garden, he had seen the adjoining fields enclosed and made pleasure grounds; and in all whereof he discoursed he had been a great part, for in out-door operations he had been a leader. According to him, Mr. Budgett had no greater delight than to be surrounded by a host of busy men; he would circulate among, he would animate them, would chide the idler heartily, and heartily encourage the worker. " Why, Sir, I do believe as he would get, ay, just twice as much work out o' a man in a week as another master." Sometimes a lazy labourer on the grounds or farm would be set all astir by the words, " Remember the gothic door." And when Friday night came, a stranger would see a practical comment on that enigmatical text. In a certain part of the wall surrounding the grounds was a door, called the gothic door, by which the men went out at night. On a Friday evening Mr. Budgett would be found standing by this door, sometimes holding a little basket filled with minute packages in paper, sometimes showing an uncommon bulkiness of pocket. As the men passed, a package was slipped into the hand of each, and one would find that he had a present of five shillings, another of three, another of half-a-crown, and so on—each discerning in his gift an estimate of his diligence; and "to a boy," said my aged informant, "he would give sixpence." You may imagine that such a narrative would kindle the narrator. "Ah, Sir, he was a man as had no pleasure in a muckin up money: why, Sir, he would often in that a way give, ay, I believe twenty pounds on a Friday night—well, at any rate, fifteen pounds."

"But would he give anything to a man who had been lazy?"

"Yes, Sir, he would gie him something, but he would soon get rid on him."

This was perfectly true; he could not bear a lazy man. Tact and push he delighted in and would largely reward; but if he could not bring a man up to his mark he would let him go. The statement above given on the testimony of the old man is perfectly correct, only that the sum bestowed in this manner seldom exceeded twelve or fourteen pounds per week. But this twined a sacred bond between men and master,—made many a cottage glad,—led many a labourer, when he saw his master in the house of God, to feel that he had given him cause to join all the more heartily in praise, —led the family of many a labourer, as they turned away from worship and saw the family of the master going to their own abundant home, to feel that they too were going to a good Sunday dinner.

Even the horse of a prosperous man is better cared for than the horse of the struggling and the poor. But full often the labourer finds himself in an establishment where wealth is gushing in amain, but not one driblet ever reaches him beyond the hard wages which would be his were prosperity far away;—no token of kindness, no gentle pledge that when gains are counted, the instruments employed to win them are remembered. With such hearts as men have in them, it is not matter of amazement that this state of things should prepare them for all sorts of seduction, for all sour theories about the enmity of capital to labour, for all blind ambitions about organising labour, sharing profits, and equalising position.

Lous Blanc's elaborate endeavour to organise labour had not a very flattering end. Four days of mortal fighting—fellow-townsmen breast to breast, beard to beard, shooting, stabbing, stoning,—merchant and mechanic, tailor and grenadier, journalist and blacksmith, cook and artilleryman, shoeblack and senator, barber and cuirassier,—the father in a blouse behind the barricade, the son in a uniform before it, the inhabitant of the first floor charging, the inhabitant of the second floor repelling the charge,—boys, women, white-headed men, all raging in one wild slaughter, all quelled "in one red burial;"—that was the way the national workshops wound up. I saw that, and I wish never to see the like again. Though new attempts to organise labour may easily have a better beginning, it is not plain that they will easily have a better end. The relation of master and men is natural, safe, manageable; and to make a community of workers so organised all our own world admits of, you need only to make masters all they ought to be. That is no small task, most surely; but on any other arrangement of society you will find a very similar task at hand. If you are to dispense with masters, and propose universal partnerships as the way to make all miseries take their leave of society, you will just find that instead of the task of making every master all he ought to be, you have the task of making every man all he ought to be; which in the long run will prove, I dare say, quite as considerable an undertaking. Emile de Girardin has no Gospel to preach, but he sometimes says a true thing. When lying in the *Conciergerie*, he wrote, "The English love liberty, the French love equality." He was right; and in that difference you have a key to much of what passes in the two nations. The English do love liberty, and will have it; but beyond that they have no faith in equality, for if men be free they cannot be equal except in this, that real liberty is the only equality attainable. Set about making two men equal, and at once they cease to be free; set them free, and in a day they cease to be equal. Equal in stature, in strength, in health, in mind, in emotional enjoyment, in power over others, we can never be. God has settled that. And as to making us equal in circumstances, it could only be effected in appearance by most grinding tyranny, and even then would be hollow and unreal. Providence has a deep system of compensation which invisibly affects a near approach to equality, where men are only free.

"Well, friend," I said to the driver of a cabriolet crossing the Place de la Concorde, some time after the republic had been established, "how do you like the republic?"

"Ah! Monsieur, the republic is a very fine thing; but—business does not thrive; I used to earn twice as much as I earn now: you see there are now no rich people, they are all gone. And that is not bad enough; but they now demand the republic democratic and social. I do not quite understand it, but they say we are all to be equal. Now, I do not like that; for most of the other cabmen spend their money in drink, and it would not be just to take what I earn and give it to them to spend so. I have always been careful. I have one son: I have saved money to educate him; he is now at a college; I mean him to be an advocate. And who knows? —my son may be a great man. Now, would it be just, in order to make us all equal, to force me to give up my earnings to men who would drink them, instead of keeping them to educate my son? Why should they try to make us equal? God has made us five fingers on one hand and has He made two of them equal?" Here he held up the fingers spread abroad; then closed them, and displayed them triumphantly as emblems of his social grades. "And, why has He made them unequal? Why, to make one good strong fist." And so saying, he clasped his fist and held it up, and turned it round, to show how much better it fitted than if all the fingers had been equally long and thick.

Now society is one hand, composed of several fingers, and institutions are but a glove. He that made the fingers did not make them equal, and you need never try to invent a glove that will; you might make an iron glove, and stunt and hamper, but though all would be distorted, they would not be equal even then. If you make a glove to fit their natural inequalities, it may prove that the thumb with his large portion is just as much straitened as the little finger with his small.

I have no faith in any attempt to make us equal in circumstances, no idea that our great Father ever meant us so to be, and no relish for that style of brotherhood which would make me hanker to have as much as my brother and share all he earned. No: let me rejoice in his lot, and rejoice in my own; and if, after every honest effort, I cannot have the satisfaction of eating my own morsel, why then, if he is a brother, he will divide his with me. But I would rather burden no man. One hardly sees the wisdom of systems which are perpetually telling society that it must take care of the individuals of which it is composed. Who ever knew of a whole making up its parts, not of parts making up a whole,—of a corn-stack making the ears, not of ears making a corn-stack? Looking at this, one is much more inclined to tell individuals to serve society, than to tell society to serve individuals.

If society is bound to care for one man it is bound equally to care for another, and so on till it must care for all; and this is the end of every scheme of provision—not providing for a section, but providing for the whole community. If you lay this task of providing at the door of any collective idea,—call it nation, society, empire, or anything else,—you assign to it precisely the same work as God has divided among, not ideas, but all men alive, charging each one of them to provide for his own. On this Divine scheme, each man has a work before him; and the work has not to look to an idea, but lies at the door of an actual agent, moved by affection, by wants, and by example, to set about his duty. On the modern scheme, each man has to look to society, or nation, or something of that kind to keep him; and when you set all the men in a country to look out for society, or nation, you will find that, apart from themselves, such words represent nothing. If society is to provide, it must either be for every one or for a part. If for every one, then you put universal provision on a new footing, trusting to the regularity of a collective organisation rather than to the fruits of individual industry; instead of dividing the great labour as much as possible, you deprive every individual of the sense of his individual responsibility. But if the idea of a collective provision for every soul in a community is not entertained, then you only mean that those who do provide for themselves and their own, ought also to provide for those who do not. Now, to this we should not object, provided those who do not provide for themselves are only those who cannot; but we do most earnestly object to have men taught that they are not bound to provide for themselves, but that society is bound to provide for them: for men are so mean and selfish that large numbers will cheerfully resign the noble desire to keep their necessities from burdening others, and give themselves up to be fed and clothed, by whom they care not so only they have plenty. And the great Author of all provision has so ruled, beyond the reach of our control, that in any community where many are indifferent to providing for themselves and their own, poverty and disorder will soon make havoc. "I must look to myself," in the sense the world uses it, is the utterance of selfishness,—a man reckless of the general good, bent only on his private ends. "I must provide for my own," in the Christian sense, is the utterance of generosity and lowliness,—a man feeling that he has no right to lay on others a load he should properly bear, no right to expect from his follow men a better share in the common inheritance than fairly belongs to his efforts in the common labour. The selfish, greedy man will look for his supplies—from what source will not in the least trouble him,—and will grudge that others should be above him. The noble and humble man will desire that he should never cost society a mite, never cost another heart a care, and will rejoice to see the services of others in the toil of life more amply rewarded than his own. This is the spirit the Gospel breathes, with its system of individual provision, and it is the spirit which, wherever it prevails, makes a working, earning, contented man.

All creatures were made by a Giver; therefore, all creatures give. The dull clod gives life to the bountiful seed, the grass-blade gives beauty to the eye and food to the herd, the flower gives manifold pleasure, the trees give majesty and good service, the stones give a dwelling; the air, the rain, the ocean, the river, all give—and who shall tell how much? The bird gives its music and its loveliness, the kine give food, the fold gives raiment; the horse, the silk-worm, and all things we love to mention give, give; and, above us, every star gives though but a slender ray, and every planet gives, and that great sun gives so much, that withdraw him and all these others would give no more. And above him is the Giver who gives all these and has yet better things to give, which will make all these look trifling. God is ever giving: He has given heaven above and earth below; there given angel life,—here human life; there thrones, dominions, principalities and powers,—here grace, mercy, and peace. He gives ever; but he does not receive, except, indeed, the joy of seeing those happy whom he has enriched out of his own store.

As a man enters on this world, he enters it the offspring of the great Giver, and looking around on a whole race of brothers, his inquiry should be, What service can I do, what part can I bear, what contribution can I give?—not, What claims can I establish, and what consideration can I obtain? What can I do for all?—not, What can I force all to do for me? And to a man in this mood of heart, nothing would be more unwelcome than to tell him, You are to be kept and cared for by the toil of others; you are to be a taker not a giver. All of the Divine image that was in him would rebel—gently, generously rebel. No, no; he would not be a taker, he would be a giver; none should bear his burden, he would bear it; and if his services were of little account, still the world has many wants, and he would supply some one of them. And say not that any man's gift is small. He that fells trees for us, is his gift small? He that raises coal for us, is his gift small? He that tends sheep for us, is his gift small? He that spins or weaves for us, is his gift small? He that breaks stones for us, is his gift small? No: every one of these, if he be "a partaker of the Divine nature," and love to live not for himself but to show forth the image of God, can rejoice in his labour, that he is employed under the great Giver to perform a part in the universal giving whereon all happiness depends. Let the gift of those who give in any one of these lines be withheld for one year, and all would cry aloud under real want. Yes, my honest brother, low-seated there, this frosty morning, breaking cold stones, thou too art giving,—bearing thy part toward the comfort of God's creation! Pity thy heart should not have a sense of the office thou art discharging; it would make thy service proceed more cheerily! I cannot help feeling humbled before thee; thy toil for our common family is less kindly than mine; it is a pleasanter thing to make books for mankind than to break stones for them!

Yes, we are all sent here to give; and, in order to do that, we must not be dependent. He cannot bestow to society who lives upon society; he only gives who provides for his own. Some there ever will be who cannot make provision for themselves; let their kindred then be givers, and keep them from burdening the community. But if there is no kindred who can or will give, O then the call of the community is clear,—love them, relieve them, make them happy; let them not be outcasts from the family, but brethren in need, and therefore supplied tenderly. "If any man or woman that believeth hath widows, let *them* relieve them, and let *not* the *church be charged*, that it may relieve them that are widows indeed." Is not that law? Does not your conscience echo it? "He that will not work, neither should he eat; if any man provide not for his own, and especially for those of his own house, he hath denied the faith, and is worse than an infidel." Put those plain things together, and if man attempt to mend them he will fail. The individual is to work; out of his earnings he is to eat; if he has some of his own house who cannot work he is to give them to eat; if he refuse this he is an infidel and worse. And if there are poor whom no kindred relieve, the church must relieve them. The individual, the family, the church; the church comes last, and is to care for those, and for those only, who cannot care for themselves, who are not cared for by the family. This is God's order; and you may make fifty thousand other plans, but you will never put half so much practical knowledge of man's heart and man's need into your long plans as lies in that short one.

It is plain from the Apostle's teaching as to what families were to do, and what the church was to do, that he taught not the doctrine of community of goods. The church of Jerusalem, in its first flame of charity, made an approach to that condition, but never reached it in anything like the socialistic sense; for though they chose to sell and to distribute, "Whiles it remained was it not *thine own?* and after it was sold, was it not *in thine own power?*"—showing that no law had pronounced the community sole proprietor, but that every contributor was considered a free-will donor. And even this general selling and distributing never occurs elsewhere. The example is never quoted to incite any other church; they are called to lay by on the first day of the week, but not to sell and distribute; and when this same church at Jerusalem has need of relief from them all, we never find her first course pleaded, and other churches called upon to do for her what she had done for her own. Had they done so, soon would they have needed other churches to do the same for them; and when a day of public distress came, all being without resources (which must ever be the case where none has private property), all would have needed foreign help, as those at Jerusalem needed it, as soon as the famine came. In the passage above quoted, the Apostle plainly disapproves the supplying of any want out of a church fund, but such as cannot be met either by individual industry or family resources.

But while utterly disbelieving the theories which tempt our working classes to move for a new order of institutions, one is not surprised that the neglect shown by masters generally should induce a state of feeling among their men highly favourable to the approaches of any one who held out the prospect of a free, equal, fraternal future. The substantial interests of a community are promoted better a thousand times by the perfect freedom of industry and the universal push of individual enterprise, than it ever could be by any interference with the relations into which labour, capital, and talent naturally link themselves as the emergencies of trade may dictate. On this free principle, he generally becomes a master whose abilities enable him, in that position, to ensure the maintenance of those whose lab ourseconds his talent employs and augments his capital; and they generally remain men whose energies produce more to themselves under vigorous supervision than they would if worked only by innate impulse, or guided only by their own prudence. On this free principle, the development of industry, the race of invention, the spread of international commerce, the employment and the wealth of a people are advanced far more surely, smoothly, and rapidly, than they could be by any artificial organisation possible. But the very conviction that only derangement and want are to be expected from fettering labour in order to foster it, makes one all the more anxious to impress upon those who, under our existing system of freedom, hold the master-rank, the solemn duty that lies upon them to make in their heart and in their actions a very wide and a very manifest distinction between their men and their machinery. Do, as a man and as a Christian, do let them feel that you are their friend and brother; that you think of them, feel for them, love them; do spend time and money to make them happy. When you prosper, let them have some slight share in your prosperity; better make fifty cottages a blanket warmer for the winter, than make your own mansion a shade more splendid. If you nett five thousand on the year, what great feat would it be if one thousand went to spread satisfaction and comfort around you?—not in indiscriminate bounties; you should not distribute as a machine but as a master, giving most to those whose aid has most contributed to the result, and then (among those whose work would just have been the same and done in the same way had all been going to wreck as it was when all was prospering) choose the best and most worthy to receive the most; but in a day when much is gathered let all have a taste. One year Mr. Budgett expected that the profits would be large; he fixed behorehand on a certain sum, and said, "So much will be the well, and all that runs over shall go among *the business*." When they had proceeded far enough to see how things would turn, he said, "The well is full;" and it did run over a very large amount, and many of those below him were made well aware of it. The receipts, the profits, the gifts of that year, I do not know; but one who was a witness of it all told me enough to make me feel that in what I have written above I am not running wild with theory, but commending things which might be done. He would often say to his heads of departments and travellers, "My business! It is not *my* business; it is *ours*." All masters should try to diffuse that feeling, and thereby lead those who work with them to feel with them.

It is evident that in giving his men some reward for good service he was actuated by a sincere desire to see them advance. This he constantly evinced in many ways. One theme of his advices habitually was that they should push their way upward; he had a wonderful impression that all might prosper, and a strong desire to see them do so. He was constantly enforcing habits of frugality; he would make them if possible save a little and put it into his hand, for which he would give them five per cent., and help them on. One whom he persuaded thus to put ten pounds into his hand, had seen it grow to one hundred. With his household servants it was just the same; he could not bear to see them neglecting means of making themselves comfortable, and would in every way in his power induce them to save and look upwards.

In personal intercourse with those under him, Mr. Budgett was extremely familiar; airs and assumptions he knew not. Most would have thought him far too inattentive to dignity; but it was his nature to be open, off-hand, and at home. What a subtraction from the discomfort of this world it would be if all who have grown rich were the same. But you have often seen a man,—a pursy, stiff, important man; his clothes good, well made, fitting tightly on a front person which has a particular, contented set; his lip locked and slightly curling; his nose slightly curling too; his shoulders moving under a deep conviction that they carry a momentous head; and the head not bent forward, not thrown backward, not leaned to one side, but cast half upwards, half sideways, very slightly, as if just commencing a consequential toss:—there he is, and whenever you see him, you read, "CASH-BOX" as plainly as ever you read it on a Chubb; and in his presence a poor man feels just as he always does in the presence of a Chubb—"No access there for me!" Now Mr. Budgett never was a cash-box; he was always a plain free-spoken man, who talked with his men homely and kindly, and if they were in fault would lecture them sharply; but if he thought he had unduly hurt a man's feelings, would take a speedy opportunity of making friends with him, and if he believed it due, would beg pardon of one of the humblest. "Indeed, he was an adept at begging pardon," said one who had long been close by his side. And a right good art that wherein to be an adept, especially when inferiors are concerned.

A habit existed in the establishment up to Mr. Budgett's death which dated from an early period of its history. Every month the heads of departments and the travellers met the principals, when all spoke freely on matters affecting the concern, each being expected to state anything which he thought wanted to be supplied, altered or discontinued. The observations of each would naturally refer to his own department; but all the range of subjects was open. By this means the principals had the personal advantage of all the experience of their responsible assistants, and these had the comfort of feeling that they could say whatever appeared to them desirable on points affecting either the morality, the comfort, or the success of the establishment. All parties gained light and stimulus, and all gradually acquired a feeling of common responsibility and common interest. After these meetings the principals and travellers took tea together.

Besides this monthly meeting, it was usual, after stock-taking, to give all the men a supper. On these occasions the rewards for punctual attendance were distributed to those who had earned them, and every man who had not had one black mark received his bright sovereign, which frequently amounted to a handsome sum altogether. Thus when the commercial harvest-home came, the labourers had the harvest-home feast, and a good practical stimulus to boot for their future benefit. All had an opportunity of saying anything that was upon their heart to say.

When the fire compelled the removal of the establishment to Bristol, some irregularity occurred in these important interchanges of good feeling. But Mr. Budgett had not lost the desire to cherish between himself and his men all the sympathies of friendship; accordingly we find a local paper giving the following account of

"A BUSINESS FETE.

"On Friday last the neighbourhood of Nelson Street was enlivened by a gay and busy movement in the establishment of Messrs. Budgett. The annual festival given to their men was on this occasion provided for them at the country residence of one of the senior partners, Samuel Budgett, Esq., Kingswood Hill. Coaches, omnibuses, and carriages of nearly every description were put in requisition to carry the inmates of this hive of industry to the spot. Ample preparation were there found both for the recreation of the body as well as the mind; and the weather for the most part proving favourable, all seemed happy in exchanging the stale atmosphere of stone walks and walls for the more healthy retreat of rural scenery. At three o'clock about 200 of their business staff sat down to a sumptuous dinner in the open air on the lawn adjoining the house, when 'the good cheer' found a cordial welcome and a hearty dispatch. This being ended, the party was soon joined by their wives and friends, to spend with each other the remainder of the day. Athletic exercises, games, and other amusements were then indulged in upon the spacious grounds, whilst a select band of music in attendance kept up the mirthful sound and 'made the welkin ring.' The pleasure grounds, fruit garden, and shrubberies were all thrown open to the company, and no scene could portray a happier appearance of self-enjoyment and social union. In the evening from 300 to 400 assembled for tea under a large covered building, after which several animated speeches were delivered by the gentlemen present, among whom were the clergy and ministers of each denomination in the village. A beautifully mounted silver inkstand, procured from Mr. W. Hodson, Broadmead, by the united contributions of each assistant in the concern, was then presented to the eldest son, Mr. J. S. Budgett, as a token of their sincere respect and attachment. The day closed too quickly upon these mutual pleasures, when all returned with a recollection of their social and commercial union. We cannot do better than recommend a similar experiment to all who wish to cherish in their business one common feeling of interest which ought always to exist between employers and the employed."

The Rev. B. Carvosso gives the following note of the same meeting:—

"Not long before I left Kingswood, he got all his commercials, clerks, porters, labourers, with their families to Kingswood, to dinner and tea. There were about 400 of his people present, two clergymen, an Independent minister, and two Wesleyan ministers. He gave a lengthened address which appeared to me of an extraordinary character; —I have often wished notes had been made of it, and it had been printed. Of the kind I think it was a masterpiece, both for its matter and manner. Except on that occasion I never heard him come out in a set public address, but the talent then displayed convinced me of the grasp of his mind, and how greatly some had mistaken him."

Now, what is there impossible in all this; and what could be more helpful to the good feeling of the whole community than its frequent imitation? To see all the inhabitants of that huge store packing themselves into vehicles with all the glee of a festivity; driving away to the country scene of their master's residence, of their own former labours, gathering on the fair lawn, round a table where every good thing abounded, porter and waggoner, clerk and salesman, traveller and cooper, errand boy and principal, all sitting down in hearty kindred; while five ministers come to honour the meeting of different grades, and show the meeting of different sects. Then, the repast over, the men betake themselves according to taste, unrestrained and unawed, some to saunter round the grounds, some to sports; while the music stirs them, and their wives, their mothers, their sweethearts arrive to share the pleasure, and presently to share a grateful treat of tea. And the principal and his sons amidst it all seem the chief pleasure-takers of the day. But after tea it proves that the men, having learned that the eldest "of the young gentlemen" is about to make a home of his own, have resolved that the treat of the day shall not be all on one side, and therefore a pretty silver inkstand, bearing grateful words, is presented with expressions that honour all parties, and tend more to cement all. Then good wholesome speeches are made by one and another—master, man, and strangers—without our national absurdity of toasts; and the energetic architect of this prosperity throws his whole heart into words meant to help his men to be wise, to prosper, and to gain eternal life. One would greatly like to have those words; but they are not;—they are gone, and he that spoke them;—yet mayhap they live in the life and heart of some youth who that day heard them.

Now, those who wail over the festal boards of feudal times may take both a consolation and a hint as to their own age from a scene like this. Wherein is this commercial fête inferior to a muster of rough men, used to rough deeds, and clattering with rough weapons—men whose dreams are of foray and feud. These men of trade are better clad, better housed, better fed, better taught, have far more of freedom and of opportunity to rise if the ability to rise is in them; and they are employed not in broils, but in ministering to the daily wants of their neighbours. They are a better, more useful, and more comfortable race incomparably than the old wassailers of chivalric days; and that merchant may look upon his retainers with an honest satisfaction, for he and they are doing a milder, worthier work far than the lords and the followers of ancient times. Such a scene, too, suggests the way wherein the relations of commerce may be elevated above that leaden materialism which too generally pervades them, and imbued with some moral warmth, some kindred and mutual feeling. I have lately been delighted to hear of several cases wherein manufacturers adopt this practice of annually giving their men an entertainment; and it cannot be too strongly recommended, for such cases are yet very rare. We have heard of mind among the spindles, and do let us try to get some heart among them also.

The year after the one in which the gala just spoken of took place, another was given in a large room in the warehouse. The room was decorated with all manner of evergreens, devices, and mottoes. These were chosen by the men, and indicated their varying taste,—the religious man, the man of business, the lover of a pleasantry. The meeting left such a relish in the memory of the men, that some of the mottoes then used had been preserved, and were put into my hand. The first that meets my eye was germain enough to the place:—

PERSEVERANCE
SURMOUNTS
DIFFICULTIES.

The next which turns up seems to have come out of a practical head:—

MAY POVERTY BE
ALWAYS
A DAY'S MARCH BEHIND US!

This is followed by one which seemed to catch the spirit of such an entertainment:—

UNION OF OBJECT,
UNION OF EFFORT,
UNION OF FEELING.

Here is one emanating evidently from a mind in which the work of life and the presiding power of God were seen in their fit connexion:—

THE BLESSING OF THE LORD MAKETH RICH.
IN ALL LABOUR THERE IS PROFIT.
WHATSOEVER THY HAND FINDETH TO DO,
DO IT WITH ALL THY MIGHT.

This I find followed by one whose author seemed to be moved by the fact that the gentleman to whom they, at the last meeting, presented the silver inkstand, was now about to bring among them a wife and a party of new relations, in whose presence and connexion "with the house," all felt, and with good reason, a personal honour:—

THE SINGLE MARRIED,
AND THE MARRIED HAPPY!

Following this, comes one with a specially florid border, which tells a good tale of master and men:—

THE THANKS OF THE ESTABLISHMENT
ARE TENDERED TO
MESSRS H. H. AND S. BUDGETT AND CO.,
FOR THEIR
GREAT LIBERALITY
IN PRESENTING
£100
TO THE SICK FUND,
AND FOR THE GENEROUS MANNER THEY WISH IT
APPROPRIATED.

And the last that lies on my table is well worthy to be blazoned on such an establishment:—

DILIGENT IN BUSINESS,
FERVENT IN SPIRIT.

The room thus prepared according to the best taste the house could command, the men were met by their superior, his family, their new connexions from the great metropolis, and some other friends whose presence was an honour. Refreshments were plentiful, tempers were blithe; and after a while Mr. Farmer, of Gunnersbury House, the father-in-law of the young master, was called to the chair, and a flow of good feeling was interchanged by all parties. The speaking was not confined to the "platform," but the men were called upon to speak freely, and used the liberty with both spirit and discretion. According to their turn of mind they spoke of the hand of Providence displayed in the progress of "the business," of the importance of true religion, of purely business topics, or of some matter calculated to raise a smile. Fine feeling, pleasure, cheerfulness, good counsel, and piety ran through the whole proceedings. Many a hearty laugh was there, and many a useful impression. The speakers were of all grades; the oldest and the most respectable men in the establishment, the younger clerks, the working men of different branches, and even the boys being represented. One of the leaders of the house heartily congratulated "our young master," expressed their pleasure at seeing so distinguished a gentleman in their chair, and especially their pleasure in seeing so many *ladies* with them; yet, the while, in good home tones, to which all kindly hearts echoed, declared that after all, his own fireside treasure was not to be bartered for any of them. The burden of several speeches was on the rise of the business; and over and over have I heard the regret expressed that no report had been taken—a regret wherein, certainly, I share. One man had a metaphor which appears to have made a great impression, wherein the business was a gun and the different agencies answered to the different parts of the gun; but of all his "admiring hearers," I have met with none who could put together the stock, lock, and barrel, although they declare that the gun went off with great éclat. Another man, in rich Kingswood accent, said that once when a boy he had come up out of a pit on a winter morning and found the ground covered with snow. He began to *rowl*, and rowled till he had a great big ball, O ever so big, till he could rowl no more; but he called another boy or two and they rowled and rowled till their ball was montrous big; then they did a leave it there. The thaw came and all the snow did melt away, but their ball did stand, and after none of the snow was to be seen nowhere, the ball was there a standing still. Now, Mr. Budgett was just like he: he had a begun and rowled and it grew bigger; then he did call first one and then another, and they rowled and rowled, and here they were all o' em; every one a rowling as hard as they could, and he didn't know how big the ball would grow afore they had done rowling; and he was sure that just like *their* ball, it would stand when a great deal of others was all melted nowhere.

Now which was it more rational,—to gather his men and spend such an evening with them,—or give a ball and supper to a party of rich people, and introduce them to his new alliances? Which was the more likely to spread real happiness, good feeling, good principles, and good living? With such scenes before us, and with the impression they have plainly left on those who partook of them, is it not altogether gratuitous to consign the different ranks of commercial life to hopeless alienation? They may meet, may eat and drink together, may kindle up good feeling, and may thus form ties which will unite men and master, give a heart to their intercourse, and render all parties happier in their lot. But the man who would hold such festivities with full success, must not be a large gentleman who will magnificently meet his men "from a sense of duty," and speak in great tones of the mutual interests of different ranks, and be mightily condescending. All that will only leave things where it found them. The man who would do this duty rightly must do it from the heart, because he loves his men, delights in seeing them happy, and feels that they have a claim on his best attentions. With a heart so prepared, he will have a winning cordiality which will go further than even the good fare.

The habit of daily prayer in the establishment, which we noticed in our first chapter, had existed from the beginning. When the business was only retail, all were gathered together as a family; and when it branched out into an extensive concern, a portion of the premises at Kingswood was set apart as a "chapel," and still stands there serving many sacred purposes. In Nelson Street this admirable habit was maintained, and there also a room devoted to this purpose. More than once I have taken part with the men in their united devotions, and that with delight and thanksgiving. You could not help feeling that a better tone must be created amongst those men by this daily pause in their haste, this hearing of the Holy Word, this bowing at the awful yet gracious throne. One of those who knew every joint of the establishment, who had risen with it and loved it as if it were his own, (a feeling, by the way, which I found more among the servants of that establishment than among those of any other with whom I have ever conversed,) remarked how this practice tended to induce among the men order and regularity of life, even where decided piety was not the result. "Besides, you see, Sir, in this way the men get to pray for the blessings of God on the business, and there is a great deal in that. Many would like to get to the elevation we have reached, but they cannot without the same blessing."

In the Christian Miscellany for 1847, is the following account, written by one then living at Kingswood, the scene of which you will have no difficulty in recognising:—

"EXAMPLE TO MERCANTILE ESTABLISHMENTS.

'Not slothful in business; fervent in spirit.'

"On the 2nd of November, 1846, after a drive of several miles from the country, at half-past seven in the morning, I dropped unintentionally into the extensive and busy warehouse of ———, in ———. I heard singing, "the voice of rejoicing and salvation," in one of the upper rooms. The senior clerk said to me, "Our men are engaged in morning prayer: will you not step up and see them? Do, Sir." At once deeply interested, I ascended, and entered a room thirty-five or forty feet long, furnished with benches, having comfortable backs, closely placed, and at the upper end was a table and a large fire. How was I surprised and delighted to find from fifty to one hundred, (for every seat seemed occupied with its complement,) chiefly porters in their white frocks, all sitting in the stillness and seriousness of family devotion! At the table sat an interesting, devout labourer, giving out one of our beautiful hymns with a tenderness and pathos that touched my heart; while the singing was conducted with a sweetness and harmony that charmed and edified. The Hymn-book was offered to me; but I declined it. After singing, I was again requested to lead their devotions. The Bible lay open on the table at the twenty-fifth chapter of St. Matthew. I read the appropriate parables of the virgins and the talents. We then fell on our knees and worshipped the God of all commerce in earth and seas; when every man rose to attend the call of duties. I felt it no common privilege to join with those praying porters and devout clerks; and the scene, so good, and coming so unexpectedly, I assure you, Mr. Editor, has left an impression on me I shall not soon forget. Is not this an example to all commercial establishments; an example worthy of general imitation? Here is a noble room for the daily worship of God in the heart of a range of warehouses, and the large number of hands employed therein have a regular portion of time allotted them for that holy purpose. Nor is time whiled away here; the porters and clerks are all required to be on the premises at six o'clock every morning, or pay a small fine in case of delinquency, as well as forfeit the master's daily pecuniary reward for punctuality. Some of the men live four miles distant; but the habit of punctuality is so established, that certain of them have never been once subject to the forfeiture through a long course of years. Precision, order, energy, and exactness are principles engraved on every department of the vast business here conducted. But everything is 'sanctified by the word of God and prayer;' and therefore it is no matter of astonment to those who have faith in the Bible, that the energetic and worthy proprietor of this exemplary mercantile establishment, in addition to his having much peace and piety among his men, has risen from small and low beginnings to great wealth and prosperity. 'Him that honoureth me, I will honour.' A WESLEYAN MINISTER."

Ah! say, if all the good men in the world went into *your* warehouse every day in the year, and all the day long, would they ever witness a scene which would make them thank God? Would they ever see anything to prove that you wished to teach your men that they had souls to prepare for life eternal? The blessing of which my good friend to whom I referred above spoke was surely upon that establishment in answer to prayer. Mr. Carvosso says:—"I have heard some of his neighbour tradesmen speak as if he rose by magic, and the matters of Nelson Street were an affair of legerdemain. 'He sells,' said one to me, 'cheaper than he buys; I know he does, from what he has bought of me: there is some deep mystery in his affairs.' So spoke a man of business not *his friend.* Well, I will not say that the *spell* of heaven was not upon him: 'There is that scattereth and yet increaseth; there is that withholdeth more than is meet, but it tendeth to poverty.' Joseph was 'a prosperous man,' by the peculiar blessing of God; so was Samuel Budgett."

On witnessing the scene at "family prayer," it immediately struck me that a man of the world would expect such an establishment to be prolific of hypocrites; therefore I asked the senior just alluded to, if he could remember many cases having occurred in the course of his service, wherein men professing religion had played foul with the firm. The question was new to him, and gave him some surprise:—"Well, I have been about twenty-five years in the house, and we have had members of the different churches—of the Establishment, Independents, Baptists, Quakers, and many Wesleyans,—and we have had a few cases of pilfering and dishonesty; but I do not remember any case of that happening with a man who was a *member* of any church." He then detailed one or two instances of dishonesty and detection. At a subsequent interview he said, that he believed one of the persons he had named had been taken by another of the men, only a week before his detection, to a class meeting of the Wesleyan body; but that was all the approach he had made to membership. This fact is very remarkable: the blessing daily invoked was not fruitless; the moral tone maintained was powerful in restraining; and doubtless much was due to Mr. Budgett's firm opposition to all imposture, and keen insight into men. Had he been slow to discover or lax to punish deception, without doubt he would have reared a numerous race of fair-faced impostors; but under his eye false pretence shrank and despaired. The result is one that religious masters should well ponder; every ruler ought to be a terror to evil doers, as well as a praise to them that do well. That is the example set by the great Ruler and his counsel to all rulers.

We before alluded to a system by which Mr. Budgett had transgressors reported to him; and whether the complaint was respecting business or character, the defaulter was sent for into the private office, and had to confront the master alone. His words of rebuke were generally short and telling; but in a grave case he would take much pains to make a favourable moral impression on the man. To boys he would often, besides advice, give a book, such as James's 'Young Man from Home,' or 'A Father's Counsels to a Son.' You may remember the old man who told of the money-givings at the gothic door: I asked him, "Did he ever speak to you about your soul?" "Often, Sir," was the pensive reply, as if the tone reproached a too heedless hearing. The bare fact of having, in case of fault, to go alone into "the private office," was no small poise against transgression, and this personal contact with the master must have had far more effect than any rebuke by deputy, or a punishment without such moral application. If any man repeatedly transgressed, "He will never do us any good, the sooner he is off the premises the better," was the conclusion, and he must be discharged. Indulgence to wrong doing is no kindness to an individual; and to a community it is ruinous. Cruelty could not desire anything more than rulers who would treat good and evil alike. In a community where offences rise, punishment is not the work of cruelty but of goodness; the suffering of the culprit being the protection of the community from universal corruption and misery. Too great severity and too great laxity both show an unfit ruler; but total laxity is the greatest plague to which family, town, or nation, could be subjected.

You will gather, then, that as a master Mr. Budgett expected full tale of service,—expected order, zeal, and industry; that he carefully trained his men to the most useful habits of business, and strictly repressed irregularity or ill conduct; that he rewarded diligence, provided for their relief in sickness, brought their hours of labour within a moderate limit, proved their friend in time of need, and encouraged them to rise; that he was familiar in intercourse, and loved to meet them in temperate but cheerful festivities; that he did not forget they were immortal, but took means to lead them to remember their Creator, to cultivate the godliness which "hath the promise both of the life that now is, and of that which is to come." In all this, has he not left a lesson which many masters may study with advantage?

To the Rev. John Gaskin, Rector of St. Cuthbert's, Bedford, who was for years Incumbent of Kingswood, I am indebted for the following beautiful sketch, which will throw a clearer light on many of the points touched in this chapter, and on Mr. Budgett's character generally. The reader will prefer it in the free style in which it has been furnished for my use, rather than if moulded into formal quotations:—

"I ought, perhaps, to introduce my remarks by admitting that my acquaintance with Mr. Samuel Budgett commenced under circumstances of very strong prejudice against him. The origin of this feeling is not a matter of importance to any. My only motive in making the allusion is to do justice to the integrity of character, the amiability of disposition, the forbearance of temper which ultimately broke down so formidable a barrier against close and loving friendship.

"At the time of which I write, and for several years afterwards, the business premises of the Messrs. Budgett stood on Kingswood Hill. I imagine there could not have been, even then, less than a hundred pair of hands in their employ. Of these parties, some were under articles of apprenticeship—youths of respectable parentage, with whom handsome premiums had been paid, and whose temporary home was in the family of one of the partners; others were young unmarried men, having, generally, apartments in the village; others, again, were heads of families, occupying houses in the neighbourhood. You can easily conceive with how much solicitude my attention was directed to this very important section of my parishioners; and how largely my heart was relieved from anxiety on their account, as time passed on, and revealed to me the extent to which their best interests were provided for by those on whom the responsibility so immediately rested.

"I have spoken of prejudice in my mind. This was partly produced by the remarks of persons who, I afterwards discovered, had yet to learn the motives which should actuate Christian masters in regard to those whom God had brought under their influence. The process under which my mind was disabused of the prejudice which had been thus inspired was the most favourable for all parties. My first correct impressions of the internal arrangements connected with this 'gigantic hive,' as it has been called, were gathered *out of doors* in my ministerial intercourse with the families of those who were employed in it. I have a clear recollection of the very first incident of the kind that occurred to me. My call was at the dwelling of one of Mr. Budgett's clerks. I had had frequent interviews with him, but on this occasion he was from home. His wife took the opportunity of thanking me for the interest I appeared to take in her husband, and earnestly expressed her gratitude for the kind providence which had directed their steps to Kingswood. They had formerly been in business for themselves, and their circumstances had been those of comparative affluence; but they had experienced sad reverses, and these, I subsequently learned from the husband himself, were mainly to be attributed to his own irregular habits. For months they had been without a home; every effort to procure employment had failed; for days together they had scarcely had food; and, to use the poor woman's own words, 'when we came into this house, we had scarcely anything around us but the bare walls.' Mr. Budgett, she informed me, had promised, through some friends, to give her husband a trial, and it was this which had brought them to Kingswood. 'I shall never forget,' she said, 'my husband's feelings when he first came in after having seen Mr. Budgett for the first time. He wept like a child—indeed, we both wept, for it was so long since any body had been kind to us. Mr. Budgett had been speaking to him like a father, but what affected him most was this,—when he had signed the agreement, Mr. Budgett took him from the counting-house into a small parlour in his own house, and offered up a prayer for him and his family.' In a short time after this, (I think she said the very next day,) Mr. Budgett's sister, 'Miss Elizabeth'—had come down, and after a few delicate inquiries about furniture, bedding and clothing, arrangements had been made for placing them in circumstances of comfort. Mrs. —— added, that from the time of her husband's having entered into Mr. Budgett's employment he had been a different man; all his tastes seemed to have undergone a change: their means were limited, it was true, compared with what they once had been, but they were now in the enjoyment of a happiness to which they were strangers when they were surrounded by what they used to regard as the comforts of life. In concluding her story, she remarked, 'Mr. —— always says that the secret of Mr. Budgett's success in business lies in his true religion.'

"And Mr. —— was right. Never have I witnessed such a remarkable instance of a firm of mercantile men, being guided by the Saviour's injunction, 'Seek ye first the kingdom of God and his righteousness, and all these things shall be added unto you.'

"As circumstances brought me into more frequent and closer communication with the heads of the firm, I had better opportunities for accurately observing the internal arrangements of their establishment, and the principles by which they seemed to be guided in every department of its operations. The more I saw the more I admired, and the longer the time I have had for revolving my growing impressions the more I am satisfied that they were fairly deduced. It was scarcely possible to enter the premises without being struck with the marvellous tone of order which pervaded every part of the busy scene. I recall, at this very moment, the manner and exclamation of an intelligent youth, who, while spending part of one of his vacations at the parsonage, happened to be with me when I was calling on Mr. Budgett. On entering the counting-house I missed my young friend, and when I stepped back to look for him, I found him standing in the middle of one of the warehouses, gazing in an attitude of utter astonishment. When he caught sight of me, he lifted up his hands, and exclaimed,—

'Hoc opus, hic labor est.'

Indeed, the most ordinary spectator must have observed, at a glance, that every movement he witnessed was under the control of one head,—that every person, from the mere boy who was nimbly picking up the crooked nails by the side of a newly-opened hogshead, to the sedate clerk who was sitting over his calculations at the desk, felt that he had a work to do; and, judging from the intense earnestness of his manner, that he felt also that his interest, nay, his happiness, no less than his duty, lay in his doing that work well. If the spectator sought for the secret influence which was at work, producing this result, he must *step within*, and get such an insight into the real character of the controlling head, as might enable him to appreciate the sympathetic thrill which could not fail to be caught from a spirit earnestly at work, feeling that the work was lawful,—that it must be sustained not for self only, but for the good of others also,—and that, to secure success, it must be carried on constantly in the fear of God.

"The influence of these principles ought to have been felt from the very first day on which any person might have entered into Mr. Budgett's employ. The domestic arrangements were such that the youth, fresh from school, was taught to begin and end the business of each day in the privacy of the closet; and the same salutary lesson was taught to the entire body of the employed as far as circumstances would admit, for they were statedly assembled in a private chapel on the premises for morning prayer. I well remember how grateful to my own heart was the discovery that every youth in that establishment *had his own private sleeping apartment, with the express understanding that this arrangement was made in order that he might feel himself alone with his Father which is in heaven*, when, at suitable times, he might be disposed to retire for the reading of the Scriptures, meditation, and prayer; and well do I remember my feelings when first I heard from within the walls of that little unpretending chapel,—now how doubly dear, from the recollection that loved ones, then on earth, but now in heaven, were wont to worship there!—well do I recall the thrill of devout gratitude to God which came over my soul, when from those walls I first heard the volume of manly voice raised in holy song—

'Forth, in thy name, O Lord, I go,
My daily labour to pursue;
Thee, only thee, resolved to know,
In all I think, or speak, or do.

'The task thy wisdom hath assign'd,
O let me cheerfully fulfil!
In all my works thy presence find,
And prove thy acceptable will.

'Thee may I set at my right hand,
Whose eyes my inmost substance see;
And labour on at thy command,
And offer all my works to thee.

'Give me to bear thy easy yoke,
And every moment watch and pray;
And still to things eternal look,
And hasten to thy glorious day.

'For thee delightfully employ,
Whate'er thy bounteous grace hath given;
And run my course with even joy,
And closely walk with thee to heaven.'

What was thus devoutly commenced in the retirement of the closet, or in domestic worship on a large scale, was followed up practically in the business arrangements throughout the day. A conscientious regard to order, punctuality, and just dealing was obvious to any intelligent observer. Hooker's motto, "ORDER, heaven's first law," seemed to be the grand prevailing principle over every movement of hand or foot. There was haste, but no hurry; dispatch, but no confusion. Every one was taught that irregularity on his part might be fatal to the regularity of another, and, *therefore*, he must avoid it. PUNCTUALITY was another remarkable feature. I have known the driver of the conveyance which was sent into Bristol three times a week for the convenience of the inhabitants on the Hill, rebuked for waiting for his own master, and thus entailing inconvenience on the parties who had taken their seats at the proper time. Here, again, the lesson was constantly enforced, that the want of punctuality might inflict an injury on others, and, *therefore*, such an evil was to be diligently guarded against. Principles of JUST DEALING, also, were constantly being urged. It was carried into the minutest matters, and, like all besides, enforced on the principles of the Saviour's 'golden rule.' I have known a young man expostulated with for using more twine than was necessary in making up a parcel; and another person's servant admonished that the time he was spending in gossip was his master's—not his own. I was once passing through one of the warehouses with Mr. Budgett, when he observed a young man cutting paper for bags in a manner which incurred loss of time and waste of material. He pointed out to him the mistake in the kindest manner, folded the paper and cut a considerable quantity of it himself, and having thus demonstrated his point both in regard to material and time, he remarked, 'Of course it will be wrong to *me* should you recur to your former method in this matter; and I know you would not wish to injure your employer even in so small a thing as this. But see the injury you will do *yourself*, should you ever have a business of your own, and not have acquired the most economical method of doing things of this kind.' On another occasion I was with him,—he was passing through the 'Fruit-room' with his usually quick step,—when his equally sharp eye caught the balance of a pair of scales which were being at that moment used: the poise was against the customer.

Never shall I forget the sharpness of the rebuke which that young man received. Months had elapsed between this incident and the one I have just named, for they were during two separate visits from Bedford to Bristol; but I immediately contrasted in my own mind the severe tone of the rebuke administered when the interest of another was affected, with the mild and gentle remonstrance when only self appeared to be concerned. I may just add here, that severity was by no means congenial to his nature; indeed, the gentleness of his temper stood out in marvellous relief from the general energy of his character. On the occasion alluded to, when, some hours afterwards, we were walking together in one of his shrubberies, he stopped short, and said, 'I have been thinking a good deal about my manner this morning with ———. Do you think I was too sharp with him?' I replied, 'Well, I confess I should have been afraid of you for the next six months, if you had given me such a *rating;* and I am sure you would not wish any of your young men to be afraid of you.' 'You're right!' he rejoined; 'I was too sharp; I've done mischief: I see it all. I've not only made him afraid of seeing me, but—' and he lowered his voice, and changing his naturally quick mode of speaking, he added very solemnly, 'I have brought a reproach on Christianity!' and then, with a look of peculiar meekness, he said, 'My Saviour never *so* rebuked *me!* I've done wrong; I'll send for him into the counting-house the next time I go into Bristol. I'll repeat to him how wrong it was of him to be so careless, and I'll tell him *how wrong it was of me* to speak so harshly to him.' Those who knew my dear 'Uncle Samuel,' will have no difficulty in realising to themselves what must have occurred in the private counting-house when he next went into Bristol.

"You know the astonishing influence which Mr. Budgett always seemed to hold over those in his employment. The secret of that influence was to be traced to their personal attachment to him, and the master-spring of that attachment was to be found in the living sympathy which every one in the establishment, from the very stripling to the man of hoary hairs, knew he had lying deep in his employer's breast. I have found him poring over the sheet of card-board containing the names of all the persons in his employment. 'Here's a task!' he would exclaim, as I entered the private counting-house. "Come, I hope you can stay; you're the very man I want; sit down; you'll help me essentially. I'm canvassing this list of names one by one, and considering what I shall have to say to each. I must see every one who is named here. Some I shall have to commend—that's always pleasant to me. There's ——; he's a truly valuable fellow—always punctual, always correct; call for that man's books at any moment, you won't find a figure unposted;—and accurate to a stroke of the pen, why you won't find an *i* undotted; what is more, he's a good man,—indeed, you always see the two things go together. I intend to make that man a present at stock-taking, and I hope I shall be able to give him something worth his acceptance. There again; there's *your* 'little friend.' His head grows wiser, and his heart grows better every day, but his body does not grow a bit bigger. Every word you used to say about him seems to be coming true. I sometimes look at him as he is standing before me by the side of half-a-dozen full grown men, and I think, If all you great fellows were rolled into one, the mass of you would not be half as really great as little ——. And here's a little fellow we have in the yard: he was in your school. He's as sharp as a needle. I hope he will prove to have good principles. I think he's truthful. I shall bring him out of the yard by-and-bye, and place him where I can see more of him. If he proves to be as well principled as he is active and intelligent, he shall learn the trade, and we 'll try to make a man of him.' 'Yes,' he would emphatically add, '*it 's always pleasant to commend.* But the *fault-finding* part of the business!'—and a heaviness of spirit would seem to come over him, softening, for the moment, his sharp, keen eye—'how I wish you would relieve me of this! But no; it is a duty for which I am responsible to God, and I will discharge it myself.' He would then proceed with the names which he had ticked with his pencil; he would continue his comments as he went on, but in a tone intimating a sadness of spirit corresponding with the difference of character which he was now noting; and occasionally he would ask my opinion with regard to the positions he intended to take in his reproofs or his encouragements. It was but seldom I made a remark in reply, beyond one of mere pleasantry. When, however, I did offer a suggestion, such was the humility of the man, it was generally adopted, and always acknowledged in a manner far beyond its worth. For example:—In one instance he was proposing to point out a certain youth in the establishment by way of example to another. I ventured to remark, that if he did so, he would probably inspire bad feelings towards his *beau ideal* in the breast of the boy he wished to benefit. He caught at the idea in a moment. 'You 're right,' he said; 'I see I must not do it; and yet I am almost sorry, because ——— is just the boy I could wish the other to imitate; for his age, and the length of time he has been with us, he is all I could wish him to be. But, as you very properly observe, it will be an ill requital to render him, by any act of mine, the victim of envy or bad feeling. What shall I do?' I mentioned to him a method that Cecil sometimes pursued in the pulpit, and advised him to adapt it to the case before us. 'Keep A,' I said, 'steadily in your mind, but don't name him; describe all the excellences with the love of which you would inspire B, and to the cultivation of which you desire to provoke him; only take care to assure him that you have seen all this in a boy not older than himself. If you leave him under the impression that your standard of excellency is only to be found in a man, you will probably repress any little disposition he may have to make the effort you require; but let him see that the model you propose for his imitation is really a boy of the same age, and under the same circumstances as himself, and he will feel and own that he has before him a standard which he may and ought to reach.' Most warmly he thanked me, and added, 'I shall make that hint tell in more cases than this. But Cecil! Cecil! I've heard that name. Who was he?' I explained, and told him of a little book of his—'Cecil's Remains'—which was always lying on my library table. His more intimate friends will anticipate what followed:—'*That's* the sort of book I like, *sharp, short, and decisive,*—order it for me, will you, the next time you go to your bookseller's.

"I have said how thankfully my relative received the smallest hint that he might turn to the advantage of those in his employment. This was the more remarkable in one who stood so little in need of counsel on this score. Indeed, he was superior to any man I have ever known for his penetrating insight into character, and for his ability to deal with the specific case before him. He would call a young man aside, in a few minutes draw from him the acknowledgment of the very failing he had observed in him and which he wished to correct, and then, having kindly but pointedly shown him the consequences of such a failing through life if not remedied, he would dismiss him with a few simple but pungent words of advice—advice of such a nature, couched in such terms, and breathed in such a spirit, that it would probably never be forgotten. The diffident and desponding would leave his presence encouraged and cheered; the vain and conceited would return to the counter or the desk humbled; and yet each would equally feel that he had a friend in his master, capable of appreciating, ready to approve worth of the lowliest and most unobtrusive kind, but no less skilled in detecting and faithful to rebuke the smallest delinquency. In some instances he seemed to *create*,—I need hardly remark that I use the word in its qualified sense,—he seemed to create the very virtue he wished to promote by giving a youth credit for it, and to crush the very vice he deplored by leading one to suppose that he thought him incapable of indulging it. And all this, I am most entirely persuaded, was done with such simplicity of heart and such singleness of eye, that he might have justified himself in the spirit and the very words of the Apostle, 'Being crafty, I caught you with guile.'

"I shall add a few words on another point, illustrative of the deep interest which Mr. Budgett cherished towards those he employed in regard to the comfort of their homes, the vigilance with which he would observe and read the very countenance of a man when once he became apprehensive that he was in trouble, and the delicacy and tact with which he would reach the truth and apply the necessary aid. In these particulars it is probable that I knew more of him than any one beyond his own family, during the whole period of my residence at Kingswood. Many of his frequent, hasty visits to the parsonage were on errands of love of this particular kind. I was often his almoner,—with a strict injunction that no reference should be made to him in the matter—where he wished to send relief to some unhappy family, the head of which he had been obliged to discard. He would sometimes—especially if he thought he had placed me in a difficulty—run back to me in the library after he had reached the bottom of the stairs, to remind me that the money he had placed in my hands 'the last time he had seen me' *was my own*, that I was to do whatever *I thought proper with it;* in a word, that 'Samuel Budgett had no more right or control over it than Maurice Britten, Jack Rawbones, or old Bedlio.' But the real interest he felt in a case of which he thus professed to have washed his hands was seen when, on the next occasion of our meeting, he would inquire into the minutest particulars of the interview. I remember one case in which he had met with the greatest annoyance, and in which we had every reason to believe there had been an attempt to injure the commercial credit of the firm; when I described to him the excitement of the party on receiving his bounty, supposing that it had come from myself, he wept even to the audible sob, and almost in an agony expressed his wish that he 'dared to make the family happy by taking the poor fellow into his confidence again.' Shortly after I came to reside at Bedford, I received a letter from a person in his employment, explaining to me the difficulties in which he found himself from circumstances which he could not control, and asking my advice. The letter reached me when I was on a bed of sickness. I felt that the most direct mode of assisting him was to communicate the facts to his master. I therefore simply inclosed the letter in an envelope to 'Uncle Samuel,' only expressing my conviction of the respect he had for the writer as a man of real worth and integrity, and my assurance that his case was in proper hands the moment it reached the private counting-house in Nelson-street. In a few days afterwards, I received a second letter from the party, telling me, in terms truly touching, that Mr. Budgett had called him aside, made him take a seat, and asked him to tell him all that was in his heart.. To be brief—the tale of sorrow had been told, and the sad heart had been relieved to its full content.

" On the very last visit I paid my dear relative, we were in his library, and our attention was called to a poor man in whom I felt an interest, by some object of his craft that caught the eye. 'Poor fellow!' said Uncle Samuel, 'he has been in sad trouble; but,' with his brilliant smile he added, 'he is out of it all now; he is as happy as a prince; his house is as nice as a new penny, and his face as cheerful as a harvest moon!' He then told me that he had observed the poor fellow looking very melancholy, so much so at last that his heart quite ached as he passed him in the yard. He sent for him into the counting-house, and after he had made him feel a little at ease, had drawn out of him all his troubles. The sickness of his wife had entangled him in debt; he could not eat, he could not sleep; his life was a misery to him, and he had exclaimed with a pathos that sunk deep into my dear relative's tender heart, 'Master, I am in debt; every time I go near the river, something bids me fling myself into it, telling me there's water enough to rid me of all my troubles, and that if I don't I shall be sent into the prison there for debt!'

"Deeply affected, he inquired of the poor man the name of his creditors, the amount of their respective claims, and the peculiar circumstances which had led to the contraction of each liability. Having ascertained these particulars, and perfectly satisfied himself that the man had not forgotten the precept of the society of which he was a member,—'Not to contract debt without at least a reasonable prospect of discharging it,'—he asked him whether freedom from these liabilities would restore to him peace of mind. The question was answered by a sort of sickly smile, which seemed to indicate a perfect despair of such a consummation. 'Well, come,' said the master, 'I don't think things are quite so bad, ———, as they appear to be to you. See here, my poor fellow, you owe ——— pounds: it's a very large sum for a man like you, to be sure; and if you had run into debt to anything like this amount through extravagance, or even thoughtlessness, I should have regarded it as an act of dishonesty on your part, and I *might* have felt it right to discharge you. But you are to be pitied, and not to be blamed. Cold pity alone goes for nothing, so let us see how you can be helped out of your troubles. Now, do you think your creditors, considering all the circumstances, would take one half, and be satisfied? Here's Dr. Edwards—his bill is the heaviest; if we can get him to take one half—' 'One half, master!' exclaimed the poor man, 'but if they *would* take half, where's the money to come from? I 'arn't got a shilling in the world but what's coming to me Friday night; and when I take my wages now, I 'arn't any pleasure in looking at the money, because it 'arn't my own; it should go to pay my debts, and I'm obliged to use it to buy victuals. I think in my heart I shall ne'er be happy again.' Still more sensibly affected by the poor man's manner the longer the interview lasted, my kind-hearted relative begged him not to distress himself any more; he said that a friend of his had given him a sum that was quite equal to one half his debts, bade him return to his work, order a horse to be put into harness as he passed through the yard, and brought round in ten minutes; and told him to be sure to make himself as happy as he could till he saw him again. He immediately drove round to every creditor the poor man had, compounded with them for their respective claims, and obtained their receipts in full discharge. On his return, the poor man's state of bewilderment was indescribable. He watched his master unfold the receipts one by one without uttering a syllable, and when they were put into his hand he clutched them with a sort of convulsive grasp, but still not a word escaped him. At length he exclaimed, 'But master, where's the money come from?' 'Never do you mind that, ———,' was the reply; 'go home and tell your wife you are out of debt, you are an independent man. I only hope the creditors have felt something of the satisfaction in forgiving you one half your debt to them, that we know God feels in forgiving our debts to him for Christ's sake; I have said that much to all of them.' But the puzzling question had not yet been answered, and again it was put,—'But master, where's the money come from?' 'Well, well; I told you a FRIEND had given it to me for you. *You* know that Friend as well as I do;—there now, you may leave your work for to-day; go home to your wife, and thank that Friend together for making you an independent man. But stay, ———, I had almost forgotten one thing. I called to see Mr. P—— as I drove through Stoke's Croft; I told him the errand that had carried me away from home all day, and he gave me a sovereign for you to begin the world with.' The poor fellow was too much affected to say anything more. The next morning, however, he appeared again, but after a most complete failure in a valorous attempt he made to express his thanks, he was obliged to leave the counting-house, stammering out that 'both he and his wife felt their hearts to be as light as a feather.' 'What a luxury there is in trying to make a man happy!' said Mr. Budgett, when he had finished his story; and I am sure he found it so at all times. It must be remarked, also, that an act like this was not, with him, one of mere *munificence*—a gift out of abundance which would never be missed; it was one of pure *benevolence*—it was cordial, it reached every sensibility of his heart, and he would spare neither trouble nor fatigue till he had accomplished his object. One other remark, and I have done. An incident of this kind was never related by my relative from any feeling of vanity; he knew that the relation of it would gratify me or the few friends to whom he might mention it in the confidence of social intercourse, and his own heart seemed to revel in the renewed pleasure it gave him to picture to himself afresh the joy which had been occasioned to a fellow-creature whom he had thus been permitted to assist. He would fervently bless God who had given him the ability 'to do good unto all men, but especially to them who are of the household of faith:' and truly, he loved 'to bear another's burdens,' to 'mind not' *merely* 'his own things, but also the things of another.'"

CHAPTER VII.

IN HIS OWN NEIGHBOURHOOD.

> "Wouldst thou be rich, give unto the poor, thou shalt have thine own with usury:
> For the secret hand of Providence prospereth the charitable all ways;
> Good luck shall he have in his pursuits, and his heart shall be glad within him;
> Yet perchance he never shall perceive, that even as to earthly gains,
> The cause of his weal, as of his joy, hath been small givings to the poor."
>
> TUPPER.

UNTIL an incredibly recent date, the neighbourhood of Kingswood was uncivilised and lawless. When Mr. Budgett first came there his brother had begun to war against its barbarism. The place is singular: it does not form a town, nor yet a group of villages; but over an extended surface of undulating and naturally beautiful ground you have an endless labyrinth of lanes—turning, winding, intersecting, branching in all directions; so that if a stranger set out to walk three miles, he would probably spend a day in the journey without a guide. By the sides of these lanes lie the cottages, some of which are comfortable, but the greater part, and especially the older ones, very wretched. About a mile from Mr. Budgett's house lies a place called Cock Road, in commemoration of its game cocks. This was a den of robbers who lived only by plunder,—sallying out to Bristol, Bath, Gloucester, Hereford, and even as far as Manchester. Hundreds of persons are living who remember when it was unsafe to pass alone in the open day. One told me that he had seen farmers come with constables on search for lost property, and their own pigs were displayed dead before their eyes, while the robbers laughed in their face; but they dare not touch them, and could not identify the pigs, as they were skinned. William Lintern, an old inhabitant of the place and a fellow labourer of Mr. Budgett's, says that one of his earliest recollections is of paying a penny to see two brothers, who had been hung, lying in their coffin; for the bodies had been given up to their relations, and they turned them to account by making them a show! In this family were, I think, five sons and one daughter; two sons were hanged, three transported, and the daughter had three successive *husbands*, who were all transported too.

Mr. H. H. Budgett, with great public spirit, addressed himself to the dangerous task of subduing this tribe of marauders. For a time he struggled alone, but he eventually obtained co-operation and the ringleaders were punished, the rest kept in check. A Bristol paper, speaking of Mr. Samuel Budgett's death, says:—

"Not many years since, Kingswood was known as the haunt of some of the most depraved and desperate race of men living, often becoming a pest and annoyance to this city. At that time the elder brother of the firm commenced business there. He for many years stood alone, though constantly harassed by the fear, as well as on one or two occasions actually exposed to the attack, of these lawless ruffians. His endeavours to produce a change were seconded by a few liberal and judicious individuals of the city and neighbourhood, so that the most notorious offenders were either detected or driven out of their hiding-places. It was not possible, however, to eradicate the rude and vicious elements which hovered round this district. But since the erection of the church, the building of two or three places of worship, the opening of several schools by various denominations, (in most of which the late firm took a liberal and active part,) many of those evils have been subdued, and much good has been accomplished. By a benevolence thus unsectarian in feeling, though in matters of opinion joining in preference to the old Wesleyan body, his good name and deeds will long be fragrant in the memory of this locality."

The Cock-Roadites as they were called, were a universal terror; and a book, detailing the operations of "The Bristol Methodist Sunday School Society," which Wm. Lintern kindly lent me, shows that it was considered a feat when a school was formed in their vicinity and filled with their children. That good work was begun by Mr. Henry Budgett; and co-operation in it was one of the first efforts of his brother for the good of the neighbourhood. The school was opened in July, 1812, when he was about eighteen; and the first day, to their surprise, seventy-five children came, of whom fifty-eight did not know the alphabet. The entry in the book of the committee is curious:—"Many of these, children of the first-rate characters in the singularly notorious tribe of Cock-roadites, some of whose fathers are now in prison—many of these poor children, with their parents, are entirely dependent on a system of robbery and plunder for their support." The school throve; a school-house must be built; and in calling for subscriptions, the committee gave the following character of the place:—

"Cock Road, a place in the immediate vicinity of Bristol, has been from time immemorial, and still is, inhabited by persons, the majority of whom are notorious for *robbery, plunder, and all kinds of illicit practices;* daring and systematic in their proceedings beyond description, they trample with impunity upon all laws, human and divine, set at defiance every principle of justice, make themselves a terror to the surrounding neighbourhood; and *this within four miles of the second city in the empire.*"

Labouring among these children of robbers, Mr. Budgett spent the Sundays of his riper youth. I was at that school the first Sunday after his funeral, and heard much of his toils and zeal. "A gracious man!" said his old coadjutor, already named, "a gracious man! O, how he would labour! All that he did will never be told." His duty in those early days was to visit the absentees, and bring them, if practicable, to school. To get over the greatest possible amount of ground, he would bring a pony and dash about from cottage to cottage among the lanes; he would talk to the people, kneel down and pray with them, stir them up to send their children to school, and then away. Thus, often, he would pass a Sunday without dinner; sometimes, perhaps, getting a morsel of bacon or a potato in a cottage where he called. "And he often told me these were the happiest days of his life, the Sundays he spent that way."

Some delight to tell us of the power of nature to mould and ennoble man; but where could you find—whether on the Himalayas, in the isles of Polynesia, among the forests of North America, the snow fields of Greenland, the plains of Australia, or any other scene whereon nature displays herself in beauty or in grandeur—a single tribe which has been left to her sole teaching that has received an education worth anything, either for this life or a life to come? "The children of nature" have been much glorified; but her children all the world over are a very ill-conditioned and ill-behaved race, the most pitiable beings the world upholds. If they were all assembled—Esquimaux and Bedouin, Bushman and Dyak, New Guineaman and Chocktaw, Veddah and Feejean—it is likely that on surveying them you would be of opinion that nature had made amazingly poor progress in the instruction of her own peculiar family. Nature is a sage and inexhaustible book for him whom revelation has taught to read; a clear, sonorous, and multiplying echo where revelation lifts up her voice: but without a teacher, the book cannot explain one of its own letters; without a voice, the echo is mute.

In Cock Road, nature had a fair aspect and a long opportunity. She was left undisturbed for generations to teach with her stars, and trees, and nightingales, her flowers and her storms. A poet, looking on those winding lanes, would have sung about guileless hearts and innocent homes; while those lanes were the hiding-place of thieves and murderers. More teaching took place in that Sunday School in the first year, more which tended to fit those children for useful lives here and glorious lives hereafter, than had taken place through all the beauties of nature from the time of the Cock-Roadites became a tribe. The school prospered, and the people improved. The two brothers and their fellow-labourers had reason to rejoice.

In the biography of William Allen (both in the original life and the shorter and more serviceable one lately published by the Rev. James Sherman), an allusion will be found to this school, which he visited while staying at Clifton, calling at the house of Mr. H. H. Budgett. He bears testimony to the needy condition of the place, and to the zeal bestowed upon it. The labours which Mr. Budgett commenced thus early, he prosecuted with diligence throughout life, not confining himself to Cock Road, but lending hearty aid to many neighbouring schools. His power over the children was great; he was ever on the watch for some anecdote or illustration that would help him to catch their attention; his addresses were both familiar and authoritative; he would, with amazing promptitude, obtain silence till the tick of the clock was heard by all; and he had a pecu liar delight in giving the children a treat and seeing them all happy.

To the good work wherein his soul delighted, he early trained his sons and only daughter, as also the pious and intelligent of those in his employment; so that every Lord's-day a numerous band of labourers went out from his own house and those of his dependants. An honoured friend of my own has given the following beautiful sketch, referring when he wrote it chiefly to a member of the family, now in a better country. It was Whitsuntide in the year 1849, and my friend was visiting at Kingswood Hill:—

"The enjoyments of the week were entered upon with great zest. The beautiful valley of the Avon and the undulating hills around Kingswood and Hanham which bordered upon it, were clothed in that soft, rich green which throughout this part of the west is so attractive and refreshing a feature; the hedge-rows in all the lanes were dusted over with the blooms of wild flowers; the new-mown hay was yielding its perfume; and all our best singing birds in the plantations were in full tune. No trifles, any of these, to a grateful and susceptible nature; but the chief charm of the scene to a Christian, an English heart, in this general holiday, was the excitement connected with the Sunday School festal anniversaries. The boys and girls clothed in their best attire were skipping along the road and bye-paths, greeting their teachers, and hasting to join a procession which must first move to the house of God and then back again to some place of innocent recreation. The grounds at Kingswood Hill were opened on one of these days for the recreation of the members of the Wesleyan Sunday School. The day was fine, and the enjoyment unalloyed: Edwin did all he could to enhance that enjoyment. The hilarity of the children called forth his own. There were moments when he was playful as the young fawn which ever and anon was throwing up her heels in the face of the different groups as she bounded by upon the grass."

One of the last services Mr. Budgett rendered to Kingswood was to build a noble room for a day school, at the cost of some eight hundred pounds; which has been placed under the Wesleyan Educational Committee, and will doubtless long serve as a beautiful monument to its founder, as a source of light to the children of the vicinity.

He had early felt a strong desire to preach to the heathen, and about the period of his marriage he began to labour as a local preacher. One who had lived in the vicinity all his life, and who insisted, "You cannot say too much of that good man, sir; you cannot say too much of that good man," told me that he heard him preach his "trial sermon" as a local preacher, and was so impressed with his power, that he told him he thought he ought to have been in the ministry; on which he informed him of his early leanings, and the causes which had fixed his lot in trade. In the later years of life he was often so deeply affected with a conviction of unworthiness, that when appointed to preach in some of the neighbouring places, he could not venture on the holy service, but would procure a substitute—often one in his own employment.

Thus in early life, before he was able to be of much temporal service to his neighbours, he did what in him lay for their spiritual welfare; but as his property increased he did not couple apparent zeal for men's souls with indifference to the wants of their bodies. He was a large and hearty giver; but he strongly desired to make his gifts strengthen rather than enfeeble the self-helping energy of others. On this account he preferred employment whenever he could invent it; and the house, the farm, the grounds, the premises, were all laid under tax for this end.

Mr. Carvosso, who was an eye-witness of his efforts in

this line, shall give an idea of the scale they sometimes assumed:—"He was surrounded by the poor, and every way disposed to do them good. Discrimination he certainly had: he knew what was in them, and was not to be readily imposed on. That he might not maintain them in idleness, during the scarcity of bread in 1846 and 1847, he spent thousands merely to employ them, engaging some 150 extra hands for small wages, and on Saturdays adding scores of pounds to the earnings of those who had families, that they might have enough to meet domestic wants. In meeting the wants of his poor neighbours by preparation of *soup*, he was foremost, both in his own gifts and in soliciting from the rich; and in this way he was mighty, almost resistless, so that the poor were double debtors to him."

Pursuant to his desire to help men to earn, he *often* made the substantial present of a horse; and in the case of a respectable widow, he offered either twenty pounds or five pounds and a horse. When he suspected that a man, instead of employing the horse to maintain the family, would sell the horse and waste the money, he would bind him by a promise to pay,—never intending, however, to call for payment unless his generosity was abused. In one case, a man to whom he gave a horse under promise of paying eleven pounds, was reported to him two days after as carousing at a public-house with money obtained by selling the horse. He at once had him looked after: he had sold the horse for thirteen pounds, and had already spent about two in his frolic; the remaining eleven were of course taken back.

A young man, the brother of one his of servants, had fallen ill in London while working as a tinman. After suffering long in the hospitals, he came into the country; but ill and feeble, he could not return to work in town. Mr. Budgett gave him fifteen pounds to set up in a neighbouring village. Part of the same family were going to America; he gave them thirty pounds; and to make it sit lightly, told them to buy land with it for him, and write him word how it got on; perhaps he would come and look after it some day. One day, in driving along the road he took up a man, and soon found out all about him, which was usually the case; for somehow he led people to disclose themselves till they were almost as open with him as he was wont to be with his own friends. This man proved to be on the point of emigrating, but with scanty means. After being satisfied as to the truth of his statement, he gave him fifty pounds, but, I believe, coupled with some conditions of repayment if convenient.

A man, with whom he often dealt for horses, had been robbed at a fair. In his despair he made an attempt upon his life. Mr. Budgett, hearing that he was lying dreadfully wounded, hastened to see him, warned him, encouraged him, and prayed with him. The poor fellow was in utter despair, both as to his soul and as to this life. Mr. Budgett assured him that as soon as he was able to go to business again he should have enough to set him on his feet. He recovered: and when asked how much would be necessary, said—Eighty ponnds; but he would wish to pay it back if ever he was able. On these terms the eighty pounds were at once given.

Besides endless detached instances of benevolence such as these, he zealously promoted the visiting and relief of the poor by a regular organisation after the model of the STRANGER'S FRIEND SOCIETY—the oldest of our visiting charities and the best. In this he laboured heartily, giving influence, time and gold. His own leisure for visiting was not such as to satisfy him; therefore a paid visitor was employed. And one of his neighbours, who laboured in this good work, told me that he would now and then ask him how they were get ting on in his district, and put two or three sovereigns into his hand, whether he would or not, to be given away. "Besides," he said, "I never came to him yet with a case of distress that he refused; and what was strange, he would never say, 'I will give you so-and-so,' but would ask, 'Well, how much do you think I should give?' And whatever I said—five shillings, ten, or fifteen, it was all the same—he gave it at once."

This statement struck me as precisely coinciding with one which had been previously made by his old neighbour and intimate friend, the Rev. John Glanville. He remarked that in all the applications he had made to Mr. Budgett, he never once knew him to say, what we so commonly hear said by those who remember their own charitable acts so well, "I have had so many calls lately." *No, not once in all those years had he heard those words out of his lips;* but whenever he went, found, just as my other friend had found, that when he mentioned the case he was asked, "Well, how much do you think I ought to give?" And whether he said ten pounds, fifteen, or twenty, that sum was forthcoming.

Mr. Carvosso says,—"In the course of my ministry, I have only met with two rich men who remembered the poor through their ministers. One was the late venerable Wm. Carne, of Penzance; the other, Mr. Budgett. Mr. Carne would occasionally put a sovereign into my hand in reference to wants the sight of which a minister cannot well shun. Samuel Budgett went further; now and then he would drop into my hand a five-pound note, intimating that I must permit him to bear some part of the expense entailed on me by visiting the poor and distressed."

One does meet with but few who thus help one to *enjoy* visiting the wretched; for when you see staring want in some of the sad corners of this huge London, it is cheerless to produce the one lean shilling which alone your own purse can furnish. But a few have given me the luxury of seeing dull eyes lighten up with gratitude to God and to an *unknown* friend. There is something touching in putting a half sovereign into the hand of a poor woman who needs it, is worthy of it, but had no hope, and saying at the same time, so as to remove all sense of uncomfortable obligation, "It is not from me; a friend has given me something to dispose of." I never went to a Christmas dinner with such pleasure as last year (1850). After a number of visits, at each of which I deposited in a poor but worthy hand enough, from the purse of a friend, to make the Christmas plentiful, one bright coin remained, and the Christmas morn had come. It was not comfortable to go to dine with that in one's pocket, yet better to keep it for a day or two, than give it away at hazard. Just after morning service, a name is mentioned; and I see, even now, the poor woman lying on that small bed in that close back room, with her feeble fire and her empty pot. She was a widow; she had children, and long, long had she been lying there; worthy, godly, with a trusting heart and a joyful hope of glory, she had lived through her illness she scarce knew how. God, by the hand of his children, had fed her. That day the barrel of meal and the cruse of oil seemed to have failed; her stores were all void. Had the friend whose money I put into her hand seen her look, and heard her blessing, he would have gone to his Christmas dinner with as light a heart as I. Rich men! why, if you will not visit and relieve the poor yourselves, should you not employ those who would?

From what has been said of Mr. Glanville, it will be seen that Mr. Budgett did not confine his charities through ministers to those of his own denomination. On the day of his funeral, the Rev. Mr. West, the Moravian minister at Kingswood, told me, that before coming out, he had observed his servant in tears, and asked her what was the matter. "Oh!" she said, "they are going to bury Mr. Budgett: he was a good friend to my poor father and mother; he would now and then give them a sovereign to get things to sell for their living."

With some men, money is cheap; with some, labour. You will find one ready to give; but he *cannot* visit, *cannot* teach, *cannot* go personally on any errand of goodness. Another man will work, but is slow to give. Each of these is a benevolent man with one leg: Mr. Budgett had both legs. Before he had much to give, he had begun to work; after he had much to give, he persevered in working.

One Sunday evening he was preaching at a neighbouring village. As he came home, he saw a number of youths lolling about under the hedges in a lane—wild, rough, ignorant, idle, ill-mannered, with bad looks, bad habits, and every stamp of the accomplished good-for-nothing. His heart yearned for them; he thought how they had been passing that lovely summer Sabbath. He went up to them, and in his own neighbourly way, began to converse. He told them he was happy, and he should like to see them happy. "You have minds, and I should like to see you improve your minds; you ought to have something to think about, and to employ you usefully." So on he chatted till he had obtained some little hold of their attention. "Now," he said, "if I gave you a good tea, would you like to come and take it?" "O yes, O yes," was the cheerful answer. "Then come up to the vestry of Kingswood chapel to-morrow evening; we are going to have a little meeting, and you shall have a good tea." This was a *tea-meeting* of the tract *distributors*. He paid for tickets for his new friends, who did not fail to be there; and after they had done their endeavour upon the eatables, he came up to them, and said, "Well, have you had a good tea?"

"'Ees, thank 'ee."

"I suppose you know many young men just of your own kind, who go about the lanes on a Sunday night like you?"

"O 'ees."

"Do you think if I promised them a good tea they would come?" He was encouraged to hope for their company on such terms; and soon his brother class-leaders had a hundred tickets in their hands, to be given to the worst young men in the neighbourhood, with a promise of a bountiful treat if they came to the great room on Mr. Budgett's premises, which served for a chapel and all good purposes. The tickets were taken rather shyly, for they knew well enough that Mr. Budgett was not gathering them without some religious end. So they said they did not want to go to Budgett to be hooked in for a prayer-meeting, or something of that sort. However, the "good tea" went far. At last a compromise suggested itself to the youths; they would go, take the tea, and then "bolt" before there was any chance of troubling them about religion. This stratagem, however, was met by a stratagem on the other side. The room was crowded; above a hundred came, and such a set of guests has seldom met under decent roof—all shades of vice and recklessness were gathered there to feast, and run away from good advice. It was plain that the ringleaders were in one corner, for thence proceeded all manner of odd and boisterous rogueries. To this point one of "the young gentlemen" betook himself, sat down beside the chief, made one of the party, and talked as familiarly as if he were quite on their side. The hero he selected had travelled and sailed as a stoker, and therefore was a notability among his associates. Neither the hospitality nor the cordial feeling had any effect upon his coarse and headstrong badness. He tried in all ways to disconcert his unexpected comrade, and would not by any means tell him his name. After vain attempts to tame him into sensible conversation, his young host said, "I hope we shall spend a pleasant evening. What do you think we ought to do by way of enjoying ourselves?"

"*You* had better get up and make us a bit of a divarshin."

Just then the repast was coming to a close, and the preconcerted move began to be made; but before they had got out of the way, Mr. Budgett ran up into the desk, and said, "I have asked you to come here for the purpose of doing something for you—something that will be of use to you. Now, just as a start, I will give you, among you, fifty pounds, and you must make up your minds what you will do with it."

The wild rogues were thunderstruck; they meant to run away from a prayer-meeting, but it was quite another thing to run away from fifty pounds. Hats that had been taken up were replaced, and feet already at the door turned back. No sooner had the offer been made than one of Mr. Budgett's sons, making himself as one of the party, said, "Fifty pounds! that's something; why, there are about a hundred of us, and suppose we divide it amongst us, there will be half a sovereign a-piece." This proposition would probably have been very acceptable to the company; but another, who was in the secret, at once rose and objected, saying he thought it would be very foolish to throw away such a sum as fifty pounds in that away; they had better put it to some use that would do them good for a long time to come. This was adroitly argued until all seemed to come into that idea; then came a proposition to found a society for study and mental improvement, to be called the "Kingswood Young Men's Association." After due discussion, this was carried by vote, and Mr. Budgett was appointed treasurer. The youths had been insensibly led by the tact wherewith the affair was managed to take an interest in it; and when the final arrangements were placed in the hands of a committee, several of them, to their great exaltation, were placed upon the committee with the friends who had so cleverly conducted the first meeting. It was arranged that the weekly rendezvous should be the vestry of the chapel on Sunday evenings after the service. This seemed to the young men a very natural gathering place; but it was just the point which secured Mr. Budgett's object of withdrawing them from their demoralising rambles on Sunday evening, and getting them to the house of God.

So far the success had been perfect; but now it remained to be seen how many would meet at the chapel. About sixty came; these were regularly met on Sunday night after the public service for religious instruction, and in the week for secular instruction. A good library was bought with the original donation, occasional lectures on scientific subjects were delivered by some of the masters of Kingswood school, and year by year a tea meeting was given at which rewards of very substantial books were distributed.

The success in this case was highly encouraging; but Mr. Budgett saw that to make it decisive a similar association must be instituted for young women; because the habit of Sunday evening strolling prevailed equally among the young people of both sexes, to the moral damage of both. By similar means this also was effected; and thus a large number of youths and young women were weekly gathered in the house of God, and afterwards separately occupied in receiving profitable instruction, while they had also good opportunities and strong incentives to self-cultivation. At the annual gathering of the Young Females' Association, Mr. Budgett was wont to regale them with tea and strawberries. A gentleman of taste and education, who has heard him address them on such an occasion, states that he had a most remarkable art of gaining their attention and interesting them in his views. He was especially struck with his power of making it appear to them, that if only godly and in earnest, they might rise to circumstances of comfort and opportunities of usefulness. I believe that these associations cost him annually about fifty pounds; but he had his reward in the improvement of many, and the clear conversion of some.

He also instituted a catechumen class for young women, which he regularly met. This was a very favourite engagement with him, and so interesting did he make it, that, at the time of his death, it was attended by about forty, some of whom had indeed passed from death unto life, and all of whom evinced intense grief at his loss.

Have you ever seen a shoddy mill? It is a curious sight. You find a multitude of rags and tatters gathered from all the winds; here a patch of Irish frieze, there a shred of tartan; scraps of women's shawls, of men's pantaloons, of flannels, horse rugs, stockings; threads, snips, and morsels; blue, black, green, and all hues; English, Welsh, German; a strange heap of the offcast and the defiled; hopeless things that no housewife could work up, that no shivering wretch would look to for comfort. Yet there they are for restoration. See how that teethed and terrible machine makes them look more hopeless still; rends up even rags, tears up tatters; champs, wrests, slashes, and flings them out at last fibres and choking dust. But next comes the oil can, and oil, abundant oil, with working and turning, till the heap begins to look like some caricature of wool. Then the spinning-frame, and, lo! the tatters form to yarn once more; then the loom, where the tatters turn to blankets, druggets, pilot cloth, and even what would pass under *your* eyes as decent broadcloth. This shoddy covers many a respectable floor, flourishes in paletots of low caste, and goes out in blue blankets to New Zealand to clothe the Maories.

Now, society has its shoddy, its offcast rags, its hopeless tatters, polluted and displeasing to look upon and very undesirable to touch. The respectable world has passed them by; they have lain in corners and grown viler till they corrupted away, the receptacles being ever filled up with new offcasts. But God's Gospel in the hearts of men has set them to search for these refuse, and to work them up again into the texture of society. The ragged school is the shoddy mill; and many a poor unpitied and unpromising tatter has been recovered to a creditable place among men. Mr. Budgett's contrivance was a shoddy mill, and some right good pieces has it yielded. The same *substance* is in all men, and the lesson of the shoddy mill is, that none are too bad to be rescued. Only do not begin to flatter the rags and say, You are fair and beautiful at bottom; you only want air and sun, a little dye, and a proper brushing to match the most serviceable cloth. Nay, they must be torn to pieces—rent right up, or they will only be rags though you give them all the air and sun, all the dye and brushing imaginable. The offcasts of men are just so: you will never make good citizens of them by nice speeches and wise lessons; the evil that is in them will survive a great deal more than that. They are bad at heart, deceitful and desperately wicked to the core of them; evil is bound up in their impulses. They must be heart-smitten, torn to the quick; their souls pierced through and through with sharp agonies of penitence, with such wounds from a hand we see not as made brave king David roar, with inner throes that will rend all their desires from their old vile objects, with godly sorrows working repentance—leading them to cry, as men cry whose whole soul is in movement, "Hide thy face from my sins, and blot out all mine iniquities; *create* in me a clean heart, O God, and renew a right spirit within me!" And the creating hand thus invoked from chaos will move; "God who caused the light to shine out of darkness" will shine "in their dark hearts to give the light of the knowledge of the glory of God in the face of Christ Jesus." That face is the face of a Saviour, a friend who actually does deliver a poor man from the foulness of his breast. This face seen, this deliverance felt, the glory of God breaks in upon the repenting sinner as the light shooting first athwart chaos, and inside his soul love, joy, and peace rise up a new creation.

Ye that laugh at this, what Gospel have ye preached? What tribe of Cock-Roadites have ye ever tamed? What refuse of our cities have ye ever restored? Ye say man's heart is good; let this Earth you live on, every inch of it, and every age of it, rise up and bid you not lie. Do you not hear it cry, "See, see all the tears which moisten me,—the groans I echo—the curses, the rages, the murders I witness—the hearts that are gnawing, burning, breaking—the wrongs that are doing—the graves that are digging: hear the voice of ten million miseries, and dare you utter the gibe, 'heart good!' What! all this filth and shame which cover me come of good! this robbery in Cock Road, this abomination in St. Giles, this human flesh and blood gluttony in bright Polynesia,—all this come of good! From what darker abyss of evil are you sent forth that you look on all this outflow of the heart of man, and looking pronounce it good?" No, the all-searching God said long ago that man's heart was evil, and all the story of this earth monotonously echoes "Evil!" Denying it you deny revelation, history, your own heart's ways; denying it you cut yourself off from all hope of seriously helping man. "Make the *tree* good;" that is the right lesson: you say "train the tree, enrich the soil, let the aspect be sunny,"—all very well if the *tree* be made good; but if you persist that the tree does not need grafting, you may transplant to the sunniest spot, train, dig, manure, and fence, but your tree will bring forth crabs. You cannot get good fruit by collective culture: your walls, and suns, and drains, and manures are very good, but each *individual* tree must be grafted—cut right away from nature's stem, set bleeding in another—or all your collective culture ends in crabs. "Make the *tree* good:" your institutions are walls and aspects, your education is training; but each man is as individual as each tree, he must be "made good," cut off from his fallen nature, grafted all tender, wounded and penitent into Christ; and though all the trees of the garden had been so grafted and you alone remained, yet you should bear but crabs. Go, then, go ye that have a heart to rescue the outcasts of men, go teach them, clothe them, feed them, heal them, do all love can do for them; but let your voice ever cry, "Repent and believe the Gospel;" let your heart ever pant to see them smitten with grief at their sinfulness, and hasting to Jesus to wash them from their sins in His own blood.

Another of his favourite labours was giving away good books and tracts. He seldom went out for a drive or a walk, but he provided a supply and gave them freely. He had a room of considerable size occupied with book shelves whereon lay all manner of volumes and of tracts, from the tiniest child book up to respectable duodecimos. All these were his stock for distribution, and were replenished by purchases of ten pounds' worth at a time.

In all the concerns of his neighbours he took a lively interest. In cases of family broils, his mediation was often called in. He would place the disputing relations in different rooms of his own house, first hear one, and then another, till he had got to the rights of the case; and keep him from the rights who could? With him equivocation was useless he *would* track it out. When he had mastered the case he would propose his terms of reconciliation, and often succeeded in effecting a permanent healing where there had been most painful sores.

Over the prospects of young persons he watched tenderly; and when he saw them in danger of forming wrong connexions for life, he would with prompt and persuasive kindness interfere. Not confining his solicitude to his own children, or to the respectable youth of his own circle, he cared and watched for the humble and the servant, and with a rare power over the will, succeeded in saving not a few from ill-judged and ungodly marriages. This testimony I have had not only from observers, but from parties who felt the life-debt they owed him, for a service which few men could have performed.

His desire to raise all about him was constantly showing itself. Take one illustration out of thousands:—Coming out of a hair-dresser's rooms, he paused in the shop and looked round. "O, you sell brushes, and things of this kind?"

"Yes, Sir."

"Well, I suppose you sell to every one that comes?"

"No, indeed, Sir."

"But *I* should. At all events you try to sell to every one that comes?"

"Well, no, we do not, Sir, one doesn't always think of it."

"But you ought: you have your family to provide for, you should have tact and push; if I were in your place, I would sell to every one that came, and you ought to try."

"Very well, Sir, suppose we begin with you," making a show of displaying some wares.

"Yes, to be sure, why not?—let us see." To work he

sets, and by way of encouraging the hair-dresser he buys brushes, combs, and such commodities to the extent of thirty-five shillings. It is not pleasant to go into a shop where they force you to buy or to be uncivil, and the thing is sometimes pushed intolerably; but the fact stated shows Mr. Budgett's desire to see others thriving.

Thus dwelt he among his own people, rising up under their eye, spreading employment on all hands, giving an example of industry and of success, teaching, preaching, visiting, relieving, helping, mediating, advising. And among them he staid. When he grew far beyond them he did not find out that Kingswood was unhealthy, and that Clifton or Bath was the only place his family could breathe in. No: he clung to them and their wants. He saw their rudeness, but instead of securing the polish of his children by taking them far from the poor colliers, he endeavoured to raise and bless the colliers by sending his children among their cottages and employing them in their schools. But in all his efforts for them, the soul was his end, though, after the example of Him who loved souls most and bought them dearest, he gave for the body all that he could give. The individual conversion of the soul was his object and his hope; he knew that every man whose heart was changed from sin to holiness did more for the elevation of a neighbourhood than a hundred other appliances. The deep interest he felt in every token of spiritual life is evinced in the following letter to the young and beloved friend, whose notes have been and will hereafter be of great value to us:—

"*Bristol*, *April* 1*st*, 1845.

"MY VERY DEAR FRIEND,—We have a great work going on here. I would try to give you some account, but I am just now pressed for time, and you will be more delighted to come and spend a week with us and see for yourself, and we will give you some heart-cheering accounts. Some of the stoutest rebels have been constrained to cry aloud, yea, to roar for anguish of spirit; and God has graciously forgiven their sins and made them the means of bringing others to seek salvation. There is a gracious work among the young females, say from fifteen to twenty years of age. Do come before the week is out, and stay if it is but a few days. Just drop me a line and I will meet you at the station; or find your way to Nelson Street, and I shall feel real pleasure in conveying you to Kingswood. I think we have added above two hundred and fifty to the society, and old professors are much quickened. The work appears to be deep and genuine, and likely to go on; but you must come, and I hope very soon.

"I am, my dear friend, most affectionately yours,

"S. B."

Among his benefactions to Kingswood stands the noble chapel close by which he lies. He did not raise it from his own funds, but he raised it by stimulating others to combine with him in his gifts and labours. He would have it, and he would have it free from debt. In Bristol, in Bath, in London, in Liverpool, he begged and was rebuked, and was successful. To a man so busy, whose time was precious as diamonds, it was no small matter to take the tedious drudgery of begging; but he had set his heart on the work; what he said in his own business he said in his master's business, "Never attempt, or accomplish." Local feeling was against so large and expensive an edifice; but he inspired others with his own desire till he enlisted their hearty co-operation. Towards the last he resolved on concluding the matter by one great meeting, and prepared tea for above twelve hundred. His "tact and push" so raised excitement regarding this meeting, that persons crowded from Bristol in omnibuses, cars, vans, and all vehicles available. At the last, tickets were besought on any terms, and fourteen hundred sat down to tea. He had all arranged with military precision, so that tea was served at a fixed moment and removed in half an hour. Just at the last, a cart was upset with, I think, *fourteen gallons of tea;* but his incredible energy repaired the mischief, and the serving and removing were effected precisely as he had pre-arranged. At that meeting his heart obtained its desire; every penny for the erection of the new sanctuary was raised. His outburst of joy and gratitude was moving. At the first meeting of the trustees he laid down sixty pounds of a surplus. There it stands, that chapel, with the school-house built chiefly by his zeal and bounty; and both will hereafter ally the name of Samuel Budgett with the progress of light and of religion in Kingswood. I once heard a holy woman say, "Were I rich, I think nothing would be so delightful as to build a house for God, and then looking down from heaven, see all the good that was going on under that roof."

Several neighbouring chapels were not, like that at Kingswood, free from debt; Mr. Budgett felt toward them as toward his own. The following description of his doings for these, by Mr. Carvosso, is characteristic:—

"With respect to his *liberality* to the cause of God, he far excelled any one that *I* have met with in the church of Christ. It is true he would not give without an eye to the bringing out of the gifts of others. I first met him in connexion with chapels at a tea meeting in his own little chapel at Kingswood, the object of which was to raise funds for the chapel at Longwell Green, where his brother lived. He was in the chair. He had offered fifty pounds on conditions; and with his usual "tact and push"—to use a favorite phrase of his own—was trying to bring others up to the mark. A paper was handed him to give out for a tea meeting at Fishponds, at which it was proposed to pay off a small part of the one hundred pounds debt on the chapel there. He read it and paused, and said if the friends at Fishponds would endeavour at once to clear their chapel of debt, he would give them fifty pounds, and come to their tea meeting. The thought of the poor people there raising fifty pounds to meet Mr. Budgett's liberal offer, was, with most parties, quite out of the question—yea, *oppression* and not kindness! A few thought differently—having Mr. Budgett with them inspired hope. After tea he was voted to the chair. He made a short, telling speech. After much effort the thing was done; and it was deeply affecting to see with what glee all sprang on their feet, and with what unanimity and joy they lustily sang—

'Praise God, from whom all blessings flow.'"

Such was the effect of his influence, that before his death all the chapels in the Kingswood circuit were free from debt, with the exception of some trifle.

The zeal of Mr. Budgett for the interests of his own denomination was decided, consistent, and active, but not sectarian; his sympathies, influence, and contributions were at the command of other labourers for the good of souls. Let the following testimony of Mr. Gaskin speak as regards the Established Church:—

"It is now nearly eighteen years since, in the providence of God, I was called to occupy the important position of incumbent minister of Kingswood. Perhaps it may be thought somewhat out of place here to speak of the difficulties which I found to be surrounding me when I first entered on that peculiar sphere, presenting, as it did, ground that as yet was all but unbroken, so far as the labours of the Church of England had been brought to bear upon it. Without some reference, however, to these difficulties, the generous, unsectarian qualities of Mr. Budgett's mind cannot be fairly appreciated. In him, and in his elder brother—with whom I subsequently became so closely connected by marriage—I soon found the most able and zealous coadjutors in every good work. The inhabitants of Kingswood were, in many respects, a peculiar people; but they were open to kind treatment, and possessed many excellent qualities, for which I shall always admire them. But their peculiarities were of such a kind, that a young and inexperienced clergyman, however well-intentioned, might have involved himself in serious troubles with them, had he been left to adopt his plans in ignorance of the character of the people amongst whom he had been called to labour. If the Messrs. Budgett—men who were at the head of so large and influential a body as the Wesleyan Methodists constituted—had wished to thwart the efforts of the incumbent minister, nothing was more easy than for them to do so, without the smallest odium attaching to them, for no overt act on their part would have been necessary. They had merely to stand by and allow their young clergyman to take his own course; in all reasonable probability, before three months had elapsed, he would unwittingly have brought himself into collision with the prejudices of the people to an extent which he would never have removed. But instead of this, they rendered—without becoming one whit the less Wesleyan Methodists, and I received—without being one whit less a churchman, co-operation of the most cordial and liberal kind. Indeed, I do not recollect a single occasion of my asking their assistance in any measure I might wish to carry out for the spiritual or temporal advantage of the place, without the immense influence which a long well-spent life had given them among the people being most unreservedly placed at my command. Their counsel was always given in the kindest and most courteous manner, and their purse was open to an extent far beyond any thing that ever appeared to the public eye. To this generous and liberal bearing on the part of the Messrs. Budgett, I refer, under the divine blessing, much of the kind feeling that has prevailed among all parties in Kingswood for so many years, much of the success which has attended the efforts of the different denominations of Christians there for the best interests of the people, and much of that personal confidence reposed in me, and that personal attachment cherished for me by my former parishioners."

We have already seen on what relations he lived with Mr. Glanville, the excellent Independent minister of the place. When he was about to erect a new "Tabernacle," Mr. Budgett gave his exertions to remove some difficulty as to part of the site, attended the meeting for raising funds, spoke, offered a handsome percentage on *whatever should be raised*, and tried to elicit one great effort, as he had frequently done before, by offering, that if they raised seven hundred pounds that night, he would make it a thousand.

Such a heart was prepared to hail a movement like the Evangelical Alliance. Into its design he entered with his characteristic ardour; its meetings, hallowed and joyous to all who have taken part in them, were to him welcome "as the water-springs;" and in connexion with it he formed, as many others have formed, some of the most precious friendships of his life. When it was debated in the family whether the house should be enlarged by adding some spacious rooms, he was very indifferent, leaving it chiefly to his children to decide; but when some one observed that such a large room would be very convenient to gather the Alliance friends together, he at once said, "O yes, then let it be done." His warehouse chapel in Nelson Street had been previously honoured by a meeting of the leading members of the Alliance.

Mr. Budgett *was* "a neighbour" to the people of Kingswood; thousands of his gold and thousands of his hours were given for their weal, and to the last his care was for the maintenance amongst them of those means of grace which had been so much blessed. Dating from the time of his boyhood, he had seen a marked improvement in the place, and toward that improvement his own influence, that of his brother, and the family generally had powerfully contributed. The blessing of God on the labours of the Methodists had been the most manifest agency in this good work, and though Mr. Budgett had the pain to see those labours seriously hindered in his last months by a violent agitation, that only offered to him a new opportunity of sealing his testimony of affection to the neighbourhood, as of his attachment to Methodism, by acts of wide-hearted and wonderful munificence to sustain Methodist agencies for the future good of the people he loved.

We shall best close this chapter, as we did the last, by a sketch from Mr. Gaskin:—

"You are aware of the amazing influence he exerted whenever the interests of his neighbours demanded that it should be put forth. I shall confine my remarks here to the manner in which that influence was acquired. I do not think that it must be referred to his munificence, to his personal labours, or even to his peculiar and varied talents. We may, any of us, call to mind instances in which none of these have been wanting, and yet there has been a marvellous lack of influence. I have always conceived that his power for good over the minds of his neighbours must be referred to the gentleness of his disposition and manners, with the unqualified confidence in the integrity of his principles which he inspired. It is thus I trace the origin and growth of the influence which he exercised over me; and it is thus, I am persuaded, that the humblest of his neighbours who are capable of drawing the deduction, will account for the influence which he exercised over them. A man, whose frugal industry might have enabled him to accumulate a small sum of money for a time of need, seemed perfectly happy about it when Mr. Budgett had been prevailed upon to take charge of it; I need scarcely add that while the poor man felt that his money was secure, he knew also that the thrift and forethought of which his savings were a proof, would be well rewarded by one who loved to encourage such a disposition. The very 'hauliers' on the road between Kingswood and Bristol perceived that in Mr. Budgett they had one who differed widely from most of those with whom, by their carelessness, they were constantly bringing themselves into collision. At one point of the road I have witnessed painful altercations between these rough spirits and gentlemen who have been interrupted by their ponderous waggons: angry words from the party incommoded have called forth a volley of abusive and profane language, accompanied with a violence of gesticulation that threatened a breach of the peace; while, perhaps only a few minutes before, an interruption of a similar kind between my relative and one of the same men had terminated in a very different spirit. 'Here, Milesome,' he would say, 'oblige me by drawing aside the head of your "shafter,"—ay, thank you; never mind the "leader," I'll manage him myself. Always have your eye on your horses and on anything that is coming near you in either direction,—that's your business, you know, while you are on the road with your team,—take care to begin drawing your horses aside the moment you see a carriage of any kind coming, if you think you are in the way; it saves time, and, what is more, it prevents unkind words sometimes. There, thank you, good morning!' All this would be uttered in his usual quick but clear mode of speaking while the man would be getting his horses and waggons on one side. There would be the expression of good humour beaming from the eyes of our swarthy friend; he seemed to feel that he was treated like one of our own species, and he would acknowledge it by a respectful touch of the hat and a hearty response to the morning's salutation,—'And a good morning to *you*, gentlemen!' I remember we were called one Saturday afternoon, rather urgently, into Bristol. As we neared the gate, by the 'Fire Engine' public house, we perceived that the road was literally blocked up by 'return' waggons and horses, the drivers of which were in the public house. A boy was sent for the drivers. 'Why, is that you B———!' exclaimed Mr. Budgett, as a stout-built fellow with a face like a sweep's came rushing out of the house, grasping his heavy whip in the one hand and hastily drawing the back of the other over his mouth, fresh from the can,—'I'm sorry to see *you* there; here, come round to me,'—then, lowering his voice, he said, 'B———, my poor fellow, you have a wife and children at home. Have they any thing to eat?' 'Not much, I be afeared, Sir,' said the man, trying to force a smile into his countenance, though he evidently felt ashamed. 'Well, tell me now,' continued Mr. Budgett, 'how much have you just spent?' 'Why, threepence,—but I had it gee'd me by th' lady 'at hat t' call.' 'Well never mind who gave it you, but tell me what you spent as you went into Bristol this morning?' 'Why, threepence.' 'Well, the lady didn't give you that; but no matter how you came by the money so that it was honestly obtained. What I want you to think about is this:—By your own showing you have spent sixpence to-day on beer; if you have done the same every day this week, and I fear you have, then you have three shillings in your pocket less than you might have had; now as you go along, just consider how many little things that three shillings would have bought for the real comfort of your wife, yourself, and your children. You say you fear they have but little to eat at home now, and you have spent sixpence on yourself! Is that kind? Nay, don't make any excuse. I know you feel you have done wrong. Don't, my poor fellow, repeat it. One word more; if you persist in this habit you will become a *drunkard*, and the Bible tells you, "Drunkards shall not inherit the kingdom of God;" it will lead you into all *wickedness*, and the Bible tells you, "The wicked shall be turned into hell!" B———,' he added very solemnly, 'think of this, tell your companions there what I have said to you; and above all, pray that God may bless what I have said to you, that He may make you a more thoughtful and a better man.' Poor B——— listened; the assumed smile disappeared, his face sank almost into his bosom, and he became evidently ashamed to look at us. At the close of Mr. Budgett's remarks, he touched his hat in a respectful manner, and said with much apparent feeling, 'Thank you, Sir; it's very good for gentlemen such as you, to talk this ways to poor men like me.'

"Here is the clue to his influence over his poorer neighbours,—an influence which he was ever aiming to turn to their own advantage—an application, this, of that influence, to which they were most sensibly alive. Of this I have continual evidence in the communications I am still receiving from Kingswood. Not one out of many letters I have had from that place since his removal which has not made some touching allusion to it. 'The whole neighbourhood mourns,' says one; 'We have lost a FRIEND! I dare not trust myself to write more,' is the remark of another; 'There is a void at Kingswood which will never be filled, observes a third. For myself I may add in the words of a favourite writer, '*Moveor equidem tali amico orbatus, qualis, ut arbitror, nemo unquam erit; ut confirmari possum,* *nemo certe fuit,—sed tamen recordatione nostræ amicitiæ sic fruor, ut beate vixisse videar, quia cum eo vixerim.'*"*

Mr. Gaskin justifies this strong language by a record of Mr. Budgett's conduct as friend, which shows that he deserved such an affection as he found, and fully prepares one for the question wherewith that remarkable narrative concludes—"Will it be matter of surprise should his name be one of the last that trembles on my dying lips?"

* For I am distressed at being bereaved of such a friend,—as none, I conceive, will be to me again, and, as I can confidently assert, no one ever was;—but yet I so enjoy the recollection of our friendship, that I seem to have lived happily because I lived with him.

CHAPTER VIII.

IN THE FAMILY.

"O the blessings of a home where old and young mix kindly,
The young unawed, the old unchilled, in unreserved communion."

TUPPER.

YOU have already seen Mr. Budgett in his father's house, seen the love of parent, brother, and sister which he cherished there, seen him leave it with a rare title to the parental blessing, and seen him afterwards twice bestowing his all for his sisters and his brother. Before me lie the means of detailing his deeds of filial love for years—means singularly afforded by one detached scrap of memorandum, jotted down for a purpose that is manifest. One is almost tempted to draw aside the obscuring veil of generalities, and show the individual facts; but, perhaps that would only be to indulge one's love of displaying a most beautiful spectacle of nobleness, humility, self-denial, and faith. That such a youth should prosper no man can wonder; at least none with faith in the fifth commandment.

His early zeal for the happiness of the family did not forsake him when prosperity came flooding his coffers and enlarging his sphere. That good mother, whose whole life had been to him a gentle, wise, and saintly instruction, lived to see him far up the eminence which rewarded his faith in the commandment with promise. In a letter to his sister Jane, he thus speaks :—

"*Kingswood Hill*, *Jan.* 30, 1831.

"MY DEAR SISTER,—I am just returned from Winterbourn from beholding one of the most interesting sights this earth affords—I mean the happy, truly happy, sick and dying bed of a saint ripe for glory. Such is our dear mother. You have seen her; she is not now less happy, only less sensible of her pain, than when you left. Her soul still triumphs in prospect of the glory that awaits her, and which in all probability she will in a few days be introduced to. 'Mark the perfect man,' &c.; how is that passage illustrated in her experience! May it be equally so in yours and mine. In order to that we have only to live the life of the righteous and we are sure to die the death. I hope, my dear J——, you are making progress; remember we are no longer happy or safe than we are vigorously pressing forward. To halt is to go back. * * * *

"Your affectionate brother,

"S. B."

At the outset, we might have expected that his impulse to rise sprung really from a love of money or personal ambition, though that cloaked itself under regard for the prospects of his numerous brothers and sisters. But as he rose, as his own family increased, as new honours, new circles, new allurements came within his grasp, how did he remember those of his own house? Did he keep them at a distance? Did he never do them a kindness but when teased? Did he shun their society and leave them out of sight? Ask them: there they are clustered about him,—brothers, sisters, brothers-in-law, nephews, and nieces; ask them and see whether their tones as they speak of "brother Samuel," or "uncle Samuel," do not make your breast feel very full.

He who is what Samuel Budgett was as son and brother has written his history as husband beforehand, and we need not write it again. As a father, he ever sought to make his children happy at home; he would provide them with all means of innocent amusement—whatever the grounds could yield to give them healthful play, with donkeys to ride, curious poultry to rear and study, rabbits, guinea-pigs, and such like playmates as might entertain without endangering them. His singular openness of heart, too, showed itself in a peculiar form; he made his children, from their earliest years, his confidants and his counsellors. They knew his business affairs intimately, and in every perplexing case he would gather them round him, with their mother and aunt, and take their advice. His standing council was formed of the whole family, even at an age when other fathers would think it cruel and absurd to perplex a child with weighty concerns. But with him all such concerns, though handled with giant energy, were viewed with Christian quiet, as connected with the hand of Providence and capable of being controlled by prayer. What, therefore, others would regard with worldly anxiety alone, he would regard with solicitude certainly, but with solicitude balanced by faith. In such a temper he could disclose all his perplexities to his children without lading their spirits with worldly care. This remarkable confidence displayed itself consistently; and much earlier than usual he gave his sons a responsibility in the business, and showed a deference for their judgment most uncommon for a man whose fortune was of his own gathering. Men of that class are prone to treat their sons as children when they are youths, and as youths when they are men, as if they thought that because the wisdom of the family was born with them so with them it will die. A proof of this perfect reliance upon his children was given in the fact, that when the eldest son was only about twenty years of age, he allowed his four boys to go alone upon the continent for about seven weeks. Such a stretch of confidence could only be justified by very ample evidence that it would not be abused; but the result testified that he did not misjudge. In matters of expenditure the same confidence was manifested; and when his *will was made it was by consultation with them all unitedly.* But this confidence was as far from indulgence as can be; it was measured and calculated, and had it been abused, a strictness as measured and calculated would have immediately taken its place. Mr. Gaskin has beautifully remarked that he knew how to create a virtue by giving one credit for it, and assuming him to be incapable of the opposite vice. This mode of treatment he applied with great effect around his own hearth.

In seeking moral excellence in his children, Mr. Budgett took it as his first maxim, that they were by nature inclined to evil, and therefore, though capable of restraint and polish by education, must be alienated from their Creator and liable to run into open iniquity unless they become partakers of a new nature. Born of Adam's stock, they partook of Adam's taint; born of a race of sinners they lay under the curse of sin; but born under the provisions of a redemption whereby all families on the earth are blessed, under the reign of a Saviour through whom the "free gift came upon all men to justification of life," they were capable of being created anew in the image of God. These two things, that his children were sinful and needed a new birth, that they were redeemed and *might* be born again, were certain and serious things with Mr. Budgett. And these are the two things which all who would promote goodness upon earth, in family, nation, or world, must lay to heart. Forgetting them, men whiten the outside of the sepulchre, but the dead men's bones are hideous within. The great heresy and *ignis fatuus* of our day is the doctrine that man is good at heart; a tree to be trained, not needing a graft. Some avow it, some stealthily diffuse it, some proceed upon it unconsciously. To the whole, to the sinless, Christ has no mission. Fallen, but redeemed; prone to evil, but capable of being made holy; loving the creature, but capable of loving the Creator; under the dominion of sin, but capable of being freed from sin and made servants of God—that is the condition of all children, and Mr. Budgett happily knew it to be the condition of his.

From their early years his prayers and influence, joined with those of their mother and aunt, were directed to this one end, that God might "take away the heart of stone, and give them a heart of flesh." And in that family, so united and so open of heart, think you not there were the seeds of mighty sins, had those seeds been left to grow—enough indication of a fallen nature to cost hours of extreme anxiety, of most importunate prayer? Family altar, sabbath holiness, works of charity, friends who feared God, all these advantages were richly enjoyed by those children; but tempers and inclinations which might mar their whole life, and a forgetfulness of God which might mar their eternity, were not to be charmed away from human nature by outward agencies like these, without the close and inward acting of God's own Spirit on the heart. *You* do not believe in this close and inward action of God's Holy Spirit to make the bad heart good. You hand poor man over to a drear, chill world, without a Father nigh at hand, without a Saviour who actually does deal with his bosom and bless it with deliverance from sin. You see Divine power upholding a world to contain us, a sun to light and warm us, renewing the herbs and trees, the generation of beasts and birds for us, making all earth alive with ten million million agencies to feed and clothe and variously delight us; yet you think that the thing which is far more to us than all the rest,—the way to find a quiet, holy heart, which may dwell here in love and goodness,—is precisely the one thing He has left to be settled by the philosophers instead of providing it Himself. Not so thought Mr. Budgett; not so his helpers at home: they had a deep, fast faith that God is love, that His love is close and fatherly, that it makes man's heart its peculiar care because, man's heart, in its own joy or bitterness, gives a taste to all things here. They believed that He, the holy Father, is nigh, very nigh, and knows us; that in Christ's sacrifice the justice which would forbid his meeting with the vile is satisfied, and that when we turn to Him now, crying, "Father, I have sinned against heaven and before thee, and am no more worthy to be called thy son," he sends forth his own Spirit into our heart; who there works a wonder—a wonder which holy men of God call a "new creation," which the Son of God called a "new birth," and which makes us delight to commune with our Maker, and sets us upon battling against sin as "*seeing* Him that is invisible." That his children might thus be changed was his earnest solicitude: and in that his heart was comforted; for early, very early he saw them, as one by one they sprang up, smitten with deep contrition for their sins, turn earnestly to the Redeemer, seek his mercy, find it, and live to make his heart glad in life's warm heyday, and to cheer the hours that bordered on the grave.

The religion his children were taught to seek they were taught to practise, not only in the quiet virtues of home life, but in the active toil of piety:—at Cock Road and other schools, among the young people of the Association, in the cottages of the poor, and in every place Kingswood afforded for training them in the duties of a Christian neighbour. To his daughter, when yet a child, he thus writes, showing how he placed the one thing needful first before their minds:—

"*Bristol, February 22d*, 1843.

"MY DEAR SARAH ANN,—Your kind note I duly received by the hand of your brother James, for which I thank you. Be assured it gives me much pleasure to know that I am affectionately remembered by any member of my family, and especially by my own little daughter. I hope you are endeavouring to be a good girl. If you knew how much the happiness of those who love you depended on *your* conduct, I think that if nothing else proved a sufficient motive to good behaviour that would; but then my dear little girl knows very well that her own happiness both in this world and the next depends on her giving her heart to God. Do not, my dear child, live one hour without being satisfied that God is just now pleased with you, that is, that you have His favour; for we are happy if we share His smile, His counsel, and His care. May you, my dear child, be truly devoted to God in youth, and then you will be prepared for a useful life or fit for early death! I dare say how happy you all are. You may write to me as often as you please and I will endeavour to answer your letters. Tell me all the workings of your little mind, all your hopes and all your fears, all your joys and all your sorrows. Please give my *very kind* love to all at home, and believe me, my dear Sarah Ann,

"Your affectionate father,

"S. B."

The following also testifies how much his heart was occupied with the spiritual welfare of his children, and how he rejoiced that they were all walking in the paths of righteousness:—

"*Ilfracombe, Saturday, Nov.* 6*th*, 1847,
"*Eight o'clock*.

"MY DEAR LITTLE SALLY,—Your kind letter to mamma we duly received, and I would have written to you before now, but I have been very unwell—so weak that I have scarcely been able to read or write anything without doing me harm; but I am thankful to inform you I am now getting better, and I hope soon to recover my strength. I assure you we think and talk of you very often, and we do not cease to pray for you. What a mercy it is, my dear child, that as a family we are all seeking our happiness from one source, and that the right one. How insignificant does every thing else look when compared with this, even in this life and in the possession of health, wealth, and all that the world calls great and good; but look a little further—a *sick bed*, a *dying hour*, a judgment day, all of which will very soon be present,—and how then shall we value all beside this one thing needful, this Divine love! The Lord fill my dear child's *heart*, and then from the abundance of the heart the mouth will speak, and you will, you *must*, however unconsciously, be made useful to others.

'Tis worth living for this,
To administer bliss,
And salvation in Jesus's name.

I believe we are all as a family going to heaven. Glory be to God! * * * * * *

"Yours affectionately,
"PAPA and MAMMA."

In describing the entertainments of the Sunday School children in the grounds, we introduced his second son, Edwin In him, more than in any member of the family, appeared the stronger traits of his father's character, with touches of worth peculiar to himself. Frank, vivacious, open, with a clear head, a quick glance, a commanding look, prompt, firm action, a hearty laugh, a mellow voice, and a musical taste which on a summer eve would sometimes make the place joyful with outdoor melody; in business, a master for decision, order and authority; at home, a son in love and obedience, a brother to be admired and delighted in; in school, a teacher ever diligent; in prayer, devout, fervent, and prevailing; in the cottage, a friend to help, to warn, to plead upon his knees; among young friends, a hearty happy companion, a kindly, winning advocate for devotedness to God, who would tell of the blessings to be found at the throne of grace, and lead the way thither, and stay in long and eager wrestlings. Such was Edwin, and if all delighted in him do you wonder? If you think that I say what he was not, go and ask any who knew him, and they are many.

The summer of '49 shone bright on Kingswood Hill. All things were flourishing; the business was swelling with prosperity; new and most charming friendships had been opened to the family; the father was hale and, as men say, young; the eldest son on the point of a union wherein all must every way rejoice; the house was the scene of a long visit from an eminent servant of Christ whose mild goodness would be a beauty to be estimated there. On the lawn the whole staff of their men had feasted, the merry Sunday School children sported while Edwin was life to them all; and at Edwin's own request the boys of Kingswood School had an entertainment and an evening's play. The rest shall be told by the friend we quoted before.

"The Sabbath of July 22d found Edwin, as usual, doing and receiving good. In the evening, after a profitable day in the school and sanctuary, he united with his brothers in singing Charles Wesley's beautiful hymn, commencing,—

> 'How happy every child of grace,
> Who knows his sins forgiven!
> This earth, he cries, is not my place,
> I seek my place in heaven;

A country far from mortal sight:—
  Yet, O! by faith I see
The land of rest, the saints' delight,
  The heaven prepared for me.'

The united worshippers seemed to rise with the spirit of their theme; and when they came to the last verse but one, the sentiment was in remarkable unison with what was to follow. At that moment their father, who was just leaving the room, struck with the sweetness of the tune and at once awed and delighted with the sentiments, turned back and lingered a few moments longer, while his children were singing, in a strain in which Edwin's voice was neither feeblest nor least harmonious,—

'Then let me *suddenly* remove,
  That hidden life to share;
I shall not lose my friends above,
  But more enjoy them there.
There we in Jesu's praise shall join,
  His boundless love proclaim;
And solemnise in songs divine
  The marriage of the Lamb.'

An aspiration how soon to be realised!

"As a member of the Wesleyan Society in Kingswood, he was very regular and punctual in attendance on his class; and on Tuesday evening he was promptly there, and in his usual seat. O how well to be in the way of duty with death so near! His leader asked him, with commendable fidelity, if he could then testify that he was assuredly born again, made a child of God, and consequently an heir of Heaven. Edwin humbly, but distinctly, replied, 'I feel thankful that I do know that I am a child of God. I have had in the past week seasons of communion with Him, and desire more constantly to realise His presence, and live to His glory.' The meeting concluded, and he was in apparently perfect health, and so he retired to rest. The next morning he complained a little. About the middle of the day the symptoms increased upon him and became serious, producing, besides pain, faintness and prostration of strength. His eldest brother sent in the utmost alarm for the surgeon, and a physician besides, who for two hours resorted to every means within their power to stay the attack, but all to no purpose. He was then hurried home in a close carriage; cramp supervened, and before evening there was no doubt that the disease was cholera. At five o'clock he was assisted to bed, and asked, 'Supposing the worst should come, do you feel any fear?' 'O no,' he said, 'I feel I am safe!' and responded in the affirmative to some observations which were made in reference to having the fear of death taken away. The nature of the disease prevented further conversation, excepting so far as that he occasionally gave a brief assurance of his calm repose upon the atonement of his adorable Saviour, and that His presence was manifested to him. His mind was perfectly composed and tranquil all night, while the vital powers, notwithstanding all remedies that were used, were sinking fast; and at half-past twelve on Thursday morning, July 26th, he gently fell asleep in Christ."

This was no slight stroke; and how was it borne? That shall be told, not by me, but by an eye-witness. Mr. Carvosso says—

"The moment he either felt or saw the rod, '*I* have sinned,' was on his lips and in the depths of his heart. Hence, in the distressing loss of his lovely son Edwin, compared with the painful consciousness of his *own deserts*, the stroke of the cholera and the bitter bereavement were 'light.' The dread evening when his loved son was writhing in the grasp of the disease, leaving him in other hands, he meets his class and then takes a poor, intelligent, pious man, a local preacher, 'his own son in the faith,' and retires in darkness to the lone summer-house in his extensive lawn, and they long continued wrestling together 'with strong crying and tears,'—the personal dread of *His* wrath who is 'glorious in *holiness*' absorbing the anguish of the purest natural affection. Returning in the advanced night to his awfully afflicted dwelling, with the cry, 'My sins, *my sins*, are the cause of all this!" his *pious* children gather round *him*, and all in succession, from the oldest to the youngest, are heard pleading with God for their father's consolation and deliverance. This piercing apprehension of the evil of sin, with the powerfully healing balm of Divine grace, given pre-eminently in answer to the 'prayer of faith,' prepared him and his family for such a manifestation of passive piety as I do not recollect ever elsewhere to have witnessed. A few days afterwards, returning from the Conference, expecting on entering his dwelling to enter a cloud whose '*darkness might be felt*,' what was my surprise to find it a true dwelling of an Israelite, all '*light within*.' The darkness was outside; here they all walked in the light of the Lord, and all tears were wiped from every eye. I beheld, and was edified; I wondered, and shall never forget! Mr. Budgett not only murmured not, but was ceaseless in praises that he and his family had been dealt with so mercifully. I knew how he loved his son, and what he expected from him."

Happy in his own family, he was solicitous for the conversion of other young persons who came within his influence. That young friend whose notes we have used is an example. From the time that Methodism took root in Kingswood, there had always been a succession of lively and pious men among the colliers; and these, with flowing heart, delighted to declare at the "Lovefeasts," in their own plain speech, the great goodness of the Lord to their souls. It was not uncommon for persons to come from a distance to hear and be edified by these simple declarations of the power of grace to renew. One Easter Monday our young friend and a sister had come from Bath to Kingswood; and were descried in the chapel by Mr. Budgett, who knew their family. At the close of the service he went up to them, and at once made himself their friend, and would not be denied, but home with him they must come. He soon won their confidence, and after a while took them out for a walk, leading them away to a cottage at some distance, where a young woman was dying in Christian peace. On the way he affectionately inquired whether they had given their hearts to God, and counselled them early to seek the blessings which hallow youth and age. After they had left the cottage, they saw a crowd, and two men stripped to the waist boxing. This hideous sight, though strange to them, was only too familiar to their new friend, who at once hastened towards the spot and with great authority separated the combatants.

With this young friend he maintained a frequent correspondence, gently begging for two letters to his one, in consideration of his want of leisure. With many other young persons also he corresponded, ever urging upon them the supreme importance of piety. He was exceedingly fond of having at his own house the youth of other godly families; and cases occurred wherein these visits were the means of their conversion, while in no instance could they reside in that home without becoming more and more alive to the charms of vital and working godliness. It is not pleasant and it is not meet to write about the living: this fact excludes much we should love to tell in this chapter; but the rule is good to be silent on the virtues of those who are still here. The only case wherein one feels quite at home in praising them, is when worthy names are aspersed by unworthy tongues. Were it not for this, we might narrate beautiful instances of happy deeds done under Mr. Budgett's roof.

We may give a few specimens of Mr. Budgett's correspondence with his young friends; it will be seen how free and tender is his style, as if it were an elder brother, rather than one so much beyond them in age, and with so much of what would induce, in most men, a high sense of consequence. The first extract is from a note written to his friend oft referred to, as the date shows, only a few days before Edwin's death; and it would seem as if his thoughts were under secret preparation for the event yet unforeseen.

"*Kingswood Hill*, *July* 18, 1849.

"My dear Friend,—I might almost conjecture you had been busy in hay harvest or something else, for it seems so long a time since I have either seen or heard from you; at any rate I hope you will make some allowance for my long silence when I tell you that I have been from home, and have had company. Do you ever intend coming to see us again? You may be assured I, indeed we all, shall be as glad to see you as ever, unless you stay away so long as to make us forget you. But how are you prospering in the best things? What a wilderness does this world seem without the hope of the Gospel; how exceedingly uncertain is every thing here. What a mercy we have the Bible. Please write me with your usual freedom, and believe me, with very kind remembrance to papa and mamma, &c., as ever,

"Your sincere and affectionate friend,

"S. B."

In the following letter we see his judgment on reading religious biography:—

"*Kingswood Hill, February* 17, 1849.

"MY DEAR FRIEND,—I am of opinion that there is scarcely any class of reading more profitable to our growth in grace than choice pieces of religious biography—such as Brainerd, Martin, Fletcher, Wesley, Richmond, Bramwell, John Smith, M'Cheyne, Carvosso, Mrs. West, Cryer, Bingham, and a host of others. All good things require to be read prayerfully and in faith. Are we not too apt to think there was something peculiar in the individuals rather than in the faith by which they derived all their excellencies? The fountain of all good is as full and as free of access now and to us as ever it was to them, and we have only to exercise the same faith and all the good will be as surely ours as ever it was theirs. May the Lord help my dear friend and me to enter more fully into the gracious designs of our heavenly Father concerning us!

"I think you cannot help admiring the present beautiful weather. See how spring and summer are approaching already! The birds sing most merrily; the days lengthen very fast; the flowers are beginning to decorate the hedges and banks; the fields are increasing in verdure and beauty; and I hope you and I shall endeavour to keep pace with all nature in praising our Creator and Redeemer. Is it not cheering to think I know that God is love, and especially that He loves me? Believe me, my dear E———,

"Most affectionately yours,

"S. B."

In another note to his Bath friend, a note full of kind feeling, I find these remarks:—

"We cannot indeed too highly value time: in this I have been truly deficient. If we would rise early we must begin at the right end—that is by going to bed early, or all will be lost labour. You must have seven hours sleep. An alarum is a very good thing; but if we neglect the call a few times, like the calls of the Spirit or of our consciences, it will be ineffectual.

"I am glad you still retain love to God after seven years' experience. May it be increased seven times seven! I think nothing is so calculated to remove reserve as zeal for God and humility. We think too much of ourselves and not enough of the importance of being found faithful; may you, my dear friend, become truly simple of heart and dead to the opinion of others when it stands in the way of duty. You have not wearied me. Your letters are no tax on my time, I am always very glad to hear from you, and the more freely you write to me the more you please me.

"I have scarcely any time for Milner. *Stock-taking* is too near; I seem just as full as I can possibly be. I have for the last week been rising at five, and have as much as I can do until ten every day. My health and spirits are good. My wife is poorly, but improving: all the rest well. With kind remembrances to your family circle, I am, my dear friend,

"Yours affectionately,

"S. B."

Here we find him inciting his young friend to perseverance and faith as a teacher:—

"*Kingswood Hill, Dec.* 24, 1844.

"MY VERY DEAR FRIEND,—I am truly thankful that God has so graciously inclined your heart to seek your happiness where alone true enjoyment can be found, and that He has not only blessed but made you a blessing.

"If you are faithful, He will give you grace to lose yourself in Him, as a drop in the ocean, and your prayers will be frequently offered and graciously answered.

'Keep me dead to all below,
Only Christ resolved to know,
Firm and disengaged and free,
Seeking all my bliss in Thee.'

You will feel so impressed with the value of souls and your responsibility to God, that you will never rest until all the girls in your class are brought from darkness to light. I remember hearing of a young person who had thirteen scholars, and for several years she saw but little fruit of her labour until she was almost discouraged; but instead of giving up, she began to wrestle with God in earnest, persevering, faithful prayer; and in a short time one of the girls evinced a serious concern for her spiritual welfare, and began to inquire with deep anxiety what she must do to be saved. This soon spread through the class, and in a few months every one of the children gave satisfactory evidence that their hearts were changed. I have little doubt but that the effect will be equally encouraging on your part if you trust alone in the mighty God who has said (Mark xi. 24), 'Whatsoever things,' &c. Let this encouraging passage have its full weight on your mind, and make all the use of it you believe your heavenly Father would have you."

"S. B."

How many busy merchants, with such an establishment upon their hands, and with such indoor and outdoor calls upon their time, would take pains thus to cherish the correspondence of pious youth, partly from a design to encourage them in religious life, partly from the impulse of an ardent friendship?

His letters indicate his love of a tour. Wales, Scotland, the Lakes, and other paths of beauty were selected for summer excursions; and there, amid the works of the heavenly Father, his heart rekindled all its best emotions. Nothing did he enjoy more than a drive or a stroll amid beautiful scenery, accompanied by members of his family or a friend or two, heightening the pleasure by poetry, hymns, or animated rehearsals of God's wonderful providence in his own career. The flowers, the trees, and the singing birds would all set his thoughts in motion, and elicit warm bursts of pleasure and of worship. When on a drive, he had been telling some of the striking passages of his life to his young friend. She said laughingly but in earnest, "Why, Mr. Budgett, your life ought to be written among the lives of wonderful men." "My life!" he said, "it is no more worth writing than the life of that bird in the bush." Of his children and of their friends he was the friend—one might almost say the comrade, and in his open-heartedness often made them more intimate with his grave concerns than they could bring themselves to make him with their lighter ones. Thus, while his influence steadily opposed every thing that was evil, no coldness, no sanctimonious sharpness, no indifference to youthful zest and sensibility ever displayed itself; and yet under all this companionable familiarity, there was a basis of unrelenting discipline which was not shown, but which, if infringed upon, would yield to no pressure or appeal.

In the management of his servants, as in that of his men, he delighted to reward diligence. When any special instruction was well carried out, some little present often followed; and even when he wished to correct a fault, sometimes he managed to do it by especial commendation of a small display of the opposite virtue, or by some trifling gift. He once gave his cook a characteristic reproof on the subject of punctuality. He could not bear to lose a moment before meals. When the bell for breakfast was rung, he sat still in his library till all were assembled for prayer, then a private bell summoned him, and so not an instant was lost. It proved on one occasion that for two or three days in succession dinner was late; this, of course, was not to his mind yet he sent "cook" no message. Some friends were staying in the house, and he made the whole party agree to enter the dining-room precisely at the hour, and take their seats at table. This all did, and much to their amusement waited for a considerable time. It may be supposed that the tidings soon travelled to the kitchen. Not certain, however, that this one lesson would suffice, he issued the same order for the following day. Again the cook heard of the whole company being seated at a table without viands, and you may suppose that such a sermon on punctuality was not delivered in vain.

No one would expect ostentation in the domestic life of Mr. Budgett; while plentifulness was everywhere, plainness and economy were its meet companions. Fond of having numerous visitors—sometimes making a descent on a group of friends, and by his own irresistible determination carrying them off, yea or nay, to Kingswood Hill—he yet never desired to get a name for entertainments. I have heard many speak of heart and warmth, of domestic order, of prayer and praise, of active piety, and endless good-doing; but in looking back upon all who have talked about that home, I do not remember one who commemorated the champagne or the brilliant *soirées*. He was far more at home in giving the Sunday School children a treat, or regaling the young women with tea and strawberries, than in seeing a number of fine ladies and gentlemen lounge and prattle. Many horses as he gave away, he never drove a pair, because he thought it would be too much display. Much as he loved beauty and rural scenes, he did not buy a mansion in some of the enchanting localities within a drive of Bristol; but tried, in the act of feeding the labourers of the place, tc make Kingswood beautiful. Temperance in all things, without extremes, either in house, dress, or board, was his taste; and temperance in all these he impressed on his domestic circle. It would have been easy for him to have had nothing to spare when the poor called; but he chose rather to have nothing to spare when extravagant luxuries called. His style was far below that assumed by many merchants of half his means, yet without any prim fashion of peculiarity; and his accumulated wealth was never so great as his largesses would lead many to imagine.

Among the mercantile class, luxury is a devouring evil; it swallows down the virtues wholesale. For their means they are far more addicted to it than the "higher classes;" their houses are enlarged and decorated with the most pretentious rivalry one of the other, their tables testify against all moderation (eschewing of course drunkenness), they make haste to march to the music of carriage wheels, to feast their eyes on plush and livery buttons. The rage to make vast fortunes arises as much from the rage for display as from the cold desire to accumulate; and style is pushed up to such a height that soon a man must have an immense revenue to keep pace even with the lower circles of respectable life. This is all bad, comes of badness, and leads to badness. Yet, alas, the men we call by emphasis "good" do little as a class to cure it; the religious merchant or manufacturer of wealth is generally a very splendid gentleman. Even men whose personal carriage, whose heart, life, and likings are meek and lowly, allow their establishments to slide up into the splendours. This habit is enervating our youths, rendering family happiness dependent on superfluities, straining health and principles in a race for dashing style, setting up splendour on the legitimate throne of moderation, and icing over domestic piety with candied incrustations. Unless it is put down, where are we to look for a race of men who can do without a dinner now and then for a work of charity, or spend years in frugal habitudes and benevolent hardship? The homes of the comfortable classes are mortally unfavourable to the formation of self-denying heroic men. Among the poor, early hardship fits for subsequent privation. Among the older families, ancestral traditions, military or naval associates, early familiarity with historic enterprise, tend to make a youth spurn dependence on the indulgences which surround him. The one class gives us hardy soldiers, the other heroic officers; but the comfortable class have neither hardship nor family tradition to kindle heroism in their youth, and the whole course of their modern progress is towards a generation of creatures dependent upon every sort of luxury, and energetic only to win the gold which will buy it. The continuance of peace, removing from our eyes the examples of self-devotion which war, detestable as it is, constantly presents, renders it all the more incumbent on us to protest against habits which would turn this hardy northern island into a nursery of soft *gentlemen* who will whine and mope if they have only a warm house, with a fire, a loaf, a joint, and a cup of tea.

The outcrying extravagance and luxury of the day needs a most masterful hand laid upon it; statesmen should smite it, authors and journalists should set the pen upon it, parents should make it a fireside laughingstock, religious men should walk over it, and preachers should burn it with living coals of eloquence. It does one's heart good to see the "Edinburgh Review," in an article replete with sense and vigour, pointing to a reduction of the prevalent extravagance as the wise, safe, short path to universal plenty. "If," says the judicious writer, "the English people could all at once be induced to lay aside their luxurious, wasteful, and showy mode of life, and adopt the frugality and temperance of the Spaniards, the simple habits of the Tyrolese, and the unostentatious hospitality of the Syrians, how few among us would not find a superfluity at their disposal? We rejoice to believe that this more rational and homely spirit is spreading among us, especially in detached localities, and we *do not think that a good citizen could render any more valuable service to his country than in promoting it by argument and example wherever his influence extends.*"

CHAPTER IX.

THE INNER LIFE.

> "Truth is not local; God alike pervades
> And fills the world of traffic and the shades,
> And may be feared amid the busiest scenes,
> Or scorned where business never intervenes."
>
> COWPER.

THERE is a life the world sees, a life the neighbourhood sees, a life the family sees, a life God sees. These are often strangely inconsistent. It is pitiable when each succeeding enclosure you pass to reach the man, introduces you to diminishing charms and growing blemishes. With Samuel Budgett it was not so: the merchant who only knew him as the unparalleled "buyer," the stranger who only heard of him from some men of business in Bristol, and many who saw but his outermost character, had no remarkable impression of his worth. But those who *knew* his works in his neighbourhood, beheld wondering; those who knew his home had a profound love of the man; those who knew his closet and his heart looked upon him with feelings which few men raise in the breasts of others.

When his opening mind first cried for food, a mother was there who wisely gave it the knowledge of one great, holy God, and added in daily teaching the knowledge of all truths essential to the soul. Not only did she feed his mind with this living bread, but she moved its powers to come forth, to stretch upwards and meet its God; she did not teach the lips alone to mutter praying words where meaning was not; but bending over the earth-prone infant mind, well knowing that it could rise, yet would if left alone grovel, his mother's soul, stirring, lifting his growing soul, urged him up toward the mercy-seat.

This was the first influence on Samuel Budgett's inner life,—a firm conviction of Christian truths, a bent towards prayer. Then he had before his eyes beings whose whole lives were adjusted on the principle that they were travelling to a better country. The songs he heard in his father's house were the songs of that shining land. The genius of Charles Wesley was, to his infancy, a lark at morn, musically inviting his eye toward heaven; a nightingale at eventide, pouring upon the shades of life melody from the invisible. The necessities he heard spoken of as most pressing, were necessities of the inner man; the treasure he heard extolled as the one pearl of price, was a heart-held gift of God. He had ever something to remind him that man does not live by bread alone, but that there is a life which moulds the life of sense to happiness or vanity.

Then came the notable hour when, passing his mother's door, he heard her making supplication for her Samuel. Now, for the first time, his soul consciously cried out within him, as a living thing which felt itself poor, hungry, and nigh to perishing,—*another* voice had, this time, spoken through his mother's. The prodigal's feeling when he came to himself is the first feeling of all souls when they first awake,—"I perish;" the prodigal's hope is the hope of all souls when awake,—"I will arise, and go to my father." That little boy, in struggling thoughts and prayers, endeavoured to find God; the efforts of his mother to lift his soul up had not been vain,—now that it was awake, it knew where to fly. Then came the happy death of Betty Coles, and the walking in the fields on summer evenings, repeating hymns on death and heaven. Then, the ride by Mells Park, when his mother lay, as he feared, dying; and where he whose soul had first been urged heavenward on the wings of her soul, now rose upon his own wing, bearing her, stricken as she was, and struggled upward with his burden, till he surmounted the clouds, and beheld the sun so clearly that his heart sang. Henceforward he felt the joy of the Divine life. Then came years at school, and early trading, followed by years of apprenticeship, throughout all which the inner life appears to have been vigorous. His thirst for the means of grace was strong and steady; his Bible was beloved; his Sabbath was a day of eager hearing, eager reading, eager meditating, and eventually a day of ardent teaching and visiting; his hymn-book was passing almost entire into his memory; and his path of filial duty was trodden with self-forgetting constancy. Inside all this was a warm delight in God—a gratitude, a love, a filial fear. In spiritual tranquillity, in calm, steadfast happiness of soul, these early years excelled the years that followed; they were the most uniformly bright period of Mr. Budgett's inward life. It would seem that throughout those days of hard circumstances, he had faithfully walked with God, and had enjoyed abounding consolation. What was that, then, which, beginning as he prayed by the park at Wells, gave him happiness and virtue throughout all boyhood and early youth? Mark the two things,—*happiness* and *virtue*, the two best and purest blessings,—in fact, the collective expressions of all blessings possible; what was it which gave him a happiness much trouble could not mar; a virtue youthful temptation could not shake? It was the Comforter—the Spirit of adoption, which, entering the heart of the happy men who return from sin to Christ, "beareth witness with our spirit that we are the children of God." Our race is a race of prodigals, far wandered from the Father's house, beside themselves, and living sinfully; but O, many have come to themselves, have returned to the Father, and have been received with pardon, with tender utterances, and wealthy gifts. But you do not believe, that when God receives back the prodigal son, He utters any word of welcome which will assure and rejoice the self-reproaching heart; you say it is impossible that the soul can be told, "Thy sins are forgiven thee." What parent in the universe is without the power of giving recovered offspring a glad welcome? Even the hen can thrill her lost, when found, with notes of delight; and is the only parent who cannot tell his love and his joy into the breast of his "lost one, who is found again," the Father of all souls, the source of all light and speech? Nay, nay; God has a way into the soul of man as well as you, as direct at least, and as effectual. God has a voice as well as you, and spirit can speak to spirit, as well as lips of earth—speak condemnation, warning, or approval. When He adopts a man, forgiving him the sins that are past, He has a wondrous thing to tell him, which no earthly eye has seen, no ear has heard, and therefore no tongue can tell; and that it may be told—clearly told, He sends forth the Spirit of His Son into the man's heart, crying, Abba, Father. It is told: the soul knows that it has passed from death to life, knows its adoption, knows the thing which eye hath not seen, or ear heard, but which God has revealed unto it by His Spirit knows itself a child; and if a child, then an heir:—this is the consolation. With this consolation comes a love, which renders obedience pleasing and disobedience hateful. It is not by convincing the judgment that cheerfulness is better than repining, virtue better than sin, that God makes men really happy and really virtuous; but by moving the affections as a Father, and winning our love by displaying His love to the eye-sight of the *soul.*

But his letters written in the years succeeding the expiration of his apprenticeship, and the detached notes still left to us, indicate clearly a state of soul in which the same calm faith no longer reigns. There is not only self-abasement, but disquiet—a soul not happy, not feeling the joy of pardon, not trustingly staid upon the cross. He is plainly conscious of great unfaithfulness; not an unfaithfulness which has laid him low in humiliation only, but which has robbed him of his peace; not an unfaithfulness which has driven him to the great Mediator with a more piercing sense of his innate sin, and a more fixed hold of Christ's infinite merit, but which has withered his hand that he cannot lay hold on the hope set before him in the gospel. These were cloudy days; but whence the cloud came I have not the means of saying.

But he was not the man to coin a spurious comfort, when the genuine impress of God's approval was withdrawn—to burnish a base metal till it would glitter as if gold; he was rather one to test the true with *aqua-fortis* scrutiny, till under the test its brightness was hidden though its substance was unhurt. Such was his habit constantly; and of that self-distrusting, self-depreciating habit, full account must be taken in estimating his spiritual state. Yet with this in view, it is evident that the want of peace which marked his earlier years of manhood, contrasting with the habitual brightness of youth, is not assignable purely to such a cause, but *began* with unwatchfulness, and some clear, specific transgression. Some *religious* men are always joyful, though never watchful; their joy is not worth a butterfly.

His copious journals are gone, burnt up by his own hand; and we are not disposed to blame any man for that. Now, a few stray fragments of notes, scattered, unfinished, abrupt, disconnected—merely the faint trace of an occasional footmark—is all that has survived. One note is dated January 1, 1822, shortly after his entrance on partnership and his marriage, when all outward things were joyous. Yet he thus writes:—

"Tuesday evening, January 1, 1822.—My soul is greatly oppressed because of sin. I shall never be happy till I find a Saviour from the love, the power, the guilt, and the sad effects of sin as it respects future punishment. I believe such a Saviour is provided, but He is not my Saviour—I do not know Him; He has not saved me from my sins; but I am resolved to try if I cannot find Him, so then I will seek Him first and oftenest, and with the most diligence, for I am in danger till I do find Him. Oh, when shall I find Him! how long shall I seek Him! Lord, grant that I may never rest till I feel He is formed in my heart the hope of eternal glory. AMEN."

At the close of the week he adds:—

"Sunday, middle day, January 6, 1822.—The last week has been a very unprofitable one. I see great propriety in what Thomas-a-Kempis says, 'the beginning of temptation is inconstancy of mind, and little faith.'

"I have been suffering all the last week from want of resisting temptation in the beginning: I am now very low. But I will *arise again*. I have before me 'Hervey's Meditations,' 'Baxter's Saint's Rest,' and the Sacred Volume. I have just taken a slight view of the loss I sustained by spending my time as I have done in the past week. As this is the first Sabbath in the year, may I now begin to redeem *time*—to form an acquaintance with my Bible, &c., &c. Oh, what pleasures, what privileges, depend on the improvement of precious time! May I—yea, I feel resolved to—give no moment but in purchase of its worth. May the Lord give me strength, and teach me what its worth is."

Towards the end of the month he makes this note:—

"Thursday evening, January 24, 1822.—I this morning returned from Midsomer Norton. In my way I indulged a few reflections, and endeavoured to form a few resolutions:—

"1st, I am a guilty, and consequently an unhappy creature.

"2d, The darkness of my mind prevents my seeing its awful state.

"3d, As my mind is darkened by sin I cannot see what is my duty, or what are my privileges.

"4th, I have not power to perform even what I know to be my duty.

"5th, The longer I continue in this state the worse I shall be, till my eternal ruin be accomplished.

"Resolved—

"1st, To seek a deeper sense and clearer discovery of my awful state through sin.

"2nd, To seek to get a satisfactory evidence that I am accepted through Christ.

"3rd, To make the service of God, and obedience to the dictates of his Spirit, the supreme object of my life.

"4th, To begin to redeem time, and to be more moderate in my eating, drinking and sleeping, and to endeavour to make one word pass for two, in order that *my soul may* grow in grace and be happy; and all this would I do in humble dependence on the continual assistance of the Holy Spirit.

"And 5th, To read every day a chapter or two of Scripture according to the resolution made January 1st, 1822."

The first sign of recovered joy comes nearly two years subsequent to the date of the above notes; when looking back on the Christmas week he says, "I am pleased on reviewing it as one of the most profitable weeks spent on this earth."

Everything we can gather betokens an earnest struggle

after a life disciplined to obey accurately strict intentions as to inward motive and outward action. His views of a call to be a child of light were very clear; and setting that beauty of holiness whereto he felt called beside the poor attainments which alone he would recognise in his character, his heart sank abashed. With lower views of the Christian calling he would have beheld his own life without strong condemnation; but, in that case, the evils he now deplored would have grown, the graces he longed for would have been neglected, and his character would have gradually deteriorated till he was either a hollow professor of religion, or a full-blown man of the world. Prosperity was setting in strongly; his natural disposition urged him to absorbing efforts in trade, and here was his danger. In the heat of driving his plans, he was constantly liable to be overcome; and doubtless many of his self-reproaches were founded on real short-comings. He had not grace sufficient to be "more than conqueror;" he was often vanquished by the impulses of nature, aided by abetting circumstances; but he had grace sufficient for this —that he would not overlook, would not excuse his fault, would search it out, confess it to God, ay, and confess it to man, abhor himself on account thereof, and go in penitent supplication to a Father for pardon. The highest effect of grace undoubtedly is to keep us unspotted; but the next is to lead us to quick, deep repentance when we have contracted a stain. About his notes there is more self-examination and self-discipline, than self-forgetting regard of Christ and of God. One clear sight of Christ's redeeming glory, does more to disengage our feelings from entanglement, and to attract them to Him, than ten thousand dissatisfied verdicts upon their actual condition. Self-condemnation is just; it is invaluable so far as it undoes all self-trust and self-glorying: but if it fixes the eye upon self so much as to hinder the occupation of the thoughts by Him that is greater than we, it then becomes another form of self-importance, another feint of self-righteousness. And you will never destroy self by scolding it—so long as you are chiefly occupied about it, however occupied, it will survive; it dies only when the soul, viewing the wondrous God become a father, a friend, and a bosom helper, is absorbed in the Saviour it has found—loving, rejoicing, beholding, and imitating, till the old man disappears—the whole character putting on the attributes we adore. But better far be ever scrutinising and ever self-condemning, than make the rich mercies of the Godhead a reason for permitting an ill-ordered heart, and a vacillating holiness.

O! ye men of business, how many of you practise Mr. Budgett's habit of self-examination? You go through a thousand transactions in a week; do you sift your heart at the end? You store up your gold; do you test it lest a plague should be in it? You "have no time." Madness and blasphemy!—no time to look to your salvation, and to see whether you are serving God! Mr. Budgett had quite as much on hand as you. Here is a set of entries in pencil which affectingly testifies that the rising merchant knew he had a Judge above, and keenly searched his thoughts, words, deeds, for offences against His law:—

"Sunday evening, August 3, 1823:—

"1. I am conscious I have thought of myself more highly than I ought to think.

"2. I have sacrificed to my own net and burnt incense to my own drag.

"3. I have ascribed my success in my undertakings to my own wisdom.

"4. I have boasted of what I have received as if I had not received it.

"5. I have gloried in very many things save the cross of our Lord Jesus Christ.

"6. I have desired the praise of men and taken pleasure in it.

"7. I have repeatedly given way to foolish desires.

"8. I have often and repeatedly given way to inordinate affection.

"9. I have indulged spiritual and bodily sloth.

"10. I have often allowed myself to speak, if not lies, yet what was not in the strict sense truth in the love thereof.

"11. I have practised in my dealings arts which would not bear strict scrutiny.

"12. I have not laboured to do whatsoever I did to the glory of God.

"13. I have indulged my bodily appetites."

Mr. Carvosso strongly describes his confessions of unfaithfulness—not the cold, mechanical indication of avowals the heart ought to make but does not, but piercing utterances of heart-pain. Openly in the class-meeting or love feast, with many of his own men present, he would speak with flowing tears, as if his soul within him worshipped and fell down and kneeled, yea, lay prostrate with awe and contrition in the presence of the infinite love and holiness, while he abhorred his own short-comings. At the prayer-meeting too, he loved to fill his place, and far was *he* from carrying before the mercy-seat the familiar tones, and the manner habitual to business scenes: no, he was not before men now; and in that glorious presence where he knelt, all his business bearing departed, his thoughts sought a depth below the dust wherein to bow, his tones thrilled with humiliation, and his tears ran plentifully. He cannot be set before mature Christians as an example of constantly bright, placid faith, "always confident, and willing rather to be absent from the body and to be present with the Lord; but the man of business, struggling with the temptations of trade and impelled by a nature eager for commercial progress, may profitably fix his eye upon him and see one situated like himself, scrutinizing his transactions as before the Judge, and when he finds his heart too much engrossed with earthly things, making haste to seek renewed grace with prayer and tears. And this, remember, not when all the fruits you could trace of his religion were to be found in his attendance at class, at prayer-meeting, at public worship, and the Lord's holy table, with the home solemnity of family prayer; but when his services to God and man were astonishing those who were familiar with common-place piety.

But though his prevalent tone was depressed, he did ever and anon taste his Father's love till his whole soul bounded with joyous energies. When so refreshed he did not allow his comforts to expend themselves in emotion, but used them as strength for works of special difficulty. On one occasion he visited his friend Mr. Wood, at Truro, and then his soul was bewailing its unfaithfulness in much depression. The night before parting, the two friends were long engaged in prayer; the cloud broke away from Mr. Budgett's soul, joy unspeakable and full of glory entered into his heart. While waiting the next day at Hayle for the Bristol steamer, his eye was attracted by a house in which he detected signs of suspicious though numerous company. On inquiry he found it was the dwelling of an unhappy man who once had seemed to "run well," but had sorely fallen, and that a loose party were meeting for dancing and debauch. He at once made for the house; would see the master; kindly, but firmly talked with him till, wicked as he was, he consented to let his strange, gentle, but resistless visitor go up stairs. As they ascended abundant tokens of wrath were uttered, for the conversation had been overheard: a candlestick was flung at Mr. Budgett's head. The man begged him to come back and himself shrank away; but no, he would warn these poor revellers. In he went, begged them not to be disturbed.

just to go on as if he were not there, said they were trying to enjoy themselves, and that was what he always wished to do, and so spoke familiarly and kindly, till he had their attention. Then he began to reason with them "on righteousness, temperance, and judgment to come:" one by one their air and words of scoffing fell, some were soon in tears, the fiddle ceased to play, and ere he left he had led that wild company to bow before the great God in prayer, while tears, and sobs, and signs of shame told that the heart within was melted. The dance was ended for that night.

On the steamer he found a gentleman who seemed ill and lonely: he addressed him with that kind perseverance whereby, in a way peculiar to himself, he would enter into any mind he wished to enter; and finding him averse to all religious things, he spoke to him in solemn warning, blended with the glorious invitations of the Gospel. The stranger was not easily won—they parted; but during the night Mr. Budgett was called to the other's couch: he was ill; he was dying; and he touchingly owned the kindness of his new friend, opened his heart, told him his tale—a dark and sad one,—told him his name, which he had not borne in travelling, committed his watch and other commissions to his hand, and died.

It is often said that to know a person you must see him at home. There is truth in that; but it may also be said that to know a person you must see him on a journey. Many who are strict and exemplary at home, put on a loose religious dress when they travel.* Mr. Budgett did not think

* I, at one time, thought of devoting a chapter to Mr. Budgett "on the road"—referring especially to *commercial travelling* with its temptations; but my materials were not sufficient to compensate for the lack of practical knowledge: perhaps it may be touched at some other time.

it desirable "just once in a way," to visit the opera when he came to town; or to take his children to a theatre that they might "just see and judge for themselves." He did not, when at a strange hotel, where "no one knew him and the example would do no harm," stroll into the billiard room and try a game "merely for exercise." He did not, at a watering place, look round for the fashionable congregation, and shun his own people if they were poor and few. He did not say he was "come out to enjoy himself," and therefore would take no pains to do good. The religion he valued at home, he valued on the road; as in Kingswood, so in Wales, Cornwall, or elsewhere he was ever on the watch for objects of charity, for occasions to say a word to men about the Redeemer he loved. He always carried a plentiful store of books and tracts which he distributed. If he knew of a prayer-meeting or week-evening preaching in a town where he chanced to be, he would haste away, and if called upon would himself preach, though from that effort his sinking heart always inclined to retire. A close companion in journeys and at home has told me pleasing tales of his wayside good-doing.

We have already seen what impression was made upon a Christian friend by the manner in which Mr. Budgett bowed to the dispensation which called away his lovely son Edwin. In the following note to his sister-in-law we see proof of the justice of that impression:—

Kingswood Hill, July 27th, 1849.

"My dear Sister P——,—Fearing that William's note to brother William, of yesterday, might have alarmed you, I write a few lines just to say we are all well and happy in God. Our dear Edwin was prepared, and is now

'Far from a world of grief and sin,
With God eternally shut in.'

We are yet, though suffering under a most painful bereavement, a happy family: yes, the peace of God that passeth all human understanding, does keep our hearts and minds through faith in Christ Jesus. It would be impossible for us to tell you how precious Christ is to us in this time of severe trial. We have this morning enjoyed a gracious visitation from our heavenly Father while we all, the whole family, knelt and prayed that this stroke might be fully sanctified. I am, my dear sister P——,

"Yours affectionately,

"S. B."

Every season of affliction, personal or domestic, was to him a call, as if from the trump of God, to humble himself. He looked at the full salvation, the perfect love and perfect peace whereto the Gospel call invited him; with this he compared his actual graces, and it seemed to him as if he had paid too much attention to earthly things, foregoing divine joys for worldly good. His soul shook and mourned exceedingly, not from fears of future wrath, but from a distressing sight of his unfaithful service to the all-blessed Redeemer. The following letter, written during an illness, displays minutely the workings of his heart at such a time:—

Kingswood Hill, Nov. 23, 1843.

"My dear Brother James,—I forced my heavenly Father to use the rod, but I am astonished to think with what gentleness He has corrected me. The first Sunday I was unwell, I made a fresh act of faith, and ventured my whole soul on the atonement. My heart seemed to have been broken in a thousand pieces, and I felt disposed to weep my life away for having grieved my God. For the first week I held fast my confidence and felt calm as in the hands of my loving Saviour, but on the second Sabbath I grew much worse, so that I had but very little hope of recovery. I began to reason with the enemy, and let go my shield of faith; and then was truly the hour and power of darkness. I can never describe the *bitter anguish* I felt on reviewing my past life, and such horror and gloom came over my mind at the thoughts of being *but just saved as by the skin of my teeth*, or of *appearing before my Maker as an unprofitable servant*, or perhaps of being a wandering spirit cast out from God for unfaithfulness to roam in endless circles of despair, as well-nigh turned my brain. My agony of mind was such that I thought I was dying, and really fainted away. I then recovered, and tried to recover my shield of faith; but on Monday morning, Satan was again permitted to buffet me, and the conflict was extreme. My dear sister Elizabeth then came to my assistance, and said I was doing very wrong—that I ought to come to the Saviour as at first I came, and that she believed I should recover, but that if I died I was safe for heaven. I immediately took courage and said, 'Lord, I did believe and was happy, and thou hast said, "Whosoever cometh, &c., &c.," I come, I believe—I *will*, I *do* believe, &c.' My heart seemed melted to tenderness, and the name of Jesus was exceedingly precious. Sister Elizabeth then said, 'Cannot you now put in your claim for the blessing of full salvation? Remember the promise, "I will circumcise thy heart, &c., &c."' I said, 'I am suffering all this because I would not take the necessary pains to obtain that blessing when that very promise was so often and powerfully impressed on my mind; and as it was so *clearly my duty* to *obtain*, to *enjoy*, and to *preach* that great and glorious Gospel privilege to others, I could not hold fast even a sense of my acceptance with God, or overcome various temptations to sin,—and it is of the Lord's mercies that I am not consumed:' but when sister Elizabeth said, 'Put in your claim just now,' I made a violent effort and said, 'Lord, thou hast said, "I will circumcise, &c., &c.:' now fulfil thine own word. I hang upon thy word; thou wilt do it. I dare believe.' I did not struggle long before my heart seemed deeply humbled, filled with love unutterable to God and all mankind. I, however, could not entertain an idea that God could spare my life; and though I felt safe and happy, I could not feel willing to die even to go to heaven with such a consciousness of unfaithfulness up to the eleventh hour, and earnestly prayed, '*O spare* me a little, that I may recover my strength before I go hence to be no more seen.' On the following morning my dear wife came into my room with the Bible in her hand, saying, 'I have just opened upon this passage.' See Isaiah xlviii. 9, 10. Never did Scripture so *powerfully* impress my mind. I said, 'It is the word of God to me, in answer to his servant's prayers: I shall not die but live.' From that time I never entertained a doubt but I should have another opportunity of preaching salvation—full salvation by Christ Jesus to every one who will put in their claim for it. My mind has since been kept in perfect peace, and I have been gradually recovering. Now, my dear brother James, my object in being thus minute in the description is, first, to lead you, as you would avoid the gloom, the horror, the anguish, such as no tongue can tell, of an unsatisfactory state of mind on a dying bed, or the more tremendous consequences of being hurried out of time into eternity; as you would enjoy this life tenfold more than you possibly could without it; as you would be unspeakably happy, safe, useful, and rising daily in refinement and elevation of character; and as you would have a glorious entrance administered to you among the saints in light; in a word, that as you would escape hell and gain heaven securely, you at once give the Lord your *whole* heart, and accept his full salvation: this, my dear brother, is much easier than doing it by halves. I am, my dear brother,

"Most affectionately yours,
"S B."

From all this it is manifest, that while Mr. Budgett's piety was not uniform in consolation, it was habitual in intensity. For the last few years of his life he withdrew to a great extent from active business engagements; and then in the library he diligently improved his leisure by studies all tending to ripen his knowledge of God's holy Word. He read, he corresponded, he prayed—passing happy days of quiet self-culture, varied by active usefulness out of doors. Methodical in everything, he was methodical in his closet; and the following table will indicate how he daily mapped out his hours. Some of the scraps of paper under my hand are evidently notes of duties to be got through in a certain day; and as he thus arranged beforehand what he meant to accomplish, so in these *time tables* we see him taking note of what he had actually done. We give one page, the first of a year, containing the record of a fortnight. You will be able to trace in the abbreviations, Cock Road, the Catechumen Class, and other favourite duties; the last abridgment I cannot explain.

1849.	January.	Townsend's O. Testament.	Townsend's N. Testament.	Genesis.	2 Chronicles.	Ezekiel.	Baxter's Saint's Rest.	Milner's Church History.	Josephus's History.	Time in Library.	Memorandums, &c., &c.
		Vol. 1.	Vol. 1.								
Sunday	7	1	1	7	5	10	92	119	156	4	Chapel, Covenant, Sacrament and home.
Monday.....	8	2	2	8	6	11	..	132	166	9	Home all day.
Tuesday....	9	..	3	9	7	12	..	...	185	4	Bristol, home & Yg.Men.
Wednesday.	10	..	4	10	8	13	..	...	...	2	To Mid. Norton.
Thursday ..	11	..	5	11	9	14	..	...	...	4	Home from Norton.
Friday.....	12	..	6	12	10	15	..	134	...	5	Bristol and home.
Saturday...	13	..	7	13	11	16	..	...	...	5	Bristol and home.
										33	
Sunday	14	..	8	14	12	17	..	...	...	1	Home, C.Rd., Catn Class and Chapel, Mr. Carr.
Monday....	15	..	9	15	13	18	94	134	190	4	Bristol and home.
Tuesday....	16	..	10	16	14	19	..	145	...	4	Bristol & home & Yg. Men's Association.
Wednesday.	17	..	11	17	15	20	..	...	...	1	Bristol (Oldland Hall) home and Class.
Thursday ..	18	..	12	18	16	21	..	...	...	2	Ditto & Chapel & Two Committee Meetings.
Friday.....	19	..	13	19	17	22	96	...	...	6	Home.
Saturday...	20	..	14	20	18	23	98	...	...	8	Home all day. Mxs.
										26	

That grace which most steadily manifested itself in him was love; his heart, penetrated with a sense of God's bounty in providence, of his mercy in redemption, was ever open, ever warm, ever tender, and claimed kindred with all hearts. Hence his delight in promoting the happiness of others; hence the joy wherewith he devoted to that end the property gained by his ceaseless exertions. The sum of his benevolence can never be known: he did not until late in life fix on a proportion of income as the minimum of his gifts; when he did, the proportion was one-sixth. Of course he did not resolve to give away only that, but to give away that at least. Had he been doubtful as to the extent of his givings, he would unquestionably have fixed a proportion earlier; but he knew well that all he had was *tithed*, and more. One week he kept account of all he had given; it amounted to sixty pounds; and he kept that account no more, but that week was considerably above the average. A man with a heart resistlessly desiring to do good, may go on without fixing a proportion, and yet certainly bestow a fit amount of his gains; but they are few who would not be astounded at the small proportions their givings bear to their income, if they tested them for a year. Most men need, for their own sake, to fix a minimum, and that minimum should not be less than one-tenth. I have known many who early in life have adopted this principle; and where it has been steadily maintained, a blessing seems ever to follow it. We are not so addicted to doing good that it comes upon us by accident; and as God bountifully gives, we should *deliberately resolve* that we will "honour God with our substance, and with the first fruits of our increase." The work of charity to men's souls and bodies, of gratitude for God's bounty, is too sacred to be left to chance and impulse: regular and calculated reserves should be made for such outlay, if we would not live to ourselves, but to Him who died for us and rose again.

From the intimate knowledge of Mr. Gaskin we shall draw our last glimpses of his walk with God:—

"The friendship which subsisted between Mr. Budgett and myself through so many years, was cherished under circumstances peculiarly favourable for observing closely action as springing from motive, and motive as aiming at an end; and without the smallest reservation I must add, that never have I witnessed aught more consistent and pure than the busy life of this member of the Christian church. Our standard of inference here, must, of course, be the rule prescribed by the Saviour, 'By their fruits ye shall know them;' and, judging from his entire deportment, we see how largely my relative's heart must have been penetrated with Divine grace. Amidst influences usually accounted unfavourable to such a result, how successfully was the spirituality of the soul maintained, and how beautifully did the whole tone of the outward life testify to the principles which were cherished within! The secret was this,—his best hours were spent with God. When I was his neighbour, it was his custom—and I doubt not the habit was preserved as long as health permitted—to be in his library by five o'clock in the morning, for the purpose of reading, meditation, and prayer; and he has often, in conversation with me, regretted that he did not feel himself physically equal to an earlier commencement of this part of his daily occupations. To those who could thus follow Mr. Budgett from the exercise of his closet, it was no marvel that he should be so securely carried through the ungenial atmosphere which hung over him as a *man of business*, and the bustling scenes amidst which he was called to act so large a part. He was eminently a man of his Bible, and a man of prayer; while 'diligent in business,' he was 'fervent in spirit, serving the Lord.' Imbued with such influences as those which we have seen him constantly cultivating, and guided by such principles as those which we have seen him constantly exhibiting, there was nothing in the active engagements of his commercial life that could mar his spirit, or divert his soul from the path in which he delighted to walk."

CHAPTER X.

THE LATTER END.

"By death and hell pursued in vain,
To thee the ransomed seed shall come;
Shouting, their heavenly Sion gain,
And pass through death triumphant home."

WESLEY.

MR. BUDGETT had now reached a point when earth might well seem a pleasant home. He was prospering amazingly, with the certainty (as men would say) of yearly prospering more; his family were grown up, and their prospects smiling; the prejudices which had hung around his sudden rise were disappearing; respect, attention, love, were coming thick upon him; wider and higher circles were doing homage to his excellence: abundant leisure for mental feasts and benevolent labours was at his command; and, only fifty-six, he might yet for years rejoice amid the fruits of his toil: so that one, looking at him about the fall of 1850, might have said, "If Samuel Budgett is not to be envied, who is?"

It was about the November of that year, when walking up a hill in Bristol, that he complained of a difficulty of breathing. Then, ascending stairs became a weariness; a new weight hung upon his agile step. Day by day strength failed; the system betokened decay; the heart was affected; dropsy was feared;—the Successful Merchant had lived too fast. His master energy which had crushed so many difficulties had been doing its work on his own frame, which soon became a witness that over-activity is not to be indulged without shivering a man at last.

Prone ever to self-reproach, slow to behold the full con solation of the Gospel, the first days of his illness were days of mourning: not the mourning of selfish fear, which shudders in presence of its just doom, without sorrow for offences; but the mourning of a heart which felt itself infinitely indebted to the Redeemer's undeserved mercy, and could not forgive itself for having loved Him so little and served Him so imperfectly. His soul was especially weighed down by this;—he had seen, felt, and been drawn toward that full salvation which our glorious Saviour has wrought out for his followers; the glory of an intimate fellowship with God had been open to his eye, and he had stopped short of it, had followed at a distance, had served with a divided heart, had consequently oft faltered and stumbled in his course. Unmeasured self-accusation, outgushing grief for his ill return of the Saviour's boundless love, open humiliation and sorrow thrown fully before friend or minister or children, prayers of piteous abasement, and tears flowing copiously, marked the early scenes of his last sickness. While many who had been far higher in their professions and far less abundant in their fruits were entering the valley of death with an easy acknowledgment that they had been "very unfaithful," Samuel Budgett was pouring floods of contrite sorrow on the feet of that blessed Saviour who had forgiven him so much and had been so unworthily requited. But, though our God seeks the sacrifice of a contrite heart, He delights not in the wailing of joyless self-reproach. In that is neither bliss for His creature nor glory for Himself. He reveals Himself as *freely and abundantly* forgiving all who contritely come to Him through Christ; and such glorious mercy is not fitly owned when, unmindful of its balm, we persist in only bemoaning our sores. This was Mr. Budgett's danger, and from this cause he passed days of gloom. But prayer was made for him continually, and friends strong in faith were ever reminding him of the love infinitely stored up in the Redeemer he adored. That Redeemer, though He permitted sorrow for a while (as if to show that in sickness all earthly comforts do not suffice, even with good hope of restoration), did, ere long, shed abroad in the heart of His servant a plenteous consolation which well showed that parting with all the enticements of earth is not hard to him whom Christ makes joyful.

It has been my task to show you (indistinctly and poorly, it is true) the Successful Merchant in his childhood, in the early trials of his way, in his swift ascent to wealth, among his men, among his neighbours, in his family, and in his closet. Mayhap, in following him, you have learned that a man may fear God, be benevolent, laborious in good works, a reader of his Bible, a follower of inward and spiritual life, and yet the while fill up a man's full place in trade and earn a prime reward. Now we have reached the moment when he and death first stand openly face to face. It is hope and fear no longer: the hour has struck, his work is done, the market is closed for ever; purchase and sale, profit and loss, are things of the past. He is facing a world where there is no money, no bargains, no store and stock of earthly good. There he lies now, in that chamber, between the world of bustle and the world of retribution; while this home, these possessions, these friends which his warm heart knows how to value, stand by, like the relations of an emigrant by the ship side, awaiting the moment when he shall glide away to the unseen country.

Just at this point I am happy to withdraw and leave you with him. The friend who had written from his own lips notes of the recollections of his childhood, would fain have completed the story of his life ere he went hence. For this purpose she came to his side; but it was vain now to seek recitals of the past. The present, however, was full of lessons, and was daily noted. This, then, enables me to lead you into his chamber, and leave you there: and if you are little wiser and little better for your fellowship with me, God grant that it may not be so as to your fellowship with him!

"On Monday, March 10th, the first morning after dropsy made its appearance, he said, 'I was not sorry last night to discover my legs were swollen, it will only hasten me home the sooner.' In the afternoon of the same day, on returning from Bristol, after hearing Dr. Symonds's opinion, he expressed his willingness to depart, and said, 'I dare say there will be a desire to say something of me after I am gone; but *mind*, let there not be one word said or written to extol the creature. *Mind* "I am a sinner saved by grace," "a brand plucked from the burning."'

"At the same time he remarked, 'My family, how I love my family! I never valued my family as I value them now; if I am permitted, I shall often like to meet you in this room, when you are assembled together.'

"Friday, the 14th, he sent for Miss ———, and said, 'I sent for you to tell you how happy I am; not a wave, not a ripple, not a fear, not a shadow of doubt. I didn't think it was possible for man to enjoy so much of God upon earth. *I'm filled with God.*'

"On stepping into the carriage he stopped and said, 'How is Mrs. ———?' On receiving a reply, he said with solemn earnestness, 'O ———, "seek ye *first* the kingdom of God and his righteousness, and all other things shall be added unto you."' During the ride, he spoke on various subjects, and much enjoyed some verses that were repeated, frequently joining in. A member of his class who saw him, came and congratulated him on being out, hoping he was better. Mr. Budgett said '*No; I feel I am going home.* I should like to have met you all *once more*, but tell them all to meet me in heaven.'

"Monday, the 17th, he said to Miss Budgett, 'I have passed a pleasant night, but feel myself getting weaker. My stay on earth will be but short. I shall soon arrive at home. It gives me great pleasure to think we shall be an unbroken family in heaven. My father's family are many of them gone; the rest are on the way. My own family, part of them, *are* in heaven. Yes, I have some dear children in heaven, *and so have you* (meaning spiritual children). It gives me great pleasure to look on ——— and ——— ———, because I know they are trying to serve the church, and when they have served their generations on earth, they will join me above. O, how thin does the veil now appear which separates earth from heaven!'

"The same day, to Mrs. M———, speaking of the uncertainty of his present state, he said, 'Who would not rather, being brought to this point, *go.*—I am resigned. *I have not a paper to sign, not a shilling to give away, not a book but any one may comprehend in ten minutes.* I feel as if I were a poor sinner saved through my dear mother's prayers, the prayers of my friends, and my own poor feeble prayers offered through Christ. He cannot cast me off, but has gently guided me through the wilderness, and is keeping me there till I am perfected through suffering.'

"The same day he saw Mr. ———:—'I am glad to see you, my dear friend. How hard it is in life and vigour to bring our minds to believe that we must suffer. But the Lord has seen fit to bring me to a death-bed. I this day hang like a little child in a brook, catching hold of a branch that is thrown out to save it; only there is this one difference in my case, I hang upon the branch of Jesse's stem. Christ will keep me; I am safe. The day of mourning is better than the day of rejoicing. God has blessed me with prosperity in life, and were he to see fit to spare me now, I should have a fairer prospect of prosperity than most before me; but I give all up. I would not alter my lot if it were in my power to do so for any earthly advantage. The blood of Christ is all to me. I hang upon the atonement.'

"In the afternoon, being a little restless and unable to sleep, he lay for some minutes apparently very uncomfortable, when in an instant a sweet smile lit up his countenance as he exclaimed, '"Why should a living man complain?—a man for the punishment of his sins?"' and then burst forth in praise to God for the mercies which he enjoyed, notwithstanding he was so great a sinner. Soon after he raised his hands and said, '*Glory! glory! glory!* I want to shout the praises of God.'

"The same day his son —— asked if he would like any message to be conveyed from him to the Young Men's Association. He said, 'I am too weak to say much; but tell them to take the advice I used to give them. I feel for them as my own sons, and they may become as happy and as useful as they are. If they will hold together and try to help one another they will be sure to prosper. I wish them to be provided for after my death as they were before, and I leave it to my sons to do so. Tell the young women of the Association the same.'

"On Tuesday, the 18th, he saw Mrs. H—— and said, 'I am glad to see you, I should like to have lived a little longer if it had been for your sake, but you'll not want an earthly friend. My sons will be to you what I have been. I have told them all about it, and they will be kind to you.' He inquired if she had anything to say to him: on her replying she only wished to thank him for all his kindness, he said, 'I wish it had been more, but I know it has helped you. Good-bye! The Lord be with you: cleave to Him and He will be a friend; yes, He will be *your* friend, your husband, your support. He will guide you in passing through the troubles of this life. He will be your shield, your defence, and your *exceeding great reward.* The time is passing away: we shall *soon meet.*' The same morning Mr. and Mrs. ——— came. After some remarks to Mrs. ———, he addressed her husband:—'My dear ———, *you* have still to cope with the difficulties and trials of business. I look back on all the way I have been led, and feel it is your privilege "to walk unburned in fire." Cleave to Him; keep close to Jesus. Every morning, before you leave your room, inquire, Lord what wouldst thou have me do? And every evening ask yourself, How much owest thou unto thy Lord? *Keep short reckonings with Him;* go forward, and your path shall be as that of the just, shining more and more into the perfect day. I think I may have a little more suffering before I go, but I am willing to bear it. Good-bye! "May the peace of God, which passeth all understanding, keep your hearts and minds in the knowledge and love of God and of his Son, Christ Jesus our Lord!"'

"On Sunday night, March 23rd, before he was undressed he said, 'Let us spend a few minutes in *silent* prayer, I think I can hardly bear praying aloud. Pray, my dear friend, that we may to-night experience the presence and blessing of our heavenly Father. Ask that I may obtain a settled calm and quiet sleep.'

"After he got into bed, he lay for some hours in a most delightful state of mind, occasionally giving vent to his feelings in expressions, a few only of which can be remembered. It was observed, 'You feel that your heavenly Father can make you *enjoy* affliction.' 'O yes,' he said, '*I do now;* I don't feel myself like a sick man, I feel I am luxuriating in God's presence; but I believe he means soon to take me.' It was remarked, 'Well *yours* will be the gain, *ours* the loss.' Mr. Budgett replied, 'Yes, I know to me it will be gain, unspeakable gain,—and you will lose a friend, but not *much* loss; I have not been so spiritually minded as I ought, and this has been *your* loss.' Again he said, 'O, what a peculiar feeling I have this evening: it is delightful. I feel as I did the other Sabbath evening with ———: then it was a solemn eventide. The room seems *filled* with God.' Presently he said, 'I feel as if God were now present, willing and waiting to receive my heart, that He may become my ALL, and give Himself to me more fully. Come, Lord, take away the last remains of sin, make me ready for heaven and fit me for crossing the Jordan.' Thus he continued in fervent ejaculations till from complete exhaustion he fell into a doze. Waking in two or three minutes, he said, 'I felt overpowered and dropped asleep, and when I awoke I thought (pointing to the curtains) all this was my tomb; but the room around me was so bright—*it was dazzling brightness, too great to bear.*' Continually he repeated, '*I'm very comfortable—too happy.*' Then again, 'This is a most remarkable time, I feel a solemn sense of the presence of God; so calm, so beautiful.' Then did he almost unconsciously slide into prayer—'Lord, I am thine, thou art mine. I have made a covenant with thee, I would not break it for a thousand worlds. Lord, keep me, baptize me anew, help me to rejoice more fully in Thee, give a still clearer witness that I am wholly thine.

"Jesus, my great High Priest,
Offered His blood and died;
My guilty conscience seeks
No sacrifice beside.
His blood for me did once atone,
And now it pleads before the throne."'

Afterwards he broke out—

'"O, here is rest and calm repose;
Here all my sorrows cease;
For Jesus meets my spirit here,
And kindly whispers peace."'

"Wednesday evening, April 2nd.—For the first time he was carried up stairs. On the way he said to the men who carried him, 'I am quite ready to be carried down whenever my heavenly Father sees fit. Thank God, I have a hope beyond the grave.' On being seated he said, 'Wait; I want to tell you on what my hope is fixed. *Listen.*' He then repeated his favourite verse,—

'"Jesus, my great High Priest, &c."

I thank God for such an assurance:—

"I the chief of sinners am,
But Jesus died for me,"

and not for me only, he is willing to receive *all*—any may come. See, this is the way all *must* come, through Him. "This man receiveth sinners still."'

"Tuesday, April 8.—At Weston-super-Mare, the Rev T——— called. After some remarks had passed respecting his health, Mr. Budgett said, 'Well, you know there is not *really* any more uncertainty about my life than yours, or any other person's; you may be gone in an hour or two, or so may I: but I have no great desire either way; for me to live is Christ, and to die is gain; but if I might choose, I would rather depart and be with Christ, which is far, far better.' He then repeated, with an emphasis never to be forgotten,—

'"Thou Shepherd of Israel and mine,
The joy and desire of my heart
For closer communion I *pine*,
I LONG to reside where thou art.
Ah, show me that happiest place,
The place of thy people's abode,
Where saints in an ecstasy gaze,
And hang on a crucified God."'

As he repeated these lines the tears streamed down, plainly indicating that more was really felt than could be expressed. The next day when dressed, he said, 'Well, I'm glad we are going home to-day; I shall not have many more changes; this I expect will be my *last* change, till I am removed to that beautiful little place they call the tomb: yes, I feel that my next remove will be to the chapel yard.'

"On Thursday, April 10th, he said, 'And so poor J. H——— is gone! Poor fellow! do you know what sort of an end he made?' On his being told nothing was known on that subject, he said, 'Poor fellow! the last time I saw him I talked to him, and begged him not to build on his health. I told him how many were called away in the midst of health. I have often talked to him on the necessity of seeking a change of heart. I don't know whether it was the last time I saw him, but it is not long since that I gave him the "Sinner's Friend."'

"Friday evening, April 11th.—Conversing with his medical attendant, he again inquired as to the probable result of his sickness, and on being told it was still very uncertain, he said,—'Well, when I look around at my family and the church, I feel as if life would still be a blessing. I am not one of those who are weary of the world, nor do I feel any sympathy with such; but when I look at myself as an individual, I feel 'twere better far to go.

"There is my house my portion fair,
My treasure and my heart are there,
And my abiding home."

But I did not feel like this at the beginning of my illness; then I felt my own unfaithfulness had been so great, I wished to be spared a few years longer that I might prepare for heaven; but I have been led to see that I can do nothing to *merit* heaven. Could I live like an archangel, still I should not merit heaven:—

"In my hands no price I bring,
Simply to thy cross I cling."

I trust *now* in the merits of my Saviour—in His atoning blood. I feel that it is "not by works of righteousness which we have done, but of his mercy hath he saved us." No, it is "by grace are ye saved through faith, and that not of yourselves, it is the gift of God." One being named who was getting old, he said, 'Oh! he has made a god of his money. Often have I talked to him and urged him to make preparation for a better country. O, what is all the world worth to a dying man? Riches I have had as much as my heart could desire, but I never felt any pleasure in them for their own sake, only so far as they enabled me to give pleasure to others: as for honour ———"

"Sunday evening, April 13th.—'I have toiled, and now others will enter into my labours.' Then dwelling on the success which had attended his efforts, he said, 'This may seem like boasting, but I feel that everything which has been well done and prospered is that in which I was prompted and guided and assisted by my heavenly Father, and that which failed was when I leaned upon my own efforts and endeavours, and then they proved weak and powerless.'

"To a young friend who was with him, he said, 'I should

like to have lived a little longer for your sake. Sometimes I feel as if I should like to look forward and trace your course through life. Yes, I should like to *mark* out your path for you; but this is wrong. *I may* not choose the *best* path, neither can you; but *I can* and do commend you to the care of our heavenly Father. *He will guide you aright.* "Commit thy way unto the Lord; trust also in Him, and He shall bring it to pass." O, "in all your ways acknowledge Him, then He will *direct* thy steps."' Soon after, looking very earnestly at her, he said, '"Let your eye be single, then your whole body shall be full of light." MIND; keep a single eye;—do you hear? In all the events of life keep a single eye.' On being told after the evening service, at which the sacrament of the Lord's Supper had been administered, how fervently he had been prayed for, he said, 'Ah, they will not have to pray for me again on such an occasion; before another month goes round I shall be in a better country.' It was said, 'How delightful is the thought that you will so soon be there! there you will have a harp of gold, be clothed in white raiment, and have a crown upon your head.' 'Yes,' he said, 'I like to hear of the beauties of heaven, but I do not *dwell* upon them; no, what I rejoice in is, that *Christ will be there.* Where He is, there shall I be also. I *know* that He is in me and I in Him. I shall see Him as He is. I *delight in knowing that.* I have no dread of death; I have not had for some time. I wish one of you would write to Mr. Wood; give him my love, and tell him I thank God almost every day for his visit here. Since that first night he was with me, I have had *no fear;* the enemy has assaulted me once or twice, but only for a short time.'

"Wednesday, April 16th.—On seeing Mrs. ———, after a few observations, he asked, 'How many children have you in heaven?' She replied, 'Nine.' On which he said, 'O, what a happy company! I look forward to see my father and mother, my sisters,—and some of my dear children are there. Yes, and I believe my dear wife, and the rest of my children, and every one of my relations, will meet me there. I look upon myself as the *most unworthy*, when I consider the many privileges I have enjoyed, the light I have received ever since I was a child. I know I have always felt something of the hidden life, but I have not always lived *so closely* to God as I should; for this I humble myself before Him. I am glad to see Mr. ——— seeking after God; he is altered, but I want to see him *decided;* nothing else will do: even he can't escape the shafts of death. "Be ye therefore ready, for at such an hour as ye think not, the Son of man cometh."'

"The same afternoon he saw Miss F———, to whom he spoke most sweetly of the many mercies and comforts he enjoyed, recapitulating many of them to her, whilst his heart seemed overflowing with gratitude. Soon after he repeated,—

'"My God, I am thine, what a comfort divine,
What a blessing to know that Jesus is mine," &c.

That was brother Henry's favourite verse. How many times he repeated it during his last illness! But this is my favourite,—

"Jesus, my great High Priest," &c.

How much is contained in that verse! How full, is it not?'

"Saturday, the 19th.—He said to S—— A——, 'Just now I woke up all in a turmoil, wondering who would take care of *Society* matters when I am gone, and then I thought of my own spiritual cares; but I can cast them all upon my Saviour,—

"E'er since by faith I saw the streams,
Thy flowing wounds supply,
Redeeming love has been my theme,
And shall be till I die."

As to the circuit affairs, I leave them all with W—— ; they need not trouble me any more.'

"To his son William he said, 'You are entering life under very different circumstances, with regard to temporal things, to what I did; pursue the same course I have done, and your way is made: let there be this difference, where I have followed trifles, you follow the dictates of the Spirit; wherein I have followed my senses, you cleave close to God, and all will be well. If you do that, in twenty years' time, if you should be spared, I shall look down upon you, and I shall see you respected and beloved by all the neighbourhood.' That text was repeated to him, 'I have fought a good fight,' &c. 'Ah,' he said, 'I can't say with the Apostle, "I have fought a good fight;" for I have not. I have been unfaithful; but there is an atonement through Jesus. I can say, I have almost "finished my course; henceforth there is laid up for me a crown of righteousness, which the Lord, the righteous Judge, shall give me at that day."'

"Saturday morning, the 19th.—On being told the water was advancing, he said, 'I thank God—for that I'm glad; I believe I shall go soon; it does not alarm me. I think I shall go suddenly; but if I go in a moment it does not matter, all will be well.' In the afternoon he observed, 'How our heavenly Father paves our way down to the tomb! I seem so happy and comfortable; it seems as if it cannot be for me, as if it must be for somebody else,—I don't deserve it.' Soon after his bell rang, and on entering his room he was seated on the side of the bed, gasping for breath. He said, 'O, I thought I was *just* going; the wind, or water, or

14*

something, rose and almost suffocated me. Yes, I thought I was going.' Then added, 'I am *so happy*, so comfortable, *so very happy*.' To Mrs. J——— B——— he said, 'I am glad to see you. I have sympathized with you deeply in your affliction. Our times of meeting are growing into a narrow compass now. This may be the last time, or at most we shall not meet above once or twice more; not that I have any particular presentiment of the sort, for God may revive me again. I may be spared to *walk* among you yet, but I think not; from the rapidity with which the water seems to be rising, it will not be long; I may go off now, this *moment*, while I am talking to you; and I should not be sorry. I am as weak as an infant: now I can do nothing. Glory be to God, all is well. My temporal affairs I leave in the hands of my sons, and my spiritual affairs with my Saviour. I cannot tell you how my comforts and consolations abound.

"Better than my boding fears,
To me thou oft hast proved."

I have sunk into the arms of omnipotent love. I cannot tell you how much mercy I have been the subject of. I love you, and am thankful I was introduced to your family: thankful for my children's sake. I only regret that I have benefited so little from your society. Give my love to all your dear family, tell them they have my *highest* respect and *best* wishes that they may enjoy every blessing both for body and soul.'

"The same evening, when several were in his room, he inquired, 'Can you tell me what a debt I owe to God for having giving me such innumerable mercies and comforts? He has indeed given me plenty of this world's goods; each of my children will have ample, and my dear wife too. I have *every comfort* I can desire; *O, tell me how much I owe!* How can I pay this debt of gratitude? *There has been many a time when I have given away my last shilling* and now I have more than I could have desired, and the more I give away the more comes in; and I have more coming in than ever I had. What a mercy to have so many kind friends. I am surprised at your kindness and willingness to do so many little acts of love for me. I hope none of *you* will ever want for kind attention in affliction.

> "Kindness gives the fleeting flower
> Of life its lustre and perfume
> And we are weeds without it."

O, God has bestowed upon me far above my desires; tell me, my dear friend, how much I owe! I enjoy all these temporal blessings, and how can I repay the debt for these? But this is not a thousandth part of the debt I owe. O no; when I think of my spiritual mercies, I'm lost. When I think of my heavenly Father's goodness—a brand plucked from the eternal burning, soon to be raised to live with angels, and above all with Himself,—I feel I have

> "Riches above what earth can grant,
> And lasting as the mind!"'

Then in a rapture, and with tears of joy streaming down his face, he exclaimed, 'O, I'm overwhelmed with love. I want to fly to preach Christ to all the world. I'll praise him everywhere. Can I be lost? O *no, no.* O, I want to preach Christ. I am overburdened with love and gratitude.'

"Sunday afternoon, April 20th.—To Mrs. P——— he said, 'Tell Mr. P——— that I come saying,—

> "Jesus, my Great High Priest," &c.,

and tell him to come in the same way, and there is no time to lose. Nothing I have ever done, and nothing he has ever done, can save him. No, we must come as poor worthless sinners to Jesus,—

"That only ground of all my plea."

You don't know what mental suffering I had at the commencement of my illness. The adversary came to me, and tormented me with fears of all kinds; he showed me my great unfaithfulness, told me I had deceived my friends (not designedly I know) with a good moral exterior, whilst my heart was not right within. I know there was truth in it all, and was distressed beyond measure, but I was enabled to say,—Lord, I am a sinner: God be merciful unto me; I am lost, but Christ hath died. From that night I have had *no fear*. The sting of death is gone. I had some fear of death at the beginning, because of my past unfaithfulness; but the merits of Christ are all-sufficient. Now I enjoy a *sweet calm*:—

"I bless the day that I was born."'

Then, as in a rapture he exclaimed, 'O, I can't describe my happiness. I bless God that He created me, that He has spared me, and that He has pardoned me. I thank God that you and I were ever acquainted, that I ever saw your dear sister, and that I was ever united to her. O, God has been very gracious to me. I praise Him for the past, what He has done for me! I praise Him for the present, what He is now doing for me! and I praise Him for the future, knowing what He will do for me.'

"One of his nephews coming to see him, he said, 'Well F———, how are you? I have heard that you have been poorly, I am glad to see you better again. Are you come out of the affliction as gold purified?' He then spoke to him of the necessity of a change of heart, of the simplicity of the plan of salvation, and of the depth of the love which Jesus Christ had manifested towards us. Once or twice he asked him whether he did not believe in the love of his Saviour,—His willingness to save all who came to Him. Then endeavouring to explain the way of faith in Jesus Christ, he said, 'Suppose that you wished to buy some sheep of me and had paid the money, and I had promised to let you have them; you would believe they were yours though they were in my field, as much as if you had them in your own, because I had promised them: so you must believe that God will give you the blessings you require of Him. Now, take your bad heart up stairs, don't take it down to the breakfast table; but take it up at once and give it to God. He will then accept it and make you as happy as I am in my affliction. Do go and fall on your knees and ask mercy while it is offered, and you will be sure to obtain it.' Having thus earnestly urged him to come to Christ at once, he said, 'You will be happier yourself, and you will return home under a different influence, be useful to your uncle and aunt and Sarah.'

"In the afternoon he sent for Miss Budgett (Mrs. Budgett and Mrs. Mees were already there) and said he felt better and should like to receive the Sacrament of the Lord's supper—a wish he had several times before expressed, but from weakness had been prevented. He then told Miss B. he should like her to question him closely, lest he should have made any mistake on the subject, and for her to read and pray with him. She then read to him the 23d Psalm, and the hymn commencing,—

'And let this feeble body fail,' &c.

After this, all his family being assembled, the two ministers, Messrs. Clay and Kevern, came, and the solemn ordinance was administered. During the service Mr. Budgett's mind seemed fully absorbed by the solemnity of the occasion. He several times added his loud 'amen' to the petitions presented to the throne of grace, especially during the concluding prayer. The service was greatly abbreviated in consequence of his extreme weakness, and it was feared, brief as it was, that his feeble frame would be exhausted by the effort required; but after its conclusion, the rapture of his spirit seemed to give strength to his body, and he requested a hymn to be sung. On a fear being expressed lest it should prove too much for him, he reiterated with great ardour, 'Sing, sing.' The Rev. Charles Clay then gave out three verses of—

'Behold the Saviour of mankind,'

during which time Mr. Budgett, seated on the side of his bed, his countenance beaming with almost angelic joy, his eyes streaming, his chin quivering with emotion, and his hands upraised, to the astonishment of all joined most heartily in the singing,—reminding one of some old prophet, or the patriarch Jacob, surrounded by his family, giving them his last blessing. He appeared in a perfect ecstasy of joy and triumph, and continued to utter the most joyful expressions of faith in Christ and hope of heaven.

" Some of his expressions were to the following effect:— 'O, I see such a fulness of merit in the atonement of my Saviour.' 'I am a poor vile sinner, but the blood of Jesus avails even for me.' 'I have been unfaithful; my only regret is my own unfaithfulness. If I could live over again, I think I should be more faithful; but that is all past and forgiven.'

" He then quoted his favourite verse,—

'Jesus, my great High Priest,' &c.

and said, 'There I rest; Satan cannot drive me from this For many days he has not been permitted to molest me,' and then described with much energy his last conflict with the adversary of souls. His son James said, 'We shall all soon meet in heaven.' 'Yes,' he replied (looking round upon his family), 'yes, thank God! He has not left a wish ungratified, a desire unsatisfied, either temporal or spiritual.'

"He also said, amongst several other similar exclamations, 'This is the happiest day of my life—the happiest hour. I am ready to go this moment, or ready to stay. O, how would I preach if I could preach now!' He bade his ministers a very affectionate farewell, and on one of them repeating the lines,—

'I the chief of sinners am,
But Jesus died for me,'

he fervently responded to the sentiment, and added, '*I never asked for joy, I always thought myself unworthy of it;* but He has given me more than I asked.' It being said, 'He giveth exceeding abundantly above all we ask or think,' he replied, 'Thank God—thank God!'

"After the ministers had retired he requested that another hymn might be sung; on which Edwin's favourite being selected—

'How happy every child of grace,'

he said, 'Yes, and Edwin will join us.' He again united most heartily in the singing, and proposed to have another hymn, when it was again suggested it might prove injurious to him. 'O no,' he replied, 'there is no chance of my recovery, nothing will hurt me now; I am going home; nothing *can* hurt me now, and I thank God I am ready to go this moment, or am willing to wait longer. If it were put to my choice now, whether I would live for a few years longer to enjoy increased riches and multiplied friends, or whether I would go home at once, I would no more choose than I would go into a foreign country that I know nothing about.' Then turning to his son Samuel—'Samuel, be faithful, my boy; I could have wished to live a little longer to watch your progress. Preach Christ; let nothing discourage you. You have not seen your best days, only follow the light imparted. Let your eye be single, and your whole body shall be full of light.'

"Addressing himself to Mrs. ———, he assured her of the happiness he had in his own family, the pleasure he felt in being connected with her family, his first thoughts on seeing her, &c., &c.; but his own expressions cannot be remembered: indeed, but a faint idea can be conveyed of that solemn but joyful hour. Altogether it was such a scene as is seldom witnessed on earth. It was the full triumph of faith. An impression was made on the minds of all present which can never be obliterated. The language of all seemed to be, 'How dreadful is this place; this is none other but the house of God, and this is the gate of heaven.'

"Tuesday, the 22nd.—'O,' he said, 'I want *rest;* this pain and suffering make me long for rest.' Mrs. J——— said, 'This will no doubt make the heavenly rest more sweet.' 'O yes,' he replied,

'"Sweet as home to pilgrims weary,
Light to newly open'd eyes,
Flowing springs in deserts dreary,
Is the rest the cross supplies;
All who taste it, shall to life immortal rise."'

He then said, 'I believe that had I but been faithful my life would have been spared. O, my dear friend, take care to make sure work for heaven; attend to the most important end of life; remember it is said, "Seek ye first, &c." I am sure religion will never make a man less successful in busi ness. No, I believe he who has the one thing needful will excel the most in business.'

"Wednesday he inquired of F——, 'What day is it?' She replied, 'Wednesday.' On which he said, 'But what day of the month is it?' On his being told, the twenty-third, he observed, 'Ah, F——, the first week in May you will all be in deep mourning; yes, by the first week in May you will all be in deep mourning.' In the afternoon he was carried down stairs, and, seated in the pony carriage, rode round his grounds. He was very observant; and seeing some docks in the grass said, 'These should not be; after the next rain get half-a-dozen men, and have them up. You know the way, J——.' On passing, he pointed, and said, 'That tree bears a beautiful yellow pear; it is a good sort; you notice them, but I shall not be here to taste them.' The carriage being stopped that he might enjoy the fresh air, he took the opportunity of speaking to L——, and urged upon him the great importance of making sure work for eternity—speaking to him with that energy which showed how deeply he felt the importance of the subject. Then turning to J——, he said, 'I've been talking to L——; I feel anxious that this affliction may be blessed to him: it has been to me, and I want it to be to him also.' On returning, he said to J——, 'These fields look pleasant, don't they, J——? I am glad to go and leave all so comfortable for you to enjoy; *but remember the end.* O let a right use be made of the enjoyment.'

"In the evening he saw Mr. J—— B——, and after speaking of some temporal and pecuniary matters, he expressed his gratitude to God for the comfortable circumstances in which he should leave his family. . . .He then spoke of the different appearance the garden, grounds, and fields presented from what they did when first he came to Kingswood and from the time when he bought the land, and of the goodness of God who had enabled him to make such an improvement. He described the wilderness of spelter works and cinders which covered the ground, and said, 'Often when I was apprenticed to your uncle H———, have I come down here on a Sunday after chapel, and, sitting on a flag between the old walls, renewed my covenant with God whilst His love was abundantly shed abroad in my soul. I used often *literally* to stop my ears as I came from chapel, lest any sound should draw off my mind from the sermon I had heard; and after thinking it all over as I sat on the stone, I committed to memory some piece of poetry out of one of the old Methodist Magazines every Sunday, and little did I then think that land would one day become my own and be so altered.'

"Thursday, April 24th, he saw Mr. P———, and said, 'Ah, we cannot always have health; no man can always have health. But it is a mercy to feel these light afflictions are but for a moment, and will work out for us a more exceeding weight of glory, whilst we look not at the things which are seen, but at those which are not seen. Yes, we must look at those which are not seen. We must be *earnest* in the pursuit of them. O, my dear brother, I have thought of you very much; I have thought of you with an intensity of feeling. You are kind, honourable, and well-disposed; but I feel in looking back that I have not always possessed that spirituality of mind which I should: you have seen the want of it in me, and I ask your forgiveness. I entreat you *now* to seek religion. "Seek ye first the kingdom of God and his righteousness, and all these things shall be added unto you." Without it life is lost; there is no enjoyment without it. *O, seek for it at once!* Now is the accepted time; now is the day of salvation. Come this very day; let us at once say, "I am determined to come to the Saviour. Lord receive me now as a poor sinner. I come that I may now be saved; if I perish it shall be entreating for pardon." O, take my advice, do let us be in earnest; both of us have been too intent upon seeking this world's good, *now* let us seek earnestly for that which alone will save. To-morrow may be *too late;* to-morrow we may lose our reason. O may you come to-day and seek happiness while it may be found. This may be your last opportunity. Then come to the Saviour *now.* There is no time like the present. In a few weeks we shall be united or separated *for ever:* it is a solemn thought. The Lord bless you and your family, and secure you a lot among the blest! Every thing else is vanity. I thought four days ago that I was dying. I then felt that there is in religion—in the love and knowledge of God, a reality, a power to support in the hour of death. I could say,—

"There is my house and portion fair,
My treasure and my heart are there,
And my abiding home;
For me my elder brethren stay,
And angels beckon me away,
And Jesus bids me come."

It is quite my desire to go, not because of my faithfulness, for I feel I have not been faithful, but I fly to Christ for refuge—there I can rest and feel saved. You and I may both rest on that foundation.' Then looking earnestly at Mr. P———, he inquired, 'Have you, my dear brother, *an assurance* of your title to heaven? Do you feel that should death come *now* you have a mansion above? Are you now assured of it? O, remain not without it: we may get it to-day; we may obtain it *now.* O, seek for it; remember, "Him that cometh unto me I will in no wise cast out." O, what a blessing! I should like to pray with you for a few minutes; but am too weak. Good-bye! may we all meet at last.'

" Saturday, the 26th.—Hearing a loud peal of thunder, he said, " Hush! 'tis the voice of a Father—'tis the voice of a God!' In the evening Mr. Budgett saw Mr. S——— and Mr. P——— [I think, two of his travellers]. Mr. P——— told him many had asked kindly for him, on which Mr. Budgett observed, 'Remember me kindly to them all. I thank God all is right, " not by works of righteousness that we have done, &c.," but of his boundless love to me a poor sinner,—

"Jesus, my great High Priest," &c.

I rest there for *pardon*, *purity*, and heaven. I *long* to go; happy should I be if I were to go this night. Let us remember, my dear friends, earth is but a scale to heaven; buying and selling is of no importance except as they bear reference to eternity. The Lord make you fit and prepare you for it.' On one of them saying, 'You will soon reach the desired haven,' Mr. B. remarked, 'O yes, I anticipate it with pleasure, thankfulness, and gratitude. Such is human life. I never expected to suffer thus; but there has been great mercy shown to me even in this state. I would not choose—I must not choose; but if I were *obliged* to make the choice, I should say it were better for me to be dissolved. Heaven is my home; I am travelling there. Lord, thine only will be done.' Mr. P——— observed, 'How the power of God is exemplified in such complete submission to the Divine will.' On which Mr. Budgett said, " It is the work of God; it is the simple work of the Spirit in answer to prayer. I am astonished, because at the beginning of my illness I was fearful of death, and more astonished because of my unfaithfulness. Who would not trust Thee?—

"O God, of good the unfathomed sea!
Who would not give his heart to Thee?
Who would not love Thee with his might?
O Jesu, lover of mankind!
Who would not his whole soul and mind,
With all his strength to Thee unite?"

Jesus, thou art merciful; every good thing comes from God. Mine is a merciful affliction.' Mr. S—— said, 'Perhaps it may be interesting to you to know that your visit last summer was made useful. Perhaps you may remember, after exhorting the people in the school-room at Aberystwith, you distributed some little books, and amongst the rest, some entitled, "Come to Jesus." A lady, who had listened to a part of your discourse, met with Mr. W—— (the preacher), and begged that he would procure one for her; he did so, and as far as I can trace the result, it was made a great blessing to her, and proved the turning point in her religious experience.' Mr. Budgett said, 'The Lord be praised! That evening I was under a cloud; I could not have imagined there would have been any such result; I did not appear to speak under the influence of the Spirit. He did give me a talent for preaching, a persuasive talent, if I had only used it aright; but I rejoice in hope of the glory of God. O, my dear friends, try to get all Nelson Street, all that are under your care, converted to God. I have been guilty of my brother's blood, but my sons will supply my lack. I am aware that business is very important; but compared with religion it is but as dung and dross.'

"On Monday morning, he said to Miss B——, 'You will find a couple of books in my drawer with Miss ——'s name in them. I wish when I am gone you would send them to her, and also one of those little books, "Come to Jesus," or else "The Sinner's Friend." Give her my love; tell her I am gone to heaven, and I hope she will meet me there. Tell her that *profession* without *possession* is of no value; that without a real change of heart, a firm reliance on the atonement of Jesus Christ, she cannot be saved. I have had many conversations with her, but I always thought she was quite in the dark on religious subjects. Now will you take her into *your charge*, and either see or write to her, and give her my message?'

"The last evening of his life he saw Mr. W———, who only remained with him about three minutes. Mr. Budgett, however, used that short time to the best purpose; he said, 'I am going the way of all flesh; but bless God I'm ready. I trust in the merits of my Redeemer.' Then alluding to the near prospect of his dissolution he said, 'I care not when, or where, or how; glory be to God!' This was the last time he was heard to refer to it. During the night he appeared rather restless; but most of his waking hours were employed in repeating portions of Scripture, hymns, &c. The last he distinctly repeated was,—

'With glorious clouds encompass'd round,
Whom angels dimly see,
Will the Unsearchable be found,
Or God appear to me?'

In the morning he sent for his daughter, and on her entering, said, 'I'm glad you are come, I am so glad to see you. *You understand me.*' To Miss B——— he said, 'O! sister Elizabeth, I had one or two things to say to you. I want you to give five sovereigns for me between four persons.' He then mentioned by name three persons of his class who were much afflicted; the fourth name he could not recall, but said, 'I'm very weak, I shall think of it bye and bye.' His medical attendant then saw him, and stated it as his opinion that he would most probably linger for many weeks. He felt strange, and soon after was removed into bed; but he still complained of a strange feeling, and wished the surgeon to be sent for, which was accordingly done. He sat with him for some time, but the pulse was still regular. He walked towards the fire-place, but had not been there a minute, when Mr. Budgett exclaimed, 'O dear!' and on turning round, he perceived a change had taken place. The bell ringing violently, immediately all the members of the family who were at home assembled in his room, and found him supported in Martha's arms, his heart throbbing violently. The blood rushed to his head, his face changed to purple, his eyes were half open, but he was apparently unconscious. They watched—his eyes gently closed, and without a struggle or a sound, his spirit winged its way to that haven he had so long desired to reach!

> 'They looked;
> He was dead;
> His spirit had fled;—
> Painless and swift as his own desire.
> The soul, undrest
> From her mortal vest,
> Had stepped in her car of heavenly fire,
> And proved how bright
> Were the realms of light,
> Bursting at once upon the sight.' "

Farewell, patient reader; our task is done! May God bless thee! May He give thee bright days, tranquil nights, and a happy end! And when He opens the GREAT BOOK wherein all our lives are written, O may it contain a good account of thee!

THE END.

www.ingramcontent.com/pod-product-compliance
Lightning Source LLC
LaVergne TN
LVHW020213110826
845151LV00003B/701